FREE Test Taking Tips DVD Offer

To help us better serve you, we have developed a Test Taking Tips DVD that we would like to give you for FREE. **This DVD covers world-class test taking tips that you can use to be even more successful when you are taking your test.**

All that we ask is that you email us your feedback about your study guide. Please let us know what you thought about it – whether that is good, bad or indifferent.

To get your **FREE Test Taking Tips DVD**, email freedvd@studyguideteam.com with "FREE DVD" in the subject line and the following information in the body of the email:

    a. The title of your study guide.

    b. Your product rating on a scale of 1-5, with 5 being the highest rating.

    c. Your feedback about the study guide. What did you think of it?

    d. Your full name and shipping address to send your free DVD.

If you have any questions or concerns, please don't hesitate to contact us at freedvd@studyguideteam.com.

Thanks again!

AP European History
2020 & 2021

AP European History Review Book and
Practice Test Questions
[Advanced Placement Exam Prep]

Test Prep Books

Written and edited by Test Prep Books.

Test Prep Books is not associated with or endorsed by any official testing organization. Test Prep Books is a publisher of unofficial educational products. All test and organization names are trademarks of their respective owners. Content in this book is included for utilitarian purposes only and does not constitute an endorsement by Test Prep Books of any particular point of view.

Interested in buying more than 10 copies of our product? Contact us about bulk discounts:
bulkorders@studyguideteam.com

ISBN 13: 9781628459425
ISBN 10: 1628459425

Table of Contents

//Test Prep Books!!!

Quick Overview

As you draw closer to taking your exam, effective preparation becomes more and more important. Thankfully, you have this study guide to help you get ready. Use this guide to help keep your studying on track and refer to it often.

This study guide contains several key sections that will help you be successful on your exam. The guide contains tips for what you should do the night before and the day of the test. Also included are test-taking tips. Knowing the right information is not always enough. Many well-prepared test takers struggle with exams. These tips will help equip you to accurately read, assess, and answer test questions.

A large part of the guide is devoted to showing you what content to expect on the exam and to helping you better understand that content. In this guide are practice test questions so that you can see how well you have grasped the content. Then, answer explanations are provided so that you can understand why you missed certain questions.

Don't try to cram the night before you take your exam. This is not a wise strategy for a few reasons. First, your retention of the information will be low. Your time would be better used by reviewing information you already know rather than trying to learn a lot of new information. Second, you will likely become stressed as you try to gain a large amount of knowledge in a short amount of time. Third, you will be depriving yourself of sleep. So be sure to go to bed at a reasonable time the night before. Being well-rested helps you focus and remain calm.

Be sure to eat a substantial breakfast the morning of the exam. If you are taking the exam in the afternoon, be sure to have a good lunch as well. Being hungry is distracting and can make it difficult to focus. You have hopefully spent lots of time preparing for the exam. Don't let an empty stomach get in the way of success!

When travelling to the testing center, leave earlier than needed. That way, you have a buffer in case you experience any delays. This will help you remain calm and will keep you from missing your appointment time at the testing center.

Be sure to pace yourself during the exam. Don't try to rush through the exam. There is no need to risk performing poorly on the exam just so you can leave the testing center early. Allow yourself to use all of the allotted time if needed.

Remain positive while taking the exam even if you feel like you are performing poorly. Thinking about the content you should have mastered will not help you perform better on the exam.

Once the exam is complete, take some time to relax. Even if you feel that you need to take the exam again, you will be well served by some down time before you begin studying again. It's often easier to convince yourself to study if you know that it will come with a reward!

Test-Taking Strategies

1. Predicting the Answer

When you feel confident in your preparation for a multiple-choice test, try predicting the answer before reading the answer choices. This is especially useful on questions that test objective factual knowledge. By predicting the answer before reading the available choices, you eliminate the possibility that you will be distracted or led astray by an incorrect answer choice. You will feel more confident in your selection if you read the question, predict the answer, and then find your prediction among the answer choices. After using this strategy, be sure to still read all of the answer choices carefully and completely. If you feel unprepared, you should not attempt to predict the answers. This would be a waste of time and an opportunity for your mind to wander in the wrong direction.

2. Reading the Whole Question

Too often, test takers scan a multiple-choice question, recognize a few familiar words, and immediately jump to the answer choices. Test authors are aware of this common impatience, and they will sometimes prey upon it. For instance, a test author might subtly turn the question into a negative, or he or she might redirect the focus of the question right at the end. The only way to avoid falling into these traps is to read the entirety of the question carefully before reading the answer choices.

3. Looking for Wrong Answers

Long and complicated multiple-choice questions can be intimidating. One way to simplify a difficult multiple-choice question is to eliminate all of the answer choices that are clearly wrong. In most sets of answers, there will be at least one selection that can be dismissed right away. If the test is administered on paper, the test taker could draw a line through it to indicate that it may be ignored; otherwise, the test taker will have to perform this operation mentally or on scratch paper. In either case, once the obviously incorrect answers have been eliminated, the remaining choices may be considered. Sometimes identifying the clearly wrong answers will give the test taker some information about the correct answer. For instance, if one of the remaining answer choices is a direct opposite of one of the eliminated answer choices, it may well be the correct answer. The opposite of obviously wrong is obviously right! Of course, this is not always the case. Some answers are obviously incorrect simply because they are irrelevant to the question being asked. Still, identifying and eliminating some incorrect answer choices is a good way to simplify a multiple-choice question.

4. Don't Overanalyze

Anxious test takers often overanalyze questions. When you are nervous, your brain will often run wild, causing you to make associations and discover clues that don't actually exist. If you feel that this may be a problem for you, do whatever you can to slow down during the test. Try taking a deep breath or counting to ten. As you read and consider the question, restrict yourself to the particular words used by the author. Avoid thought tangents about what the author *really* meant, or what he or she was *trying* to say. The only things that matter on a multiple-choice test are the words that are actually in the question. You must avoid reading too much into a multiple-choice question, or supposing that the writer meant something other than what he or she wrote.

5. No Need for Panic

It is wise to learn as many strategies as possible before taking a multiple-choice test, but it is likely that you will come across a few questions for which you simply don't know the answer. In this situation, avoid panicking. Because most multiple-choice tests include dozens of questions, the relative value of a single wrong answer is small. As much as possible, you should compartmentalize each question on a multiple-choice test. In other words, you should not allow your feelings about one question to affect your success on the others. When you find a question that you either don't understand or don't know how to answer, just take a deep breath and do your best. Read the entire question slowly and carefully. Try rephrasing the question a couple of different ways. Then, read all of the answer choices carefully. After eliminating obviously wrong answers, make a selection and move on to the next question.

6. Confusing Answer Choices

When working on a difficult multiple-choice question, there may be a tendency to focus on the answer choices that are the easiest to understand. Many people, whether consciously or not, gravitate to the answer choices that require the least concentration, knowledge, and memory. This is a mistake. When you come across an answer choice that is confusing, you should give it extra attention. A question might be confusing because you do not know the subject matter to which it refers. If this is the case, don't eliminate the answer before you have affirmatively settled on another. When you come across an answer choice of this type, set it aside as you look at the remaining choices. If you can confidently assert that one of the other choices is correct, you can leave the confusing answer aside. Otherwise, you will need to take a moment to try to better understand the confusing answer choice. Rephrasing is one way to tease out the sense of a confusing answer choice.

7. Your First Instinct

Many people struggle with multiple-choice tests because they overthink the questions. If you have studied sufficiently for the test, you should be prepared to trust your first instinct once you have carefully and completely read the question and all of the answer choices. There is a great deal of research suggesting that the mind can come to the correct conclusion very quickly once it has obtained all of the relevant information. At times, it may seem to you as if your intuition is working faster even than your reasoning mind. This may in fact be true. The knowledge you obtain while studying may be retrieved from your subconscious before you have a chance to work out the associations that support it. Verify your instinct by working out the reasons that it should be trusted.

8. Key Words

Many test takers struggle with multiple-choice questions because they have poor reading comprehension skills. Quickly reading and understanding a multiple-choice question requires a mixture of skill and experience. To help with this, try jotting down a few key words and phrases on a piece of scrap paper. Doing this concentrates the process of reading and forces the mind to weigh the relative importance of the question's parts. In selecting words and phrases to write down, the test taker thinks about the question more deeply and carefully. This is especially true for multiple-choice questions that are preceded by a long prompt.

9. Subtle Negatives

One of the oldest tricks in the multiple-choice test writer's book is to subtly reverse the meaning of a question with a word like *not* or *except*. If you are not paying attention to each word in the question, you can easily be led astray by this trick. For instance, a common question format is, "Which of the following is…?" Obviously, if the question instead is, "Which of the following is not…?," then the answer will be quite different. Even worse, the test makers are aware of the potential for this mistake and will include one answer choice that would be correct if the question were not negated or reversed. A test taker who misses the reversal will find what he or she believes to be a correct answer and will be so confident that he or she will fail to reread the question and discover the original error. The only way to avoid this is to practice a wide variety of multiple-choice questions and to pay close attention to each and every word.

10. Reading Every Answer Choice

It may seem obvious, but you should always read every one of the answer choices! Too many test takers fall into the habit of scanning the question and assuming that they understand the question because they recognize a few key words. From there, they pick the first answer choice that answers the question they believe they have read. Test takers who read all of the answer choices might discover that one of the latter answer choices is actually *more* correct. Moreover, reading all of the answer choices can remind you of facts related to the question that can help you arrive at the correct answer. Sometimes, a misstatement or incorrect detail in one of the latter answer choices will trigger your memory of the subject and will enable you to find the right answer. Failing to read all of the answer choices is like not reading all of the items on a restaurant menu: you might miss out on the perfect choice.

11. Spot the Hedges

One of the keys to success on multiple-choice tests is paying close attention to every word. This is never truer than with words like almost, most, some, and sometimes. These words are called "hedges" because they indicate that a statement is not totally true or not true in every place and time. An absolute statement will contain no hedges, but in many subjects, the answers are not always straightforward or absolute. There are always exceptions to the rules in these subjects. For this reason, you should favor those multiple-choice questions that contain hedging language. The presence of qualifying words indicates that the author is taking special care with his or her words, which is certainly important when composing the right answer. After all, there are many ways to be wrong, but there is only one way to be right! For this reason, it is wise to avoid answers that are absolute when taking a multiple-choice test. An absolute answer is one that says things are either all one way or all another. They often include words like *every*, *always*, *best*, and *never*. If you are taking a multiple-choice test in a subject that doesn't lend itself to absolute answers, be on your guard if you see any of these words.

12. Long Answers

In many subject areas, the answers are not simple. As already mentioned, the right answer often requires hedges. Another common feature of the answers to a complex or subjective question are qualifying clauses, which are groups of words that subtly modify the meaning of the sentence. If the question or answer choice describes a rule to which there are exceptions or the subject matter is complicated, ambiguous, or confusing, the correct answer will require many words in order to be expressed clearly and accurately. In essence, you should not be deterred by answer choices that seem excessively long. Oftentimes, the author of the text will not be able to write the correct answer without

offering some qualifications and modifications. Your job is to read the answer choices thoroughly and completely and to select the one that most accurately and precisely answers the question.

13. Restating to Understand

Sometimes, a question on a multiple-choice test is difficult not because of what it asks but because of how it is written. If this is the case, restate the question or answer choice in different words. This process serves a couple of important purposes. First, it forces you to concentrate on the core of the question. In order to rephrase the question accurately, you have to understand it well. Rephrasing the question will concentrate your mind on the key words and ideas. Second, it will present the information to your mind in a fresh way. This process may trigger your memory and render some useful scrap of information picked up while studying.

14. True Statements

Sometimes an answer choice will be true in itself, but it does not answer the question. This is one of the main reasons why it is essential to read the question carefully and completely before proceeding to the answer choices. Too often, test takers skip ahead to the answer choices and look for true statements. Having found one of these, they are content to select it without reference to the question above. Obviously, this provides an easy way for test makers to play tricks. The savvy test taker will always read the entire question before turning to the answer choices. Then, having settled on a correct answer choice, he or she will refer to the original question and ensure that the selected answer is relevant. The mistake of choosing a correct-but-irrelevant answer choice is especially common on questions related to specific pieces of objective knowledge. A prepared test taker will have a wealth of factual knowledge at his or her disposal, and should not be careless in its application.

15. No Patterns

One of the more dangerous ideas that circulates about multiple-choice tests is that the correct answers tend to fall into patterns. These erroneous ideas range from a belief that B and C are the most common right answers, to the idea that an unprepared test-taker should answer "A-B-A-C-A-D-A-B-A." It cannot be emphasized enough that pattern-seeking of this type is exactly the WRONG way to approach a multiple-choice test. To begin with, it is highly unlikely that the test maker will plot the correct answers according to some predetermined pattern. The questions are scrambled and delivered in a random order. Furthermore, even if the test maker was following a pattern in the assignation of correct answers, there is no reason why the test taker would know which pattern he or she was using. Any attempt to discern a pattern in the answer choices is a waste of time and a distraction from the real work of taking the test. A test taker would be much better served by extra preparation before the test than by reliance on a pattern in the answers.

FREE DVD OFFER

Don't forget that doing well on your exam includes both understanding the test content and understanding how to use what you know to do well on the test. We offer a completely FREE Test Taking Tips DVD that covers world class test taking tips that you can use to be even more successful when you are taking your test.

All that we ask is that you email us your feedback about your study guide. To get your **FREE Test Taking Tips DVD**, email freedvd@studyguideteam.com with "FREE DVD" in the subject line and the following information in the body of the email:

- The title of your study guide.
- Your product rating on a scale of 1-5, with 5 being the highest rating.
- Your feedback about the study guide. What did you think of it?
- Your full name and shipping address to send your free DVD.

Introduction to the AP European History Exam

Function of the Test

The Advanced Placement (AP) European History Exam, created by the College Board, is an exam designed to offer college placement for high school students. The AP program allows students to earn college credit, advanced placement, or both, through the program's offering of the course and end-of-course exam. Universities may also look at AP scores to determine college admission. This guide gives an overview of the exam along with a condensed version of what might be taught in the AP European History course.

The AP program creates multiple versions of each AP exam to be administered within various U.S. geographic regions. With these exams, schools can offer late testing and discourage sharing questions across time zones. The AP exam is offered in the U.S. nationwide. Outside of Canada and the U.S., credits are only sometimes accepted in other countries. The College Board website has a list of universities outside of the U.S. that recognize AP for credit and admission.

In 2018, 101,740 students took the AP European History exam.

Test Administration

On their website, the College Board provides a schedule of exam dates for all of the AP exams. In 2020, the AP European History exam is given on Wednesday, May 6, at 12 p.m. Coordinators should notify students when and where to report.

Students may take the exam again if they are not pleased with their results. However, since the exam is given only once per year, students must wait until the following year to retake the exam. Both scores will be reported unless the student cancels or withholds one of the scores.

A wide range of accommodations are available to students with disabilities. Students should work with their school to request accommodations. If students or parents do not request accommodations through their school, disabilities must be appropriately documented, and accommodations requested in advance via the College Board website.

Test Format

The AP European History exam is three hours and fifteen minutes long and contains multiple-choice questions, short-answer questions, a document-based question, and a long essay. The multiple-choice section is made up of reading passages from primary and secondary-source historical documents and has fifty-five questions total. This section accounts for 40 percent of the exam and lasts fifty-five minutes. The short-answer section has three questions that the test taker must analyze and respond to. This section accounts for 20 percent of the score and lasts forty minutes. The free-response section has a document-based question and a long essay question. The document-based question accounts for 25 percent of the exam score and lasts sixty minutes which includes a fifteen minute reading period. The long essay is 15 percent of the exam score and lasts forty minutes.

The exam is divided into nine units (each with 10–15 percent exam weighting) which are listed below:

Unit	Chronological Period
Unit 1: Renaissance and Exploration	c. 1450 – c.1648
Unit 2: Age of Reformation	
Unit 3: Absolutism and Constitutionalism	c. 1648 – c. 1815
Unit 4: Scientific, Philosophical, and Political Developments	
Unit 5: Conflict, Crisis, and Reaction in the Late 18th Century	
Unit 6: Industrialization and Its Effects	c. 1815 – c. 1914
Unit 7: 19th-Century Global Conflicts	
Unit 8: 20th-Century Global Conflicts	c. 1914 – present
Unit 9: Cold War and Contemporary Europe	

Scoring

Scoring on the AP exam is similar to that of a college course. The table below shows an outline of scores and what they mean:

Score	Recommendation	College Grade
5	Extremely well qualified	A
4	Well qualified	A-, B+, B
3	Qualified	B-, C+, C
2	Possibly qualified	n/a
1	No recommendation	n/a

While multiple-choice questions are graded by a computer, the short-answer and free-response questions are graded by expert AP teachers. Scores on the free-response section are weighted and combined with the scores from the multiple-choice questions. The raw score from these two sections is converted into a 1–5 scale, as explained in the table above. Scores on the exam are not norm-referenced; students receive the score they earn regardless of how many other students earn that score.

Colleges are responsible for setting their own criteria for placement and admissions. However, most universities will give credit or allow advanced placement for a score of 3 or higher on the exam.

Period 1: 1450–1648

Renaissance and Exploration

Contextualizing Renaissance and Discovery

Rediscovery of Works from Ancient Greece and Rome

While most medieval scholars focused their studies on Latin translations of scholarly works, **Renaissance scholars** focused their studies on Greek translations of works written by Plato, Ptolemy, Archimedes, and pre-Socratic philosophers. These new translations undermined the authority of medieval scholarship, which had relied heavily on Latin translations of Aristotle and Galen. New debates over truth emerged as a result of this shift in scholarship. In particular, these debates focused on scientific truth, which challenged the classical philosophical translations of the Middle Ages. The result, in some instances, was an outright rejection of medieval philosophies, which launched Europe into a new era of Enlightenment that reinforced a broader Scientific Revolution in the early modern period.

Renaissance artists also promoted new ideas based on close observation and experimentation. Their artistic perspectives, in turn, influenced scientific inquiry. These artists challenged classical views of the cosmos, nature, and the human body by using observation to accurately depict the world around them. In their artwork, they tried to accurately imitate plants, animals, and humans, and they established new standards for depicting natural phenomena. Specifically, they changed the ways in which people understood perspective and accurate anatomical proportions. As a result, they created greater interest in scientific observation and human anatomy. Many Renaissances artists, such as Leonardo da Vinci and Albrecht Dürer, were also mathematicians and engineers. While traditional conceptions of knowledge and the universe persisted, especially in the Roman Catholic ecclesiastical hierarchy, new ideas in science based on observation, experimentation, and mathematics began slowly chipping away at these old belief systems.

Exploration of Overseas Territories

Spanish Sponsorship and European Interest in Transoceanic Travel

In 1492, **Queen Isabella I** of Castile and **King Ferdinand II** of Aragon completed the Reconquista, ending the Moorish occupation of Spain. That same year, these joint rulers of a newly unified Spain sponsored the Italian explorer **Christopher Columbus'** ambitious plans to reach Asia by traveling west across the Atlantic Ocean. King John II of Portugal had already rejected Columbus's offer, but Spain's joint rulers were desperate. Portugal had established a monopoly across the West African sea lanes, and the Spanish Crown hoped to find a faster route to the lucrative Chinese and Indian markets.

Columbus set sail on August 3, 1492, with three ships, and he arrived in the Caribbean on October 12, 1492. On this initial voyage, Columbus established a small settlement called **La Navidad** in present-day Haiti and explored the coastal waters surrounding present-day Cuba, Haiti, Hispaniola, and the Bahamas. Upon his return to Spain in 1493, Columbus was adamant that he had landed on islands off the Indian coast. Despite this mistaken belief, Columbus did alter world history by jump-starting a period of rapid European exploration in the Americas. Excitement was so high that Pope Alexander VI set a boundary for Spanish and Portuguese exploration halfway between the Portuguese-held Cape Verde islands and the Caribbean islands explored by Columbus. Spain and Portugal agreed and signed the resulting **Treaty of Tordesillas (1494)**, though it was mostly ignored by other European powers.

Immediately after Columbus returned to Spain, European powers rushed to explore the "New World" and continue seeking a western sea route to Asia. Columbus continued searching for a western passage to Asia, and on his third voyage in 1498, he was again wrongly convinced he had succeeded when he was near present-day Venezuela. In 1500, the Portuguese Crown sponsored a voyage that ultimately arrived in present-day Brazil. One year later, Portuguese explorers again failed to reach Asia and explored present-day Uruguay and Argentina instead. Spain finally succeeded in sailing west to Asia, but the voyage lasted significantly longer than was hoped (1519–1522). While sponsored by Spain, the Portuguese explorer **Ferdinand Magellan** passed through the Strait of Magellan to reach the Pacific Ocean. Magellan was killed during a battle in the Philippines, but his crew successfully completed the first-ever circumnavigation of the earth in 1522. In 1580, English privateer Sir Francis Drake completed the second circumnavigation of the world, and he accomplished the feat in a single three-year expedition. Additionally, Drake explored the western coast of the Americas and claimed present-day California for England.

Northern Atlantic Crossings

European powers repeatedly sought to reach Asia by traveling across the Northern Atlantic, commonly referred to as the **Northwest Passage**. At the time, Europeans didn't know seawater could freeze, so they assumed a northern route would be fastest. In 1497, England commissioned John Cabot to search for the Northwest Passage, and his expedition landed in present-day Newfoundland. Similarly, Portugal sponsored João Fernandes Lavrador's expedition north, and he made landfall in present-day Labrador in 1499. Between 1499 and 1502, Gaspar and Miguel Corte Real led several additional Portuguese expeditions, and they mostly explored the coastal areas surrounding Greenland and Newfoundland. France also sent several expeditions in search of a Northwest Passage, beginning with the sponsorship of Italian explorer Giovanni da Verrazzano in 1524. Ten years later, Jacques Cartier explored Newfoundland and the Saint Lawrence River to no avail. However, Cartier did found New France to capitalize on the area's potential for fishing, though his settlements didn't survive. Soon thereafter, France succeeded in establishing settlements near the present-day Grand Banks of New Foundland because it offers unparalleled opportunities for fishing. In the early seventeenth century, Samuel de Champlain continued searching for a Northwest Passage and ended up exploring the Great Lakes and founding Quebec, which thrived based on the lucrative fur trade.

Merchants also tried to find the potentially lucrative Northwest Passage. In 1608, the Dutch East India Company hired English explorer Henry Hudson to find the prized sea route. Hudson explored the waterways surrounding present-day New York City, sailing along the Hudson River. On a later expedition, Hudson sailed through the Hudson Strait and explored Hudson Bay. Although Hudson didn't find the Northwest Passage, his discoveries led to the Dutch settlements in present-day New York. Hudson Bay also proved to be a profitable area for the fur trade, and the English granted a royal charter to the Hudson's Bay Company in 1670 to compete with French Canadian fur trappers.

The mass transfer of Africans and Europeans to the Americas created an unprecedented mixing of cultures and people. Early European colonists benefited enormously from contact with **Amerindians**, the indigenous people of the Americas. For example, if not for Amerindians' agricultural assistance, the Jamestown settlement likely would have collapsed almost immediately, like England's earlier settlement attempts at Roanoke. Amerindian culture placed heavy emphasis on the natural world, and Europeans settling frontier areas, especially French and British fur traders, adopted some of this lifestyle. Amerindian culture also changed through the adoption of horses and guns. Horses facilitated more nomadic lifestyles, and when combined with guns, hunting practices became far more efficient.

Commercial and Agricultural Capitalism

The European socioeconomic order revolved around agriculture from 1200 to 1450 due to the prevalence of **feudalism**. The powerful landed class of feudal nobles typically organized their land under the **manorial system**. The vast majority of European nobles served as the Lord of the Manor, and their extensive landholdings were known as **fiefs**. Peasants who lived on the fief were allowed to farm the land, but they were obligated to pay the Lord of the Manor taxes either in the form of free labor or percentage of crops. Furthermore, the Lord of the Manor held all political power, and even more importantly, created and oversaw the legal system that applied to the fief. Nobles' legal and economic dominance over the peasants is why they held such power under feudalism. Although trade and urban centers generally increased from 1200 to 1450, Europe was still an overwhelmingly agriculture society due to the number and size of fiefs across the continent.

Political Centralization

From 1450 to 1750, state power revolved around absolute monarchs who wielded absolute power. Oftentimes, **absolute monarchies** legitimized their right to supreme authority by divine right. For example, King Louis XIV claimed a divine right to rule based on God's mandate, meaning he rejected any earthly power attempting to restrict or overthrow his rule. The primary effect of centralized state power was the elimination of feudalism. Absolute monarchs replaced feudal lords with large centralized bureaucracies and militaries under their hierarchical control. The consolidation of political and economic power facilitated colonization because absolute monarchs had the military strength and financial resources to sponsor expeditions. Additionally, absolute monarchies contributed to the growth of international trade because they were able to fund navies that could protect merchants and establish trading posts.

The centralization of power and growth of empires was met with local social, political, and economic resistance. Aristocracies strongly resisted the **centralization of political power**. Under feudalism, aristocrats wielded near-absolute control over the peasantry and could defy the central government based on their disproportionate military and financial resources. As such, feudal aristocrats enjoyed tremendous political power, lucrative economic rights, and elevated social status. This changed under absolute monarchs who replaced aristocrats with a centralized system of advisers, bureaucrats, and militaries. Aristocrats regularly attempted to undermine or overthrow monarchies, but they were largely unsuccessful. Instead, aristocrats generally positioned themselves as advisers to the royal court and invested in colonial expeditions. Peasants mostly resisted absolute monarchies by protesting and rioting, especially during food shortages. They also advocated for political rights, though it was met with limited success; the notable exception was the British Parliament. Colonies resisted the expansion of empires by revolting against their colonizers, but European colonizers retained absolute power over the overwhelming majority of their overseas colonies during this period.

Italian Renaissance

Revival of Classical Texts in the Italian Renaissance

Francesco Petrarch (1304–1374) was a scholar and poet during the **Italian Renaissance**. Associated with the founding of **humanism**, Petrarch believed that man was the center of his own universe and that society should embrace human advancement and creations. Petrarch's teachings were in stark contrast to the Catholic Church's teachings. He lobbied heavily for the return of classic Greek and Roman teachings and secular law, encouraging a move away from religious teachings that restricted human growth and development. Petrarch also revived the letters of Cicero, who was a Roman statesman, philosopher, writer, and orator during the final years of the Roman Republic. Petrarch is famous for his sonnets and his lyric poetry. He is thought to be the first to develop the concept of the "Dark Ages."

Lorenzo Valla, a rhetorician, educator, priest, and humanist, contributed to the revival of Latin study through his book *Elegantiae linguae Latinae* written in 1471. This book, which was used to educate Italian youth, emphasized Valla's strong belief in Roman ideals. Valla also provided textual analysis that the Donation of Constantine was a forgery, proving the Roman Catholic Church had committed fraud in the eighth century. Valla's stark criticisms gave cover to writers and thinkers who wanted to challenge the Catholic Church's influence and reach.

Marsilio Ficino was a Catholic priest and Italian scholar who founded the Platonic Academy, one of the most influential institutions of the Renaissance. The **Platonic Academy** taught and funded writers and thinkers who sought to expand on the teachings of Plato. Ficino translated Plato's works into Latin, thereby spreading Plato's ideas into the mainstream of Europe. This led to a rebirth of Platonic ideals throughout Europe. One of Ficino's students at the Platonic Academy, Pico della Mirandola, also made great strides in promoting Plato's teachings, eventually writing the *Oration on the Dignity of Man.*

Baldassare Castiglione, an Italian diplomat, Renaissance author, and courtier, wrote the *Book of the Courtier*, which taught etiquette in Renaissance Italy. This book provided insight into the idea of a well-rounded man: deeply knowledgeable of Greek and Roman teachings, a warrior, and also musically and artistically talented. This ideal blended new teachings with the old warrior mentality of the Middle Ages. This book also outlined which medieval habits were now unacceptable, such as eating with the hands and spitting.

The Florentine writer **Niccolò Machiavelli** wrote *The Prince*, a political treatise written as a guide to ruling and examining former prominent rulers. Machiavelli's conclusions on the correct forms of government and who should rule were based on a thought process devoid of religious morality or ideals. Machiavelli's writings stated that a successful leader would be able to justify a successful ending with any means possible.

Political, Intellectual, and Cultural Effects of the Italian Renaissance

Humanist teachings during the Italian Renaissance stressed the importance of human free will and contribution to society, called "virtú." Teachings from Plato were popular, with a strong emphasis placed on living a life of reason and having a nature for happiness. By the end of the 1400s, most of the classic Roman and Greek writings had been translated and distributed, becoming a bedrock of knowledge for humanist thinkers of the time. The new teachings valued a liberal arts education of grammar, poetry, philosophy, and history. Humanists also taught the importance of serving in government or being active in civic affairs, called "civic humanism." An adequate education was thought to be one that prepared young people to be political leaders, and humanist thinkers often served in government.

Renaissance educators taught the importance of civic duty and contribution to society, leading to an increased sense of duty and creation of a stronger political entity. Latin made a comeback as a language by the end of the 1400s, and Italian states began to resemble that of the early Roman Empire. While Italy became increasingly more secular, this by no means meant that the government became nonreligious. Rather, Italian thinkers promoted that God valued human beings above all else, particularly their free will to choose. This new style of individualism brought about vast changes in Italian culture.

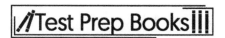

New Styles of Painting and Architecture

Funding artists was a characteristic of wealthy families as well as the Catholic Church. Churches regularly commissioned religious paintings and sculptures. Florence's influence in **patronage**, financial aid given to artists from the wealthy, led to an artistic boom that continued throughout the Renaissance. Following the decline of Florence in the early 1500s, Pope Alexander increased patronage in Rome by funding artwork. Artists such as Michelangelo, Raphael, and Bramante did projects for the Catholic Church, making the organization instrumental in the art scene during this period.

New artistic styles paved the way for great advancement of art during this era. The technique of **perspective artwork**, which rendered three-dimensional effects on a two-dimensional surface, grew in popularity. The illusion of depth with light and shadow, called **chiaroscuro**, provided a new realism to artwork. Additionally, more attention was given to the face than in other periods, focusing on individuality and emotion. In Rome, the world of art was just as influential but centered around the papacy instead. The "Renaissance Popes," Alexander VI, Julius II, and Leo X, were generous patrons of the arts.

Sculpture in the Renaissance also evolved. Drawing on Greek and Roman influence, Italian sculptures were free-standing and designed to be seen by all. They drew inspiration from humanism, with sculptures displaying nude bodies with more realism and individuality. Architecture also began to resemble Roman and Greek design. The Renaissance embraced architectural geometry and balance with the use of arches, domes, and columns to reflect classical antiquity. In Florence, **Filippo Brunelleschi** designed the Florence Cathedral's dome, the largest dome in Europe at the time. **Lorenzo Ghiberti**, another Florentine Italian artist, crafted the famous bronze doors for the Florence Baptistery. **Donatello**, an Italian sculptor, was one of the first Renaissance artists to sculpt a nude likeness of a male, a bronze sculpture of David. **Raphael**, an Italian painter, made many paintings for the Vatican and used his artwork to pay tribute to great philosophers such as Plato and Aristotle.

Leonardo da Vinci, a Renaissance painter, inventor, sculptor, mathematician, engineer, writer, and scientist, painted the *Mona Lisa*, an iconic and still-popular painting today. Additionally, his *Last Supper* was created around this time. **Michelangelo,** an Italian sculptor, architect, painter, and poet, painted the ceiling of the Sistine Chapel, still regarded as a marvel of the world.

Other styles of art arose in response to the new Renaissance artwork. **Mannerist art** started in response to these new styles of Renaissance artwork and became popular among more traditionalist painters. The Renaissance style of balance and simplicity was contrasted to Mannerism's rebellion against the more classical form. Mannerist works were often odd in shape and asymmetrical, with exaggerated features. The most famous of these artists is **El Greco**, a Greek artist living in Spain, who used unnatural figures and elongated drawings and shapes in his work.

Northern Renaissance

Human-Centered Naturalism

Ideas and advancements from the Italian Renaissance began to spread into Northern Europe, albeit much later than the Italian Renaissance. The Italian Renaissance lasted from the late 1300s through roughly 1550. The **Northern Renaissance** began to gain traction around 1650. Humanist teachings in particular became more widely known as more people gained access to Italian writing and translations. Human-centered naturalism flourished during the Northern Renaissance, which built upon humanism, and encouraged the idea that human beings and everyday life were appropriate figures for artistic expression, focusing on raw emotion and unique mannerisms.

The German humanist **Rudolf Agricola** studied in Italy and returned with a breadth of humanist teachings to spread to the rest of Germany. His teachings inspired the work of a poet named Conrad Celtis and a knight named Ulrich von Hutten. Celtis and Hutten led a humanist revolution in Germany that blended Agricola's teachings with that of an increasing tinge of nationalism.

The military conquests that extended into Italy brought humanism back to France. **Guillaume Bude**, a French thinker and humanist, as well as **Jacques Lefevre**, a French biblical scholar, brought humanist thought to the forefront of French life. Lefevre in particular was very aggressive in teaching humanism to young French students, leading to many publications of his work and inspiring future thinkers such as Martin Luther and John Calvin. These men played significant roles in the coming Reformation period.

Thomas More, an English philosopher, lawyer, and author, was a very influential humanist of the time. More served in high office, reaching Lord Chancellor in King Henry VIII's government. He wrote the influential book *Utopia* published in 1516, which described a seemingly perfect society. This perfect society, he argued, could not be achieved because of disputes over rights to land. For those problems to truly be solved, More believed, people must be willing to sacrifice individual gains for the common good.

Arguably the most famous influence during this time period, however, was the English writer, poet, and playwright, **William Shakespeare**. Shakespeare dominated the English Renaissance, with most of his works remaining famous today. His work drew from Greek and Roman culture, as well as using themes of humanism and individualism. His tragedies include *Romeo and Juliet*, *Hamlet*, *Othello*, and *Macbeth*. His other plays include *The Taming of the Shrew*, *A Midsummer Night's Dream*, *Much Ado About Nothing*, and *As You Like It*.

Spain reacted differently from its English and French counterparts. While humanism seemed to be weakening religious influence in other countries, humanist teachings actually helped to strengthen the Catholic Church in Spain. Queen Isabella even appointed a "Grand Inquisitor," a humanist thinker named **Francisco Jimenez de Cisneros**. Cisneros pushed for reforming the Catholic Church for a multitude of abuses.

Christian Humanism

The **Christian humanist movement** used early writings of Christianity to try to improve society and the Catholic Church. While still drawing influence from Greek and Roman teachings, the Christian humanists used religious ideals to shape their thinking and interpretations of societal standards. They used very early Greek and Hebrew texts of the Bible to set new guidelines for Christian behavior, and they placed an emphasis on education. These new teachings contained stark criticisms of the Catholic Church.

Perhaps the most famous of these Christian humanists was **Erasmus**, who sought to revolutionize the Catholic Church. He was a master of Greek, and he used Greek teachings to support his criticism of the Church. He retranslated the New Testament into Greek and Latin. Erasmus also wrote *In Praise of Folly*, which was the second-highest selling book for its time, after the bible. This work heavily criticized the Catholic Church and pushed for religious reforms.

Printing

Literacy rates exponentially increased after **Johannes Gutenberg** invented the printing press in 1439, and writers similarly benefited from royal patronage. **Miguel de Cervantes** received the patronage of Spanish royalty and religious elites, such as the Count of Lemos and Cardinal Archbishop of Toledo. This patronage resulted in the publication of Cervantes' *Don Quixote* in two parts during the early

seventeenth century, and it is widely considered to be the first modern novel. Daily and weekly newspapers similarly became much more common during the seventeenth and eighteenth centuries throughout Europe.

Technological innovations during the seventeenth and eighteenth centuries also fostered widespread interest in scientific inquiry. The mass production of the telescope and compound microscope both occurred during the early seventeenth century. Other inventions during this period included the slide rule, mechanical calculator, barometer, vacuum pump, pendulum clock, alcohol thermometer, and commercial steam engine. Like the developments in the visual and performing arts, inventors benefited from patronage and the overall economic boom. Patronage allowed inventors to concentrate on their experiments without worrying about making a living. The economic boom increased the amount of investment capital available to inventors, and it created a popular market for their inventions.

New Monarchies

Development of Political Institutions

From 1450 to 1750, monarchies consolidated political and economic control, which transformed the role of existing political and economic elites called **aristocrats**. Prior to this period, European nobles had enjoyed significant economic and military power under the feudal system. Feudalism was a political system where the aristocratic lords provided military support and tax revenue to the monarchy. As such, the aristocracy could better override the monarchy by withholding resources. When European monarchies centralized control over the military and economy, it undermined aristocrats' economic and political influence. Although aristocrats generally retained their hereditary titles and land, they were no longer kingmakers. In addition, aristocrats' political and economic power was challenged by the rise of powerful merchants. For example, English merchants in the House of Commons held more than twice as much wealth as the noblemen in the House of Lords during the seventeenth and eighteenth centuries.

European rulers created complex bureaucracies to consolidate political power at the expense of the aristocracy. Under the prior feudal system, aristocratic lords collected taxes and supplied troops to the ruler. This meant rulers depended on the aristocracy to exercise political power and conduct warfare. As such, centralizing political power through the development of a bureaucracy helped rulers bypass the aristocracy. Rather than relying on the cooperation of aristocratic lords, the bureaucracy allowed rulers to directly and independently pursue policy goals, such as raising revenue through tax collection. Likewise, the professionalization of militaries allowed rulers to exert power over the aristocracy. For example, the Russian tsars deployed their professional military to seize territory historically controlled by aristocratic Boyars. In addition, professionalization increased military effectiveness due to advantages in training and experience. For example, the Ottoman Empire was able to rapidly expand by developing a professional standing army before its rivals, including the Safavid Empire and European powers.

Religious Ideas, Art, and Monumental Architecture

Rulers often legitimized their power through the incorporation of religious ideas, art, and architecture. Religious ideas were commonly used to justify why the ruler deserved to lead an autocratic monarchy. Louis XIV of France explicitly proclaimed a divine right to rule. Other rulers sought a close association with a popular religion. Habsburg rulers in Spain, Portugal, and the Holy Roman Empire governed predominantly Catholic populations, so they all forged close ties with the pope. Some Protestant rulers also obtained a leadership role in the state's official religion. For example, the English Parliament passed the Supremacy Act of 1534 to name King Henry VIII as the Church of England's top religious authority.

Safavid and Ottoman emperors similarly characterized themselves as defenders of the Muslim world in order to rally support for imperial pursuits.

Art and architecture served as symbols of the rulers' power. Ottoman rulers commissioned miniature paintings to glorify imperial conquests. For example, after the Ottoman Empire captured Constantinople in 1453, a series of miniature paintings depicted Ottoman troops as righteous conquerors. Some of those paintings also compared the emperor to Alexander the Great and other famous historic figures. Architecture of this period was monumental, and it served to express the rulers' absolute power. Mughal rulers built the Taj Mahal, an elaborate mausoleum, for the royal family. Royal palaces also increased in size during this period. For example, Louis XIV oversaw the construction of the extravagant Palace of Versailles.

Generating Revenue

In order to fund territorial expansion, some rulers collected tribute and engaged in tax farming. Tribute collection most often occurred when a ruler enjoyed an advantage over some other country or community. For example, the Manchu Empire was able to collect tribute from European merchants because if the merchants refused, the Manchu Empire had the capacity to bar Europeans from trading with China. European tribute helped generate revenue for the Manchu Empire's expansion into Tibet and Xinjiang. Tribute collection was also used in the Americas, especially by the Spanish. Tribute from Amerindians is a major reason why the Spanish were able to extend their territories in the Americas from present-day California to Argentina. Under the *repartimiento* and *encomienda* labor systems, the Spanish Crown forced Amerindian tribes to pay tribute in the form of precious metals, agricultural products, and/or labor. If the Amerindians refused, the Spanish military would invade the tribe and seize all of the resources.

Tax farming involved using a private third party to collect tax payments. Compared to forming and operating a bureaucracy, tax farming was much more efficient. However, the delegation of state power to private parties increased the risk of corruption and abusive practices. As such, rulers often used tax farming to collect revenue from distant territories and colonies. For example, the Ottoman Empire's *iltizām* system granted the right to collect taxes based on a public auction. Private actors placed bids on the percentage of taxes they would keep. European rulers used a similar system to collect revenue from their colonies in the Americas. Noblemen and joint-stock companies were often granted rights to territory under the condition that a portion of the revenue would be sent back to the ruler.

The expanding role of joint-stock companies in interregional trade caused an explosion in merchants' profits, particularly due to the transfer of cash crops from the Americas to Europe. Consequently, governments' tax revenues increased, and some of that money went to funding more visual and performing arts. In general, the performances began as private entertainment for the royal members, but they were later brought to playhouses where the public could attend. The relationship between the famous playwright William Shakespeare and Queen Elizabeth I of England illustrates this trend.

At the end of the sixteenth century, an English nobleman named Henry Carey served as the Lord Chamberlain, and he was responsible for the English Crown's entertainment. Carey's patronage led to the founding of a play company called the Lord Chamberlain's Men, and William Shakespeare worked as the company's principal playwright. Shakespeare's famous plays, such as *Hamlet* and *Macbeth,* were performed before the royal family, and the plays' success fueled the rise of Elizabethan theater. Drama became a field of study in grammar schools, choir schools, and universities, which all featured public performances. Court patronage also provided funding for playhouses, cementing plays as a popular form of visual entertainment for public audiences.

Gender and Family Restructuring

Urbanization, interregional trade, and slavery notably transformed gender dynamics and family relations. The economic opportunity in cities delayed marriages as compared to traditional rural settings where people generally married upon reaching puberty. Similarly, urban families generally had fewer children. While rural families benefited from their children's labor, children placed more of a burden on urban families.

Interregional trade reduced the amount of power held by Southeast Asian women. Women historically played an important role in Southeast Asian commerce. When merchants wanted to access the local market, they often entered into temporary marriages with these women who, consequently, enjoyed extensive business connections. European merchants initially continued this practice and relied on women to access the local markets. However, European trading posts eventually grew powerful enough to conduct business independently.

Slavery caused a dramatic demographic shake-up across Africa. From 1525 to 1866, the transatlantic slave trade and Indian Ocean slave trade combined to remove an estimated 18 million people from the African continent. As a result, Africa experienced a significant labor shortage that stalled the region's economic development. Furthermore, the majority of slaves were men, which created a gender imbalance. African women filled the familial and societal vacuum, assuming traditional male roles in agriculture, hunting, and fishing.

Technological Advances and the Age of Exploration

European Technological Developments and Innovation

European countries capitalized on the discovery of previous advancements made by the Classical, Islamic, and Asian civilizations. Classical philosophers' scientific and mathematic advancements shaped how European explorers viewed the world in quantitative terms. Latin translations of the Greek philosopher Ptolemy were especially influential during this period. So, rather than understanding the world based on qualitative descriptions of people, culture, and geographic features, Europeans began plotting and navigating locations through mathematical grids. Consequently, European explorers greatly improved at cartography. Prior to this period, European maps had often placed Jerusalem at the center and organized the world based on biblical connections. In contrast, European explorers produced maps that accurately reflected locations' distance and relative position.

Similarly, Spanish and Portuguese adopted the Islamic astrolabe, an astronomical measuring tool. Islamic civilization had adopted the Greek astrolabe for religious purposes, such as locating the direction of Mecca, and European explorers applied the astrolabe to navigation. The astrolabe assisted in navigation because it calculated altitude based on the angle of the sun or North Star. The Portuguese version of the astrolabe was known as the mariner's astrolabe, and nearly all European explorers used it. Another tool that facilitated navigation was the magnetic compass, which displays cardinal direction. The magnetic compass was invented during the Han Dynasty (202 BCE–220 CE), and it was first used for navigation during the Song Dynasty (960–1279 CE). The magnetic compass was widely adopted in Islamic and European civilizations at the end of the twelfth century. The combination of maps and navigational tools exponentially increased European explorers' efficiency and accuracy.

Production of Tools, Innovations in Ship Designs, and an Understanding of Wind and Current Patterns

European explorers used their improved understanding of science and mathematics to create new tools, such as the traverse board, which calculated speed in knots. The traverse board calculated speed over four-hour increments, and sailors organized the data in logbooks to determine the ship's dead reckoning, ensuring that the ship was on the correct course.

European ship innovations also borrowed from earlier civilizations. Most famously, the Portuguese caravel used the triangular lateen sail, which was originally used by Chinese, Arab, and Phoenician sailors dating back to the fourth century. The lateen sail increased maneuverability and allowed ships to travel at greater speeds and sail into the wind. Portuguese explorers sailed caravels around the West African coast, and Christopher Columbus sailed a fleet of caravels to the Caribbean. The Spanish galleon was another popular ship developed during this period, and it used a lateen sail in combination with several rectangular sails. This extra sailing power was needed to support the Spanish galleon's enhanced size, including multiple decks. Compared to the caravel, the Spanish galleon was better able to carry heavy cargo. Spain later placed cannons on these ships, marking a significant leap in naval power.

A stronger understanding of winds and sea currents also facilitated transoceanic trade and travel. Winds were particularly important because they powered the sails. European explorers learned about the monsoon winds from Indian and Chinese sailors. During the summer, the monsoon winds blow toward India, meaning ships could travel from the Pacific Ocean to the Indian Ocean nearly twice as fast if they timed their journey correctly. When the monsoon winds reversed direction in the fall, the explorers could similarly travel at above average speeds around Africa on their way back to Western Europe. Similarly, Portuguese explorers discovered the *volta do mar*—trade winds, such as the North Atlantic Gyre and North Pacific Gyre, that could expedite oceanic travel. If not for this discovery, it likely would have been impossible for Western European countries to compete in global maritime trade. European explorers also began following oceanic currents to increase speed and ease of travel. Traveling with currents was important because they allowed trips to stay on course even if the winds didn't fully cooperate.

European Exploration and Expansion

From the fifteenth through the eighteenth century, interregional trade increased through existing trade routes. The Ottoman Empire and Safavid Empire revived the Silk Roads, reconnecting East Asia and Europe. Additionally, the Ottoman Empire consolidated power over the Mediterranean sea lanes, and the Mughal Empire facilitated trade along the Indian Ocean sea lanes. However, interregional trade was transformed after Portugal began sailing from the Atlantic Ocean to the Indian Ocean around Africa. While maritime trade between Europe and Asia increased, overland trade through the trans-Saharan caravan network declined as European powers established a stranglehold on West African trade.

European exploration applied preexisting and innovative technologies to make unprecedented achievements in transoceanic maritime reconnaissance. In 1488, Portuguese explorers first sailed around the African coast, proving for the first time in world history that the Atlantic Ocean connected to the Indian Ocean. Four years later, Columbus arrived in the Caribbean, opening up unprecedented opportunities for exploration across two continents. Within a couple of decades, European explorers had charted nearly all of North America's and South America's eastern coasts, culminating in the circumnavigation of the entire world during a Spanish expedition organized by Ferdinand Magellan. Although European explorers never discovered a lucrative Northwest Passage, the flurry of expeditions laid the foundation for settlements across the Americas.

Portuguese Development of Maritime Technology and Navigation

During the first half of the fifteenth century, Spain and Portugal were waging a holy war against the Ottoman Empire. So, the Portuguese initially explored West Africa to find a way to undercut the trans-Saharan caravan network, which was controlled by the Ottoman's North African Muslim allies (Moors). The Portuguese were able to explore this region before their European rivals due to their invention of the caravel and application of the astrolabe to navigation. However, the exploration began slowly. At the time, Europeans did not know whether it was possible to reach India by sailing around Africa, and many sailors believed in myths about evils lurking in the South Atlantic off the African coast. Prince Henry the Navigator spearheaded the initial Portuguese expeditions into West Africa, but progress was slow. In 1471, the Portuguese reached present-day Ghana and discovered a flourishing trade of gold and slaves. Seven years later, Portuguese and Spanish ships fought off the coast of present-day Ghana, marking the first European war over colonial expansion. Portugal won the naval battle and claimed possession over the West African coastal waters. Portuguese exploration of West Africa was completed in 1488 when Bartolomeu Dias sailed around the Cape of Good Hope, proving that the Atlantic Ocean connected with the Indian Ocean.

To solidify its early advantage over European rivals, Portugal built trading posts in the coastal areas it explored. The trading posts were heavily fortified, providing protection to merchants and local allies. Since they were located in coastal areas, they also benefited from naval support. Along with serving as centers of trade, these outposts also warehoused goods and provided navigational support to Portuguese explorers. In effect, trading posts served as minicolonies. Prince Henry established the first trading post in 1445, and by the end of the sixteenth century, there were approximately fifty similar fortifications in West Africa, East Africa, India, China, and South America. The Casa da India in Lisbon oversaw Portugal's burgeoning economic empire, including all of the trading posts. Portugal also occasionally granted control over their trading posts to royally chartered companies. The Netherlands, Spain, and England later copied the Portuguese model of heavily fortified trading posts.

Religion as a Stimulation for Exploration

Belief systems were at the forefront of the cultural diffusion that occurred through interregional contact. As belief systems interacted with each other, syncretism often occurred. **Syncretism** is the merging of different belief systems, resulting in changes to one of the belief systems or the creation of a new belief system. Less orthodox Christian denominations, such as Nestorian and Arian Christianity, merged with local religious beliefs and practices. On the Indian subcontinent, syncretism between Buddhism and Hinduism merged the doctrines closer together. Similar to Christianity, Buddhist doctrine was altered after spreading into new regions, especially in China.

Early Christians were a persecuted religious minority in the Roman Empire, and they struggled to gain new followers. Therefore, Christianity heavily emphasized proselytism to convert more followers and gain widespread acceptance. Following the Roman Empire's conversion to Christianity, Christian proselytizing began to spread as increasing numbers of missionaries traveled on the Silk Road and ventured deeper into Roman territories. When preaching to local populations that were entirely unfamiliar with Christianity, missionaries often discussed Christianity in the context of local religion and culture. This merging of Christianity and local religion naturally led to the development of novel belief systems.

Nestorian Christianity differed from Nicene Christianity, the form of Christianity that was ultimately adopted by the Roman Empire as the state religion. Like Arians, Nestorian Christians did not believe in the Holy Trinity—the notion that God, Jesus, and the Holy Spirit were all coequal and indivisibly divine.

Nestorian Christians primarily believed that Jesus Christ had both human and divine elements. Due to their rejection of religious orthodoxy, Nestorian Christian missionaries' flexibility facilitated their success in converting new followers on the Silk Road and beyond. Specifically, Central Asians understood Nestorian Christianity as a form of shamanism and Jesus Christ as a shaman with the most powerful connection to higher powers. Thus, Central Asians altered Nestorian Christianity through the adoption of more rituals and superstitious beliefs. For example, many Central Asian Christians believed the cross was a powerful relic that could be used to fight evil spirits. Similar to the merging of Christianity and shamanism in Central Asia, Christianity merged with religious practices in China. For example, Chinese Christian artists often combined traditional Christian symbolism with the yin and yang.

Similar syncretism between Christianity and local religion occurred during the conversion of the Germanic and Celtic tribes. Rather than adopting Nicene Christianity's orthodox doctrine, many of these tribes adopted Arianism, including the influential Goths and Vandals. Like Nestorian Christianity, **Arian Christianity** was more flexible when it came to religious doctrine. However, some syncretism occurred even when Germanic tribes adopted the more orthodox doctrine of Nicene Christianity. For example, the King of the Franks, Clovis I, famously converted to Roman Catholicism, and he claimed to fight wars against the pagan and Arian Germanic tribes. However, Clovis I believed that Jesus Christ provided him with the military strength required to subjugate his enemies—a belief very similar to Germanic pagan beliefs. Despite the mass conversion of Germanic tribes to Christianity, syncretism frustrated attempts at spreading orthodox Christian beliefs. Consequently, Christian missionaries began cutting down sacred trees that continued to be revered by Germanic tribes even after their conversion. Following the collapse of the Western Roman Empire, disputes over the true meaning of Christianity continued across Europe for centuries due to the uneven merging of paganism, Arianism, and Catholicism.

Scope and Influence of Empires

Imperial expansion between 1450 and 1750 impacted and was impacted by the diversity of the conquered populations. The Ottoman Empire's expansion into Eastern Europe resulted in mass conversions to **Islam**, and Ottoman merchants contributed to the spread of Islam into Central and Southeastern Asia. Similarly, European colonization in the Americas converted millions of Amerindians and Africans to Christianity. Trade with European powers provided African states with guns that facilitated imperial expansion, which increased the states' diversity. European powers forcefully transferred millions of Africans to the Americas in the transatlantic slave trade. The arrival of African slaves led to the development of the racial Casta system, and African slaves' agricultural knowledge supported the transfer of African crops to the Americas, including bananas, okra, coffee, rice, and kola nuts. Amerindian and African coerced labor sustained the Columbian Exchange, which supported population growth across Afro-Eurasian due to improved nutritional content and crop diversity. African slaves shaped how Christianity developed in the Americas, leading to the creation of new syncretic belief systems like **Haitian Vodou** and **Louisiana Voodoo**.

Increased trade naturally resulted in more cultural exchange as people accompanied merchants along trade routes and settled in foreign lands. Intensive cultural exchanges resulted from immigrants sharing their ways of life with native populations, and this phenomenon was particularly evident in agricultural practices. However, increased interregional contact and cultural exchange also spread diseases. Along with the spread of people, technology, and disease, interregional contact also led to the cross-pollination of belief systems. The resulting syncretism altered the regional practice of several world religions, such as Christianity, Hinduism, and Buddhism.

Rivals on the World Stage

From 1450 to 1750, European powers began sponsoring maritime expeditions to find the **Northwest Passage**—an alternative route to Chinese and Indian markets through the North Atlantic Ocean. Although European monarchies were almost always involved in the organizing and funding of expeditions, they sometimes granted royal charters to wealthy merchants to secure additional investment. These private-public partnerships helped mitigate the expeditions' risks and costs. After Spain sponsored the Italian explorer **Christopher Columbus**'s expedition to the Caribbean in 1492, Spain, Portugal, England, France, the Netherlands, and Sweden began to aggressively sponsor expeditions to find a Northwest Passage to Asia. Although the sponsored expeditions never found a Northwest Passage, they directly resulted in European colonization of the Americas. Similarly, Portugal's sponsorship of **Vasco da Gama** facilitated his discovery of a passage to Asia around the Cape of Good Hope, and European states began sponsoring more expeditions to Asia. By the late sixteenth century, Spain, Portugal, and the Netherlands had established themselves as dominant maritime powers in the Indian Ocean and Pacific Ocean.

European powers raced to establish maritime empires in the Americas to exploit the continents' rich resources. The Portuguese established a new maritime empire in present-day Brazil during the first half of the sixteenth century. Initially, the Portuguese privatized colonization, and the territory was divided into fifteen separate colonies. Portuguese noblemen funded and controlled these colonies, but they failed for a variety of reasons, including agricultural issues, conflicts with Amerindians, and disputes among the noblemen. To save the floundering enterprise, King John III placed Brazil under royal control in 1542. The newly formed central government consolidated its control by conquering the Amerindians and thwarting French attempts at colonizing northern Brazil. In addition, the government converted much of the land into sugarcane plantations, and the intense labor demands led to the importation of African slaves. In the early seventeenth century, the Dutch attempted to seize control over sugarcane production in northwestern Brazil. However, Portuguese forces expelled the Dutch in 1654, leaving Portugal as the uncontested power in Brazil.

The Spanish maritime empire was unprecedented, and it included a substantial amount of territory in the present-day United States, Mexico, Central America, the Caribbean, and South America. In order to construct this empire, Spain had to conquer several advanced Amerindian civilizations. The Spanish conquistador **Hernán Cortés** launched a campaign against the Aztec Empire in present-day Mexico. Cortés made a strategic alliance with the Tlaxcala city-state, a historic rival of the Aztecs, and the Aztec Empire collapsed in 1521. Another conquistador, **Francisco Pizarro**, conquered the Inca Empire in 1533. As a result, Spain assumed control over territory in present-day Peru, Bolivia, Argentina, Chile, and Colombia. Other Spanish conquistadors defeated the Muisca Confederation in present-day Colombia as well as numerous Mayan city-states in Central America. Spain divided its massive territories into viceroys, which functioned as provincial administrative states. Along with defending the territories, the viceroys were primarily tasked with mining gold and silver.

The Netherlands relied on the Dutch West India Company to construct its maritime empire. After sponsoring Henry Hudson's voyage to North America, the company established permanent colonies on the Eastern Seaboard of the present-day United States. These colonies were known as **New Netherlands**, and they primarily focused on fur trapping. However, the Dutch had difficulty populating their North American colonies. The most successful colony was New Amsterdam, which was located in present-day New York City. Following their defeat in the Third Anglo-Dutch War, the Dutch ceded New Netherlands to England in 1674. The Dutch also competed with France, England, and Spain in the

Caribbean, and they established several successful sugarcane plantations on a series of islands known as the **Dutch Antilles**.

The French maritime empire stretched from present-day Canada to the Caribbean. France founded numerous settlements in present-day Eastern Canada and Upper Midwestern United States. Those settlements centered on fishing and fur trapping opportunities. French explorers also explored the Mississippi River, and successful settlements were established in St. Louis, Baton Rouge, and New Orleans. However, like the Dutch, the French had difficulty populating their North American territory. France's most successful colony was **Saint-Domingue** in present-day Haiti. Saint-Domingue's sugarcane plantations outperformed the rest of the Caribbean, but it came at a deadly cost. African slaves' mortality rate on Saint-Domingue was the highest of any European colony in the Americas.

The British maritime empire included thirteen colonies in the present-day United States and numerous settlements in the Caribbean. England's thirteen colonies had incredible economic variation, ranging from shipbuilding in the New England colonies to plantation economies in the Southern colonies. Despite experiencing some initial setbacks, England was markedly successful at attracting European immigrants to the thirteen colonies. For example, in 1750, ten times more Europeans lived in England's thirteen colonies than in all of France's North American colonies. Along with a more favorable climate and geographic position, England was able to attract immigrants by offering extensive rights to self-government. Aside from the thirteen colonies, England established more than a dozen major settlements in the Caribbean between 1623 and 1750. England sent more African slaves to work on Caribbean sugarcane plantations than any other European power.

Colonial Expansion and Columbian Exchange

Connections Between Eastern and Western Hemispheres

Increased contact between Europe and the Americas naturally led to the **Columbian Exchange**, which involved the transfer of diseases, cash crops, food crops, animals, and agricultural techniques between the Eastern and Western hemispheres. Amerindians lacked immunity to Western Hemisphere diseases, resulting in the decimation of Amerindian populations. After seizing control over the Amerindians' land, Europeans built massive plantations to grow cash crops, such as tobacco and sugarcane. African slaves, Amerindian captives, and European indentured servants provided the necessary labor for plantations, and these sources of coerced labor further increased cash crops' profitability. The reliance on cash crops incentivized the adoption of unsustainable agricultural practices that led to widespread deforestation and soil depletion. Aside from cash crops, Europeans cultivated Afro-Eurasian fruit trees, grains, and domesticated animals in their American colonies. Some American foods, such as maize, potatoes, sweet potatoes, and tomatoes, were also transported to Afro-Eurasia. These foods supported explosive global population growth due to their nutritional value and high caloric density.

European Colonization of the Americas

European colonization devastated Amerindian populations, primarily due to the spread of new diseases into the Eastern Hemisphere. Diseases such as smallpox, malaria, measles, and influenza were endemic in Eurasia for centuries, but they were relatively unknown in the Americas. These diseases, which were far more common in Eurasia compared to the Americas, were often spread through domesticated animals. Repeated epidemics had ravaged Eurasia due to the prevalence of interregional trade and travel. For example, in the second century, the Antonine Plague traveled along the Eurasian Silk Road, devastating both the Roman Empire and the Han Dynasty. Similarly, in the fourteenth century, the Black Death Plague killed an estimated 100 million people across Eurasia. So, the European colonizers had

some immunity to these diseases, while the Amerindians had none. This proved catastrophic. Eastern Hemisphere diseases killed somewhere between 80 and 95 percent of the Amerindians within two centuries of Columbus's first landing in the Caribbean.

The spread of Eastern Hemisphere diseases in the Americas was accelerated by the unintentional transfer of disease vectors. Brown rats traveled to the Americas on ships, and they carried a number of pathogens and parasites. European colonizers also introduced *Aedes aegypti* mosquitoes to the Americas. Unlike native mosquito populations, *Aedes aegypti* mosquitoes are the perfect disease vector because they prefer human blood, and they spread lethal diseases, such as yellow fever and malaria, across the Americas.

Slave Trade

From the latter half of the sixteenth century to the early nineteenth century, European powers transferred goods, labor, resources, and wealth through the Atlantic system, which connected Europe, West Africa, and the Americas. The Atlantic system is also referred to as the **Triangular Trade** or **Transatlantic Slave Trade**.

Bullion, food crops, sugar, and tobacco were extracted from American colonies and sent to Europe. These resources fueled European domestic industries, which produced guns, manufactured goods, rum, and textiles that were sent to African trading posts and American colonies. African trading posts primarily supplied American colonies with the slave labor that was necessary for large-scale resource extraction. Europe also provided a significant amount of free and unfree labor to the Americas. Wealthier Europeans immigrated as farmers and merchants, but the majority of Europeans arrived through indentured servitude. In exchange for transportation to the Americas, indentured servants entered into coercive labor contracts, meaning they received little to no pay for a designated period of time.

Interracial marriage occurred between Europeans and Amerindians. This was occasionally done for political reasons, such as the marriage between John Rolfe and Pocahontas, but it was also a way for Amerindians to escape the brutality of European colonization. While Europeans were mostly unsuccessful at forcing North American native populations into labor, the Spanish instituted the *encomienda* and *repartimiento* labor systems. Since mixed race people were excluded from these systems, many native tribes sought to intermarry with the colonizers. Intermixing of Amerindians and escaped African slaves was common in frontier regions, while marriages between Europeans and African slaves was rare due to legal prohibitions, especially in North America. However, the Caribbean had a large populations of **creoles**, which refers to people of mixed European, African, and Amerindian descent.

The Atlantic system carried more than 10 million African slaves to the Americas, representing one of the largest diasporas in human history. Portuguese and African slave traders originally developed a "pidgin" language during trade negotiations, and African slaves adopted this crude form of communication as they traveled the dreaded "Middle Passage" between West Africa and the Americas. After slaves began arriving in colonies en masse, the **pidgin language** was influenced by African, European, and Amerindian dialects, resulting in a creole language that was unique to each colony. Music also merged in the Americas. Amerindians' and African slaves' rhythmic music, featuring chants, drums, rattles, and bells, combined with European instruments, such as trumpets and horns. A similar syncretism also appeared in religious practices. Europeans generally attempted to convert natives and African slaves to Christianity, but Christian practices also merged with traditional African and Amerindian religions to create a wide range of voodoo religion. Different variants of this voodoo syncretism appeared in the Caribbean, Brazil, and Louisiana.

Commercial Revolution

Global Circulation of Goods

In order to capitalize on the flourishing interregional trade of the sixteenth and seventeenth centuries, European rulers adopted mercantilist economic policies and issued royal charters to joint-stock companies. The charters provided the companies with a monopoly on a specific market or designated stretch of land, and in exchange, the companies shared their profits with the European rulers. Rulers then poured their share of the profits into funding powerful militaries and sponsoring expeditions to find new lands to conquer and colonize. As a result, there was a marked increase in European contact with American, Asian, and African civilizations. To more efficiently extract goods and resources from these colonies, merchants created new transoceanic shipping services. This led to the development of the Atlantic system, which combined preexisting commercial relationships between Africa and Europe with American colonization. Spain imported massive amounts of silver through the Atlantic system, and much of that silver was used to purchase Asian goods. As such, silver functioned as global currency throughout this period.

European merchants' role in Asian trade was limited due to the Ming Dynasty, which exercised hegemonic control throughout the region. The Ming Dynasty's government was highly complex, far surpassing its regional competitors as well as the Europeans. In addition, the Ming Dynasty fielded a powerful and modernized military, and the Chinese economy was one of the world's largest in terms of gross domestic product. As a result of their parity with European powers, the Ming Dynasty was able to set the terms for trade, and European merchants had no choice but to obey if they wanted access to the lucrative Asian markets. Consequently, European merchants mostly served as middlemen who transported goods between Asian markets and the Indian Ocean region.

Of the European powers, Spain and Portugal forged the deepest ties with Asian markets. In 1535, Portugal established a commercial port in Macau (southwestern China), but unlike other Portuguese trading posts, the Ming Dynasty forced the Portuguese to pay a substantial rent. After the Portuguese assisted the Ming Dynasty in squashing a piracy threat, they were allowed to create a permanent trading post in 1557. Still, the Ming Dynasty constructed a Barrier Gate to regulate Portuguese access and trade with the rest of its territory. Portuguese merchants purchased valuable Chinese goods, such as silk and porcelain, with gold and silver and then transported the Chinese goods to their trading posts in Nagasaki (Japan) and Malacca (Malaysia). Chinese goods were especially valuable in Nagasaki due to the Chinese embargo on Japan, which was handed down over issues with Japanese piracy. From Malacca, Portuguese traders sailed to their Indian trading posts where they primarily traded Chinese silk for Indian textiles. Most Portuguese merchants stopped at the trading post located in Goa (southwestern India), which was responsible for managing all Portuguese imports and exports to India, and then sailed back to Portugal around the Cape of Good Hope.

From 1565 until 1815, Spain operated a regular trading route between its Mexican colonies and trading post in Manilla (Philippines). Spanish merchants exported silver, tobacco, chocolate, and food crops from Mexico to Manila, and they used the silver to purchase Chinese goods in Macau. To avoid stopping at Portuguese trading posts, Spanish merchants typically transported Asian goods across the Pacific Ocean trading route. In the case of Chinese luxury items that were destined for Spain, the goods were then transported overland from Acapulco to Veracruz in order to reach the Atlantic Ocean.

Peasant and Artisan Labor

Demand for peasant labor increased from the fifteenth to the eighteenth century. The **Black Death** killed approximately one-hundred million people in Eurasia during the fourteenth century. As the global population rapidly increased in the century that followed, so did the demands on food supplies. As such, the demand for peasant agricultural labor increased to keep pace with the growing population. At the start of the sixteenth century, approximately 85 percent of the European population worked as peasant farmers. The vast majority of European and Chinese peasants lived on small farms owned by noblemen or wealthy families. In exchange for a plot on the farm, the peasants paid landlords rent either in the form of money or a portion of their crops. Most peasants had a subsistence livelihood, meaning they lived off only what they produced on the land. As such, famines and droughts caused by the Little Ice Age often resulted in disproportionate harm to peasants.

The demand for artisan labor also intensified in this period due to population growth and urbanization. Most artisans worked in urban environments, providing goods and services for European and Chinese cities' booming populations. The artisans were also responsible for turning raw materials extracted from American colonies into manufactured products. As such, artisans played a critical role in supporting European mercantilist policies, which prioritized importing raw goods and exporting manufactured products. Some artisans worked as members of a guild, while others worked independently as entrepreneurs. The level of skill varied wildly, with some artisans working with luxury items and others producing basic manufactured goods, such as textiles. Demand for artisan labor is reflected in the growing percentage of the urban population that worked as artisans which, in some European cities, exceeded 75 percent. This increased demand caused specialization within the artisanal craft economy. As artisanal work became more complex, artisans began working as subcontractors, and master craftsmen hired these specialized subcontractors to complete a single portion of a larger project.

Age of Reformation

Contextualizing Sixteenth and Seventeenth Century Challenges and Developments

Governments faced a variety of challenges when attempting to consolidate political power and expand their territories. The Safavid and Ottoman empires competed over trade routes and territory in Anatolia, Mesopotamia, and the Balkans. European powers faced stiff competitions for trade routes in the Indian Ocean, and they were forced to deal with the threat of piracy in the Caribbean. Religious rivalries in the Holy Roman Empire led to the **Thirty Years' War**, which destabilized nearly all of Europe. Peasant uprisings and food riots also threatened to undermine the legitimacy of European rulers.

Omani–European Rivalry in the Indian Ocean

European powers had a complex rivalry with Omani merchants as they competed for control of the Indian Ocean. The conflict began when Portugal achieved a decisive victory over the Mamluk Sultanate at the Battle of Diu in 1509. As a result, the Portuguese navy controlled the Indian Ocean's most valuable ports, and it was further supported by fortified trading posts in East Africa, the Arabian Peninsula, and India. In addition, Portugal controlled Muscat, the center of trade for Omani merchants. Muscat was particularly important due to its proximity to the western coast of India. In 1650, an influential Omani Imam raised a small army of Muslim troops, and they defeated the Portuguese forces at Muscat. Following this success, Omani merchants provided material and strategic support to East African towns under Portuguese control. This heavily contributed to Portugal's decline as the leading power in the Indian Ocean. Consequently, the Dutch, French, and English increased their presence in the Indian Ocean, but they similarly faced pushback from Omani merchants. Along with controlling Muscat,

Omani merchants and Mughal rulers were both Muslim, and this shared faith strengthened their economic ties. European powers navigated these issues by signing a series of treaties with Omani merchants. For example, England's peace treaty with the Omani merchants increased their access to Indian markets, which later resulted in England consolidating control over the Indian subcontinent in the nineteenth century.

Piracy in the Caribbean

Colonization of the Caribbean created opportunities for pirates to intercept ships heading toward European markets. Pirates primarily targeted Spanish vessels because they were the most likely to carry gold and silver. In response, Spain started using treasure fleets to better protect its precious cargo. The treasure fleet traveled in a convoy alongside Spanish warships. Rather than risking a direct attack, pirates usually trailed the treasure fleet in the hopes of picking off a ship that fell behind the rest. Piracy dramatically increased in the 1650s as the Netherlands, England, and France aggressively competed with Spain over territory in the Caribbean. All three countries issued letters of marque to privateers, which essentially provided state sanction for piracy. **Letters of marque** gave privateers legal permission to attack enemy ships, and the profits were split between the privateers and the government. Private businesses also financed **buccaneers**—pirates operating solely in the Caribbean—due to piracy's high profit margins. Several pirate ports developed in the Caribbean, such as the Port of Tortuga in present-day Haiti. Piracy declined in the 1730s as European powers expanded the size of their navies and permanently stationed warships in the Caribbean. England's Royal Navy was especially effective at establishing law and order in the Caribbean during the eighteenth century.

Thirty Years' War

The **Thirty Years' War** (1618–1648) was one of the bloodiest wars in global history, with approximately five million people dying as a result of the conflict. The conflict began when the Holy Roman Emperor Ferdinand II attempted to forcefully convert his kingdom to Catholicism. Protestant communities in present-day Austria and the Czech Republic refused to convert, declared independence, and formed the Protestant Union. Like the twentieth-century world wars, each side of the conflict was supported by an alliance system. Spain and Hungary allied with the Holy Roman emperor. All three countries were predominantly Catholic, and they were all ruled by members of the House of Habsburg. The Protestant Union benefited from a broad anti-Habsburg alliance, which included Sweden, England, Denmark-Norway, Brandenburg-Prussia, Russia, the Ottoman Empire, and the Netherlands. Most of the fighting occurred in Central Europe, which regularly suffered from civilian massacres and mass looting. The Thirty Years' War ended with a series of treaties referred to as the **Peace of Westphalia**. Ferdinand II lost a considerable amount of power, including the right to enforce a state religion on his territories. Under the Peace of Westphalia, local lords of the Holy Roman Empire could officially sanction a religion in their lands, but they were barred from persecuting other Christian denominations.

Ottoman–Safavid Conflict

The Ottoman and Safavid empires engaged in a series of military conflicts and trade disputes from the early sixteenth century to the eighteenth century. The Ottoman Empire practiced Sunni Muslim, and they were the dominant power on the Anatolian Peninsula in present-day Turkey, with extensive territorial holdings throughout the Mediterranean region. The Safavid Empire championed Shi'a Muslim, and they controlled territory in present-day Iran. The two empires competed over access to the Eurasian Silk Roads, and they fought over territory in Mesopotamia and the Balkans, particularly in the present-day countries of Armenia, Azerbaijan, and Georgia. These economic and geopolitical tensions grew the divide between Sunni and Shi'a Islam because both empires used religion to rally popular support. Overall, the two empires fought more than a dozen major wars against one another, with the most

decisive result occurring in the **Ottoman-Safavid War of 1623–1629**. The Treaty of Zuhab ended the war, and the Ottoman Empire emerged fully in control of the entire Anatolian Peninsula and Mesopotamia, including the valuable city of Baghdad. This represented a major victory for the Ottomans because it contained the Safavid Empire to its territory in present-day Iran and parts of the Eastern Balkan states. Although the Treaty of Zuhab didn't establish permanent peace between the empires, the territorial borders were essentially permanent.

Food Riots

Food riots increased in intensity during the fifteenth and sixteenth centuries. The **Little Ice Age** caused the Northern Hemisphere's climate to become slightly drier and colder, which increased the risk of crop failures. Consequently, peasants regularly experienced food shortages. Tensions often reached a boiling point when the government raised food prices, hoarded harvests, and/or failed to properly store the surplus from previous harvests. Food riots were a spontaneous reaction to famine, but they also functioned as a collective bargaining tool. Since food riots threatened to undermine the government's authority over a large percentage of the population, they were generally successful in obtaining concessions. As a result, food riots constituted the most common form of protest. For example, there were hundreds of separate food riots in France between 1690 and 1710. Food riots were also common in the Americas, particularly when European governments exported a harvest during times of shortage. During the early eighteenth century, the working poor in Boston erupted in protest when merchants hoarded and exported grain to England, causing widespread bread shortages and price hikes. The Boston Bread Riot applied immense pressure on the colonial and royal government. To cool tensions, the governments passed policies that lowered prices of bread, limited grain exportations, and created a public granary.

Luther and the Protestant Reformation

Martin Luther's publication of his *Ninety-Five Theses* in 1517 prompted the **Protestant Reformation**, and it resulted in the creation of multiple Christian denominations that competed with the Roman Catholic Church. Protestants favored the literal interpretation of the Bible, opposed the Catholic Church's self-declared authority as expressed through the pope, and repudiated the church's practice of selling indulgences to shorten Christians' time in purgatory. Protestant movements were active throughout Europe during the sixteenth and seventeenth centuries. Sometimes the conflict between these emergent Protestant movements and Catholic power structures led to violence, such as the Thirty Years' War that ravaged Central Europe (1618–1648). In addition, some rulers sought to increase their political power by adopting Protestantism and declaring independence from the Catholic Church. For example, **King Henry VIII** of England issued the Act of Supremacy in 1534 to establish himself as the Church of England's leader and highest religious authority.

Protestant countries often pursued exploration and colonization for religious freedom. In particular, the Netherlands and England rejected Portuguese and Spanish claims to all newly discovered lands under the **Treaty of Tordesillas**. Pope Alexander VI had originally organized the Treaty of Tordesillas to promote Catholicism abroad and prevent conflict between the major Catholic trading powers. To counter these claims, the Netherlands and England built strong navies and subsidized powerful trading companies in order to gain a foothold in Asia and Africa. Compared to Catholicism, Protestants sent fewer missionaries abroad; however, proselytizing was still common. The Netherlands, England, and Sweden also established colonies in North America, which further contributed to the spread of Christianity outside of Europe.

Wars of Religion

French Wars of Religion

In France, **Calvinism** was gaining popularity among the French nobility. **King Francis I** made efforts to stop the spread of Protestantism throughout his reign in the 1540s, but his failure only exacerbated tensions. His heir, King Henry II, suffered a tragic accident and died in 1559. After King Henry II's death, his wife, **Catherine de Medici**, wanted the throne to remain in the family for one of her three sons and wanted the kingdom to continue to be Catholic under her Valois family. Opposing her and her family, a section of Protestant nobles laid claim to the throne through **Henry de Bourbon**, an heir of a former ruling family, and wished for the Huguenots to be free to practice in France. Another contender was Henry I, Duke of Guise, from the Guise family, a staunchly Catholic family that was supported by Philip II of Spain and the Pope. Philip II and the papacy saw Catherine de Medici's family as weak and wanted to stop the spread of Protestantism.

Over the next decade there was immense fighting amongst the two religious sects, as well as numerous attempts at peace by Catherine and her sons. However, many of these attempts failed. Finally, in 1572, Henry de Bourbon attempted to ease tension by agreeing to marry one of Catherine's daughters, a sign of peace between the Huguenots and the Medici family. However, the marriage created rumors that Protestants were attempting to take over the government. In response, a slaughter of Protestant nobles ensued, and nearly 10,000 French Protestants were killed in what became known as the **St. Bartholomew's Day Massacre**.

Habsburg Rulers Attempt to Restore Catholic Unity

Charles V, a Habsburg ruler, Holy Roman Emperor, and Archduke of Austria, sought to stop Protestantism by making an alliance with Pope Leo X to try and return Europe to Catholicism. While seeking to undermine the Lutheran spread in Germany, Charles was instead drawn into fighting with Turkey and France in separate wars. In 1531, Lutheran princes in Germany formed the **League of Schmalkalden**, an alliance of Lutherans that sought to protect northern Germany from the threat of Charles V.

In a sign of the politicization of the region, Francis I of France allied himself with the League, despite his Catholic faith. The League, particularly due to its allegiance with France, did not last long before fighting erupted with Charles V's forces. What resulted was a division of German faiths. While Charles V finally defeated the League in 1547, **Lutheranism** had spread across Central Europe, forcing him to abandon his fight to restore Catholicism in Germany. The **Peace of Augsburg**, signed in 1555, allowed the free practice of both Protestantism and Catholicism. This cemented religious division in Germany.

Exploitation of Religious Conflicts

Germany saw changes in the early 1500s, as the spread of Lutheranism added pressure to the Catholic Church. Many Northern German states made the change to Lutheranism, with German princes breaking from the Catholic Church and claiming land for themselves. Neighboring Denmark and Sweden adopted Lutheranism as well. Southern Germany, by contrast, remained heavily Catholic. **King Philip II of Spain** followed his father, Charles V, in efforts to stop the spread of Protestantism, this time in the Netherlands. However, in response to taxation demands and religious pressure, William I, Prince of Orange, led a revolt. After nearly two decades of fighting, the Spanish surrendered the Netherlands, giving the region independence and marking the beginning of the decline of Spanish hegemony.

Edict of Nantes

In 1588, a brutal civil war called the **War of the Three Henries** erupted in France, beginning after Henry Guise, with support from Spain, took the city of Paris. To combat this threat, Henry III, son of Catherine de Medici, made an alliance with Henry de Bourbon, with the promise to name him the next heir to the throne. The two Henries—Henry III and Henry de Bourbon—invited Guise to the palace only to assassinate him. This angered many in France. An unruly monk assassinated Henry III in 1589, leaving Henry de Bourbon, or King Henry IV, to rule France.

King Henry IV's rule came with its own challenges, however. In his attempt to return to Paris, his path was blocked by Spanish troops who were still there to support the assassinated Henry Guise. The next few years brought more war, and King Henry IV finally converted to Catholicism to bring peace back to France. He then issued the **Edict of Nantes**, an order that allowed Huguenots to freely practice in France. He was one of the most beloved rulers in French history, establishing a strong and lasting dynasty.

Peace of Westphalia

The **Thirty Years' War** began in part due to lasting effects of Charles V's efforts in Germany, as well as the continuation of the struggle between Protestant and Catholic believers in Germany and throughout Europe. In the early 1600s, certain Protestant groups were ready to be free of Catholic rule under the Holy Roman Empire. The rebellion began in 1618, when Bohemian rebels threw two Catholic officials from a castle window, in what became known as the **Third Defenestration of Prague**. In the ensuing war, the Holy Roman Emperor, Ferdinand II, destroyed the Bohemian uprising, and the Bohemians converted to Catholicism.

The fighting was not over, however; Denmark joined the fray against Austria. General Albert Wallenstein of Austria was tasked with turning back the Danish forces. He destroyed the opposing armies, leaving Austria victorious in the region. As soon as peace was declared, however, Sweden joined the fight, and another long war was waged between Swedish and German forces against the Austrian army, with Austria again prevailing. France joined the war in 1635, hoping to defeat the weakened Catholic forces. With France's entry into the war, each side was now eager to find a compromise and end the long and costly wars. The **Peace of Westphalia** was a series of peace treaties that ended fighting among European nations and set the standard for future peace treaties among nations. The treaty also ended the **Eighty Years' War**, fought between Spain and the Dutch Republic.

Catholic Reformation

In response to the Protestant Reformation's growing threat to its global influence, the Catholic Church launched the **Counter-Reformation** to introduce reforms, roll back Protestant gains, and spread Catholicism to new regions. As such, Catholic countries leveraged their influence as major trading powers to support a new Catholic religious order called the Society of Jesus, and Jesuit missionaries traveled across Africa, Asia, and the Americas to convert local populations to Catholicism. For example, Saint Francis Xavier traveled along Portuguese trading routes in Asia, conducting baptisms in India, Japan, Borneo, and China. The desire to spread Catholicism also motivated France, Spain, and Portugal to explore and colonize the Americas. Although Europeans' colonization decimated Amerindian populations, Catholic missionaries believed they were actually saving Amerindians from eternal damnation through conversion and baptism. Furthermore, colonization served to enrich Catholic countries, enabling them to more strongly oppose the Protestant threat in Europe and beyond.

Sixteenth Century Society and Politics

With European economic expansion, as well as the ensuing Reformation and wars, life changed in Europe. Still, new systems maintained some of the existing structures. Hierarchies still existed in their traditional form, with the wealthy, land-owning nobility holding a higher place in society. These nobles, while sometimes facing tax problems from monarchies, were mostly left to control their regions and those living on their land. Religion also played a large role, as the Catholic, Lutheran, and Calvinist communities based their hierarchies on social standing in the Church.

Women's Roles
Households saw changes as well, with women contributing to household income by being milliners, dyers, washerwomen, embroiderers, or food preparers. In the Protestant faith, women were granted more rights and protections, such as the right to divorce and remarry. Women were also encouraged to read the vernacular Bible and have their own relationship with God. Still, women were mostly left out of political and economic issues, with men making decisions in state-level governing and in the home. Some women, such as Angela Merici and Teresa de Avila, were allowed to teach and spread the faith in the Catholic Church. However, women's roles continued to be debated throughout the centuries.

Regulating Public Morals
With the power of religious institutions waxing and waning throughout this period, some European countries, such as Protestant France, began to regulate morality for the general public. New secular laws were imposed to regulate private life. Bans on certain types of dancing and singing were widespread, as were strict codes outlawing prostitution and begging. Additionally, activities like the carnival were curtailed, with pageantry and eroticism of the festivals being removed. Some communal styles of leisure were kept and even merged with religious activities. When not banned, the carnival was made into a church-style pageant for the community to enjoy. Saint's day festivals and celebrations were common, with many cities uniting around religious holidays for community entertainment. Blood sports like bull-riding and cockfighting became status symbols and had a lengthy lists of participants eager to garner praise and admiration.

Rituals of Public Humiliation
At this time, criminal punishment by government involved public humiliation. These rituals, called **charivari**, were designed to discourage immoral behavior through fear of humiliation in front of peers. Stocks, devices of wood with three holes for arms and a person's head displayed in a crowded town square, gained popularity, as well as public whipping and branding, all to police public behavior.

Art of the Sixteenth Century: Mannerism and Baroque Art

Changes in Artistic Expression
As the Catholic Church sought to redefine its image in the wake of the Counter-Reformation, it turned to the world of art to aid in the reclamation of its former status as the dominant social and cultural leader in Europe. **Baroque art** became more popular, aided by support from the papacy and Jesuits as a way to retain their societal status. Baroque art emphasized emotion and grandiosity, especially in relation to the power and image of monarchs and the Catholic Church.

Gian Bernini, a famous Baroque architect, created many works that defined the Baroque structure and style. His "Colonnade" in front of St. Peter's Basilica in Rome, as well as St. Peter's Baldachin, is still regarded as some of the most incredible artwork in the world. Throughout Rome, Bernini left an impact

that carried over long after the end of the Reformation. His art kept alive the style and majesty of the Catholic Church.

Baroque painting also strived to elicit an emotional response. It used light, shade, and imagery to show holy and reverent symbols of hope. The artwork was dramatic, with heavy emphasis placed on emotion rather than detail of realism. **Peter Paul Rubens**, a Flemish painter working in Brussels, emphasized this style of painting. Rubens used many different colors and contrasts in his works. His figures were animated and larger than life. His paintings mostly featured Roman gods, saints, and angels.

El Greco, a Greek artist who worked in Spain, also used this style. El Greco used **Mannerism**, a style of painting that grew in popularity during this time. Mannerism used unnatural and less realistic faces, shapes, and colors to seek a more emotional response. His *Burial of Count Orgaz* and *Toledo* paintings are still renowned for their impact in Spain, both featuring odd figures and unnatural colors.

Another famous artist of the time was the Baroque painter **Artemisia Gentileschi**. Gentileschi became the first female artist to gain prestige and recognition following the Reformation. She painted female religious symbols and goddesses, using the Baroque style to portray the figures as majestic and mighty. Her "Judith" paintings are still held as some of the most important religious paintings in the world.

Practice Questions

1. Which of the following was NOT a factor in the changing of the European societal structure during the beginning of the Renaissance?
   a. The effects of the plague
   b. The rise of the Catholic Church
   c. Fighting amongst religious sects
   d. Increased war throughout the sixteenth century

2. Which of the following countries was NOT unified during the Renaissance period?
   a. France
   b. England
   c. Spain
   d. Italy

Questions 3–5 refer to the passage below.

> At last, the Supreme Maker decreed that this creature, to whom He could give nothing wholly his own, should have a share in the particular endowment of every other creature. Taking man, therefore, this creature of indeterminate image, He set him in the middle of the world and thus spoke to him:
>
> We have given you, O Adam, no visage proper to yourself, nor endowment properly your own, in order that whatever place, whatever form, whatever gifts you may, with premeditation, select, these same you may have and possess through your own judgement and decision. The nature of all other creatures is defined and restricted within laws which We have laid down; you, by contrast, impeded by no such restrictions, may, by your own free will, to whose custody We have assigned you, trace for yourself the lineaments of your own nature. I have placed you at the very center of the world, so that from that vantage point you may with greater ease glance round about you on all that the world contains. We have made you a creature neither of heaven nor of earth, neither mortal nor immortal, in order that you may, as the free and proud shaper of your own being, fashion yourself in the form you may prefer. It will be in your power to descend to the lower, brutish forms of life; you will be able, through your own decision, to rise again to the superior orders whose life is divine.

Excerpt from Oration on the Dignity of Man by Pico della Mirandola, 1486

3. Based on the passage, Mirandola is a proponent of what philosophy?
   a. Individualism
   b. Humanism
   c. Realism
   d. Reformation

4. Who was instrumental in the spread of humanist teachings?
   a. Francesco Petrarch
   b. Cosimo de' Medici
   c. Johannes Gutenberg
   d. Pope Alexander VI

5. According to the passage, what gift did the Supreme Maker bestow on man?
    a. The custody of all other creatures
    b. The laws of nature as guidelines to follow
    c. The ability to choose what type of life to lead
    d. The endowment of a clear visage

6. Which event was NOT a result of the Commercial Revolution?
    a. Newfound state wealth and colonial growth
    b. A "price revolution" that increased the price of goods throughout Europe
    c. Rural areas that grew faster than cities as farms exploded in size
    d. The growing middle class found new wealth opportunities

7. Throughout the Reformation, many works criticized the Catholic Church and its teachings. Which of the following was NOT one of those works?
    a. Calvin's *Institutes of the Christian Religion*
    b. Luther's *Ninety-Five Theses*
    c. Erasmus' *In Praise of Folly*
    d. More's *Utopia*

Questions 8–10 refer to the passage below.

> 31. The man who actually buys indulgences is as rare as he who is really penitent; indeed, he is exceedingly rare.
>
> 32. Those who believe that they can be certain of their salvation because they have indulgence letters will be eternally damned, together with their teachers.
>
> 33. Men must especially be on guard against those who say that the pope's pardons are that inestimable gift of God by which man is reconciled to him.
>
> 34. For the graces of indulgences are concerned only with the penalties of sacramental satisfaction established by man.
>
> 35. They who teach that contrition is not necessary on the part of those who intend to buy souls out of purgatory or to buy confessional privileges preach unchristian doctrine.
>
> 36. Any truly repentant Christian has a right to full remission of penalty and guilt, even without indulgence letters.
>
> 37. Any true Christian, whether living or dead, participates in all the blessings of Christ and the church; and this is granted him by God, even without indulgence letters.
>
> Excerpt from <u>Ninety-Five Theses</u> by Martin Luther, 1517

8. Which practice discussed in the excerpt above was one of Luther's major criticisms of the Church?
    a. Salvation through good works
    b. Sale of indulgences
    c. The interpretation of the sacraments
    d. Belief in predestination

9. What was the Catholic Church's response to Martin Luther's *Ninety-Five Theses*?
   a. Luther was executed.
   b. Luther was arrested.
   c. Luther was kidnapped.
   d. Luther was excommunicated.

10. In which country in the mid-1500s would a person likely have to choose between Lutheranism, which was based on Luther's teachings, and Catholicism for religious practice?
    a. Germany
    b. France
    c. Spain
    d. England

11. Which of the following tactics did the Catholic Church NOT use during the Counter-Reformation?
    a. Jesuit-led Inquisitions to restore order to Protestant areas of Europe
    b. A new list of forbidden books established to keep people from reading Protestant works
    c. A council established to work toward a peaceful resolution with the Protestants
    d. Church emphasis on obtaining salvation through "good works" and faith

12. By the end of the Reformation period, women had obtained what right in most Protestant communities?
    a. The right to vote in elections
    b. The right to buy and sell land
    c. The right to divorce and remarry
    d. The right to serve in the military

13. Which country in the Peace of Westphalia lost control over the Netherlands?
    a. Spain
    b. England
    c. Switzerland
    d. Netherlands

Short Answer Question

1. Use the passage below to answer all parts of the question that follows.

> Feudalism, if systematized, would seem an admirably articulated system, extending upward from the petty nobles to the king or even the emperor. The little castellans would do homage to the barons, they to the viscounts, they to the counts, they to the dukes, and they to the supreme suzerain, His Grace Philip Augustus, at Paris. Actually, of course, nothing of the kind occurs. Not merely do many fief holders have several suzerains (as does Conon) and serve some of them very poorly, but there is no real gradation of feudal titles. Conon, a baron, feels himself equal to many counts and superior to most viscounts. The mighty Count of Champagne holds his head arrogantly as the equal of the Duke of Burgundy. Of late years, especially since Philip Augustus began to reign (1180), the kings of France have made it clear that they are the mightiest of the mighty and deserve genuine obedience. Yet even now many seigneurs grumble, "These lords of Paris are only the Capetian dukes who began to call themselves kings some two hundred years ago. Let them wax not too proud or we will send them about their business as our forefathers sent the old Carolingians." In short, the whole feudal arrangement is utterly confused.

Excerpt from Life on a Mediaeval Barony by William Stearns Davis, 1922

a) Explain ONE way in which monarchies undermined feudalism.

b) Provide ONE piece of historical evidence related to the political decentralization caused by feudalism.

c) Provide ONE piece of historical evidence related to how the development of state power enriched Europe.

Answer Explanations

1. B: The rise of the Catholic Church (Choice *B*) was not a change in the societal structure because it was already established. As the medieval period ended in Europe and the Renaissance began, deep and systemic changes happened in Europe. The plague wiped out nearly half of the European population (Choice *A*), changing work and home life. Fighting occurred amongst Protestants and Catholics in many European countries (Choice *C*). Due to these religious differences, war ravaged the area (Choice *D*).

2. D: During the Renaissance, Italy remained separated into city-states without any unifying rule. In France and England, the monarchy took power and began to seize control from nobles. In Spain, two powerful kingdoms were united to create a strong new monarchy to rule.

3. B: Humanism changed the intellectual landscape in Europe. Instead of relying on God, humanist thinking enabled people to become the center of their own spiritual life. Humanists, such as Mirandola, felt that free will and human achievements were important.

4. A: Petrarch's writings and teachings supported the idea of free will and that achievements and contributions to society were to be valued. Medici (Choice *B*) was a member of the wealthy ruling family of Florence that used bribes and wealth to maintain control of the city. Gutenberg's (Choice *C*) invention of the printing press aided in the spread of humanist thought, but he was not a notable humanist. Pope Alexander IV (Choice *D*) was also not a humanist, as the Catholic Church was criticized by many humanists.

5. C: The passage states that Adam can be the shaper of his own being. This allows him to choose what type of life to lead, so Choice *C* is correct. Choices *A* and *B* are incorrect because the other creatures of nature are described as being defined and restricted within laws but that those laws do not apply to Adam nor are enforced by Adam. Adam is described as having an indeterminate image; therefore, Choice *D* is incorrect.

6. C: The Commercial Revolution brought new wealth and tax power to many states. This, in turn, led to colonial growth and expansion of new European empires. Back home in Europe, a "price revolution" increased prices and gave farmers and merchants new wealth. The middle class, made up of these farmers and merchants, grew quickly as wealth opportunities expanded with new money and trade. Rural areas, however, saw decline, as cities expanded due to trade and the decline in need for large farms with colonial trading.

7. D: Calvin's book (Choice *A*) showed the scandal in the Church and highlighted where his new ideas on religion differed from the Catholic teachings. Martin Luther's *Ninety-Five Theses* (Choice *B*) criticized the Catholic Church and its teachings and practices. Erasmus (Choice *C*) paved the way for Luther with his work, detailing the Catholic Church's inconsistencies. More, however, wrote about what a true king should possess to rule a powerful government, making Choice *D* the correct answer.

8. B: The practice discussed in the excerpt that Luther did not agree with was the sale of indulgences to pay for the absolution of sin, Choice *B*. Luther also disagree with the Catholic Church on the idea of salvation through good works and the interpretation of certain sacraments, but these are not discussed in the excerpt, so Choices *A* and *C* are both incorrect. Choice *D* is a tenet of Calvinism and was not a critique of Luther's against the Catholic Church.

9. D: Pope Leo X excommunicated Luther in 1520. He was consequently put on trial and declared an outlaw and enemy of the church but was kidnapped by Fredrick III of Germany before he could be arrested or executed. Fredrick III kidnapped Luther to allow him to be able to continue his writings.

10. A: Conflict between Lutheranism and Catholicism was rife in Germany. This was not the case in France, where Lutherans were few. Instead, France had Calvinist Huguenots. In Spain, Catholicism ruled. And in England, Lutherans had almost no hold, although there were Puritans.

11. C: The Catholic Church made many efforts to curb the spread of the Protestant faith. The Jesuits led inquisitions in both Spain and Italy, seeking to oppress Jews and Protestants in the area (Choice *A*). Additionally, a banned book list tried to keep anyone from reading Protestant works (Choice *B*). The Church also reiterated that salvation was achieved through good works and faith, in contrast to the Protestant teachings (Choice *D*). However, no council was ever established to work with the Protestants.

12. C: By the end of the Reformation, women had a larger role in society. Still, the right to vote in most elections was not given (Choice *A*). Land was also still owned by men (Choice *B*), with most women barred from owning any. Military service was also still restricted, with women expected to be homebound (Choice *D*). However, Protestant communities did finally grant women the right to divorce and remarry.

13. A: The Thirty Years' War was a long and bloody conflict that marked the end of the Reformation period and the beginning of a new age in Europe. In the treaty that ended the fighting, the Netherlands and Switzerland (Choices *C* and *D*) won independence from foreign rule over their land. England (Choice *B*) also emerged as a premier power in the region. The Netherlands gained independence from Spain in 1648.

Short Answer Response

1.

a) Monarchies undermined feudalism by centralizing the functions of government, particularly in terms of tax collection and military power. Prior to the rise of absolute monarchies, feudal lords enjoyed considerable power under feudalism. Feudal lords controlled most of the land, collected taxes from the peasants, and raised personal militaries. In effect, monarchies depended on the lords if they wished to wield meaningful power. To undercut the feudal lords, monarchies consolidated political power through the creation of centralized bureaucracies that collected taxes and developed powerful militaries. This meant that monarchies could unilaterally govern without the lords' consent and/or cooperation. Under absolute monarchies, feudal lords functioned as advisers to monarchs rather than governing partners.

b) Political decentralization caused by feudalism resulted in the stagnation of European innovation. While Europe was governed by a feudal system, the Song Dynasty developed the lodestone compass for navigation, advanced gunpowder weaponry, introduced government-backed paper currency, and invented the movable type printing press. Similarly, Muslim civilizations were at the cutting-edge of scientific discovery, particularly in terms of mathematics and medicine. In contrast, feudalism ushered in a "Dark Age" because the decentralized political system didn't have the resources to incentivize innovation, foster international trade, or develop a scientific community. For example, Europe experienced especially high mortality rates during the Black Death due to the lack of scientific knowledge and the governments' inability to institute large-scale public health initiatives.

c) As state power dramatically increased in Europe during the fifteenth and sixteenth centuries, absolute monarchies used their newfound power to sponsor maritime expeditions that enriched Europe. Prior to this increase in state power, European powers didn't have the financial or logistical capacity to carry out these expeditions. The centralization of political power increased government revenues by streamlining taxation, and monarchies financed explorers' search for alternative paths to Asian markets. These sponsored maritime expeditions enriched Europe in two major ways. First, after the Portuguese Crown sponsored Vasco da Gama's expeditions around the Cape of Good Hope, European powers built immensely profitable trading posts in East Africa, India, and Southeast Asia during the late-fifteenth and sixteenth centuries. Second, the search for a Northwest Passage resulted in European colonization of the Americas. England, France, the Netherlands, Portugal, Spain, and Sweden all established colonies in the Americas where they extracted raw resources with a coerced labor supply. Colonization fueled mercantilist economic policies, which strengthened European powers' domestic economies and spurred industrialization.

Period 2: 1648–1815

Absolutism and Constitutionalism

Contextualizing State Building

Struggle for Sovereignty

Between 1500 and 1700, modern nation-states began to sprout up all across Europe. By 1700, Europe was no longer one vast empire, or set of empires. Instead, Europe was a series of sovereign states. Indeed, the seventeenth and eighteenth centuries were dominated by two major historical forces: state-building and national rivalry. These two forces occurred in tandem; they were two sides of the same coin. This era in European history witnessed major countries—such as France, Great Britain, Prussia, Austria, and Russia—imposing their sovereignty onto other surrounding states, amassing power over other autonomous states and absorbing their populations. Small states were devoured by this process of political centralization, all in the name of a larger state's sovereignty. New forms of government—absolute monarchy, constitutional monarchy, and oligarchic republic—allowed states to claim supreme power in their own unique ways. As a result, smaller states such as Lorraine, Scotland, Lucca, and even (temporarily) Poland faded into the borders of larger sovereign states. As religious institutions lost power, political centralization became the primary method of exerting authority over local populations. Europe's states became entangled in political rivalries as powerful sovereign authorities tried to exert their power upon the continent (and beyond).

New Political Institutions

Historians argue that the sixteenth century was a turning point in European history. They claim that this era helped birth the modern state system. Proponents of this historical framework claim that this broader paradigm shift was motivated by a larger search for order, one that stemmed from the Reformation's attack on religious hegemony and the growth of modern secular ideals. The Reformation challenged notions of a single spiritual authority, which helped pave the way to the rise of a variety of modern secular states that attempted to assert their own visions for salvation. Put simply, the notion of a united Christian Europe was supplanted by the notion of secular sovereign states. In this climate of weakened Christian hegemony, Europeans began developing new political systems that favored secular order over religious order. Various new political models sprouted in this era as the aristocratic class jockeyed for power. In places like England, representative assemblies formed. Nevertheless, the most dominant political model to emerge in this era was absolute monarchy, or absolutism, which revered kings, like Louis XIV of France, as omnipotent authorities.

Competition Between Monarchs and Nobles

Traditionally, historians have regarded Louis XIV's reign in France (which lasted from 1642 to 1715) as one of the principal examples of the role that absolute monarchy played in influencing political relationships in Europe in the seventeenth century. Louis XIV's reign allowed French culture to diffuse throughout the sociopolitical affairs of most of central and western Europe. Indeed, the perceived superiority of Louis XIV's military prowess allowed his court to become a central sociopolitical force in Europe.

French language and culture began spreading throughout Europe between 1643 and 1715, as rulers across the continent tried to imitate Louis XIV's absolutist approach. Nevertheless, Louis XIV's ability to stabilize his kingdom was inextricably tied to the instability that preceded his rise to power. This instability deeply affected the reign of two key political figures in French history: Cardinal Richelieu and Cardinal Mazarin. These two royal ministers held *de facto* power in the half-century separating Henry IV's death and Louis XIV's absolutist reign. Following Henry IV's death in 1610, Louis XIII, Henry IV's oldest son, inherited the throne. However, Louis XIII (who ruled from 1610 to 1643) was only nine years old when he was crowned King of France. Likewise, Louis XIV was still a boy when he was crowned king after his brother's death in 1643. A power vacuum emerged as a result of these adolescent reigns. This power vacuum allowed Cardinal Richelieu and Cardinal Mazarin to become the unofficial rulers of France in the years separating Henry IV's reign from Louis XIV's adult reign. The turmoil of the Richelieu-Mazarin era in French history thus set the stage for the emergence of an absolute monarchy that enabled France to become a regional powerhouse from the mid-seventeenth to early eighteenth centuries.

According to primary sources written by and about Louis XIV, at twenty-three years old the king promised to never relinquish power to another soul again. Louis XIV was determined to be a real king, not just a figurehead for other royal ministers.

"The Age of Louis XIV" is defined by one overarching theory of rule: absolute monarchy. This absolutist framework was built upon an entire set of myths perpetuated by the king and his court. Emanating from Versailles was the myth of the Sun King, a royal legend that worshipped Louis XIV as the light for all his land, the source of illumination for his people. Historians often claim that this self-engineered myth fell short of the reality of the times. Nevertheless, myths often drive real changes in society. When he fully assumed the throne, Louis XIV was in fact confronted by a system fragmented by competing authorities. In spite of the centralization efforts of the Richelieu-Mazarin era, royal authority remained challenged by disaggregated provincial influences in the old estate system. Provincial nobles still maintained a large amount of local control—they had their own regional courts, they established their own sets of laws, and they still forced lesser members of the nobility into submission. The centralization efforts of the Richelieu-Mazarin era did not vanquish the esteem in which local officials were held. In fact, the financial corruptions of the Richelieu-Mazarin era helped reinforce this fractured political structure. Louis XIV, while imperfect in his approach, helped consolidate power in the guise of perfectibility. He raised the bar for royal potential by enacting a series of powerful albeit controversial administrative reforms.

Competition Between Minority and Dominant National Groups

In the sixteenth century, the Spanish Empire extended from Spain, through the Spanish Netherlands, to the Americas in the New World. King Philip II (son of Charles V of the Hapsburg Dynasty, ruler of the Holy Roman Empire) inherited this empire from his father. During Philip II's reign, the Spanish Empire began to weaken as a result of foreign wars and economic inflation. In order to finance its foreign battles, Spain borrowed inordinate amounts of money from Italian and German financiers. The empire became so financially unstable that King Philip II had to declare the nation bankrupt on three occasions. As a result of this financial instability, Spain became prone to internal revolt. One of the most notable examples of internal unrest in the sixteenth century emerged in the Spanish Netherlands, a region that had little in common with its Spanish overlords.

Spain was a predominantly Catholic nation-state, while the Spanish Netherlands was a predominantly Calvinist enclave. Likewise, the Dutch residents of the region spoke a different language from their Spanish rulers. A Dutch minority revolt was staged in opposition to the Spanish occupation in the 1560s. To make matters worse, as the Spanish economy wavered, the Dutch economy strengthened. The Spanish Netherlands were becoming a hub for manufacturing and trade by the 1560s. The prosperous middle class there became the target of Philip II's Catholic animosities. He raised taxes in the region in

an attempt to undermine the Protestant-Calvinist culture. In 1566, the Calvinist middle class revolted against the king's taxation attempts. Calvinist mobs destroyed and pillaged religious idols and paintings in Roman Catholic churches. Philip II responded by sending an army to quell the rebellion. Under the leadership of the Spanish Duke of Alva, Philip II had 1,500 Protestant rebels executed on a single day in 1568.

William of Orange emerged as a local leader in the revolt against the Spanish crown. He wanted to liberate the Netherlands from Spanish occupation. At first, he was unsuccessful in his efforts. However, in 1574, as the city of Leiden was under siege, William of Orange's soldiers desperately opened the floodgates of the dikes holding back seawater in the Leiden Low Country. The resulting floods drove Spanish troops out, shifting the momentum of the revolt. By 1579, the United Provinces of the Netherlands (seven northern provinces in the region) declared independence from Spain, paving the way to a Dutch "golden age" in manufacturing, exploration, and trade. Ten southern provinces, located in modern-day Belgium, remained under Spanish control.

The Czech minority of the Holy Roman Empire, which was a minority group (with its own language) concentrated largely in Bohemia, carried out an uprising between 1419 and 1436 known as the Hussite Wars. These wars centered around the martyrdom of a Catholic priest known as Jan Huss. A century before Martin Luther penned his *Ninety-Five Theses*, Jan Huss protested the ecclesiastical system of the Roman Catholic Church and its corruptions. In a treatise entitled *Questio de indulgentis* (1412), Jan Huss denounced the Roman Catholic Church's use of indulgences (payments for the promise of eternal sanctity). In 1414, after being summoned as a heretic by the Council of Constance, Jan Huss was burnt alive at the stake. His writings were burned along with him. This martyrdom ignited an event known as the defenestration, in which a number of prominent Catholics living in Prague "fell" to their deaths. This string of Roman Catholic deaths ultimately resulted in the Hussite War or Hussite Rebellion, which resulted in a battle between the Hussites (followers of Huss) and the Roman Catholic Church and its crusading military. The rebellion eventually ended in compromise—the Roman Catholic Church allowed the radical Hussites to read the Epistles and the Gospel in their native tongue (Czech) instead of Latin. Historians often describe the Hussite controversy and compromise as a precursor to the Lutheran Reformation in Germany.

Between 1640 and 1659, King Philip IV (King of Spain) and Gaspar de Guzman (Count-Duke of Olivares, Minister to the King of Spain) attempted to centralize power in the Spanish Empire through political reform. These power-hungry reform efforts proved to be largely a failure due to Spain's costly imperial expansionist efforts and its involvement in the Thirty Years' War. The expensive political reforms and military campaigns incited the ire of marginalized populations within the Spanish Kingdom, such as the Principality of Catalonia in northern Spain. A series of internal revolts transpired as a result of pent-up frustrations with the king and his minister. The Catalan Revolts, which affected primarily the northern principalities, created years of civil war within the kingdom. The Catalan people revolted against the occupation of the Spanish Kingdom, which they believed to be a foreign nation. The Catalan people had their own history and language, which they believed was completely separate from the history and linguistic heritage of Spain. The Catalan Revolts became a symbol of Spain's imperial decline, ending officially with the Peace of the Pyrenees in 1659. The revolt, therefore, extended over ten years beyond the Peace of Westphalia. The Peace of the Pyrenees surrendered portions of the Spanish counties of Roussillon and Cerdanya to France, leaving the Catalan minority there in a semi-autonomous limbo that did not bring about full independence from power-hungry European nations.

Models of Political Sovereignty

With the rise of absolutism, monarchy became the preferred form of rule throughout most of Europe in the seventeenth and eighteenth centuries. As religious institutions' power faded in the wake of new ideas and new discoveries, monarchical nation-states filled this power vacuum. This era witnessed the rise of absolute monarchs such as Louis XVI. It also witnessed the ultimate demise of monarchical systems as a result of Enlightenment-inspired revolutions (such as the French Revolution).

Absolutism was only one response to the religious wars and crises of the seventeenth century. As a result of this larger search for order, other political systems emerged. Two dominant political systems included constitutional monarchy in England, commonwealth republics in Cromwell's England, and republics (such as the Dutch Republic).

English Civil War and the Glorious Revolution

The English Civil War

The **English Civil War** resulted from the political struggles stemming from the influence of three historical figures: James I, Charles, I, and Oliver Cromwell.

James I

Queen Elizabeth I of England preceded James I as the monarch of England. Throughout her reign, Elizabeth I participated in a series of tumultuous political battles with Parliament. Following her death in 1603, **James Stuart**, King of Scotland, became the heir to Elizabeth I's throne. Since Elizabeth I did not have any children, James Stuart (son of Mary, Queen of Scots), her cousin and closest relative, succeeded her as the monarch of England. In 1603, he became officially known as **King James I of England**. England and Scotland were not officially unified until 1703, but James I became the first ruler to unite the two territories under one crown. Nevertheless, while technically unified under the rule of one leader, King James I's nation-state was far from politically unified. In fact, James I inherited an unstable political situation with Parliament that eventually blossomed into the English Civil War. His reign is consequently remembered as one of the most prominent examples of seventeenth-century challenges to absolute monarchy.

Accustomed to the absolutism of the Scottish kingdom, James I quickly declared that "kings are justly called gods." Understanding very little about the parliamentary customs of England, he attempted to assert his divine authority as an absolute monarch. While Elizabeth I had her battles with Parliament, believing also in her divine right to rule, she never tried to alienate Parliament with her perceived supremacy. Her battles with Parliament were mostly financial in nature. She attempted to live in the Tudor traditions of her predecessors, which established a "balanced polity" that allowed her monarchy and Parliament's governing body to rule alongside one another in England. King James I, on the other hand, outright alienated Parliament with his righteous claims to divinity. Parliament responded by refusing to offer additional monies for his expensive court and foreign wars.

King James I also ruffled the feathers of the Puritan religious contingent in Parliament. These Puritan politicians wanted to purify the Church of England of its episcopal model (a religious hierarchy dominated by bishops). They wanted a Calvinist-Presbyterian model (used by religious leaders in Scotland and Geneva) to supplant the episcopal model of the Church of England. While James I was also a Calvinist, he ultimately refused Puritan reforms; he realized that the religious hierarchy of the Church of England proved to be a solid political backbone for absolute monarchy. The Church of England's bishops were appointed by the crown and therefore indebted to the crown. The only Puritan reform passed by King James I was the now-famous common translation of the Bible into English. Other reforms

were squelched by the king's efforts to maintain absolute control over his kingdom. The alienation of Puritan politicians proved to be unwise for the English monarchy. Many Puritans had risen to a level of social nobility that allowed them to own land, control economic activities, and dominate the House of Commons (the lower house of Parliament). The Puritan gentry (landed nobility) of England established a rising chorus of opposition to monarchy, which only grew worse after James I died in 1625 and subsequently bequeathed a state of political instability to his heir, Charles I (his son).

Charles I

King Charles I rose to power after his father, King James I, died in 1625. Charles I inherited his father's conflicts with the Puritan contingent in Parliament. By 1628, just three years after Charles I assumed the throne, Parliament tried to place limitations on the power of monarchy. First, they passed the Petition of Right. The **Petition of Right** prohibited the king from levying taxes without Parliament's consent. Additionally, the Petition of Right stated that that the king could not quarter soldiers in private homes, imprison subjects without due cause, or impose martial law during peacetime. Charles I initially accepted these terms. He hoped that working with Parliament would eventually help him to finance his foreign wars. Nonetheless, he later reneged on the agreement, ignoring its terms. He believed the Petition of Right placed too many restrictions on his divine authority. By 1629, the king's relations with Parliament had disintegrated to the point that Charles I decided to outright dissolve Parliament. Between 1629 and 1637, Charles I refused to call Parliament into session. He pursued a course of personal rule that eventually spiraled out of control and resulted in the English Civil War.

The year 1637 proved to be a turning point in relations between the crown and Parliament. In that year, Charles I upset the Presbyterian Scots by attempting to impose one religion—the Church of England—upon his land (that is, on both England and Scotland). He upheld episcopal ritual and tried to force the Presbyterian Scots to read Anglican prayer books. The Scots ultimately defied the king, assembled an army, and threatened to invade England. The threat forced Charles I back into a political dialogue with Parliament: he needed finances to quell the rebellion. By bringing Parliament back into session, Charles I empowered a frustrated Parliament, affording Puritans the chance to resurrect their political squabbles with the king. From 1640 to 1641, Parliament, now back in session, tried to severely limit the royal power of the king. Throughout this session, Parliament abolished arbitrary courts and taxes collected without Parliament's consent. Additionally, they passed a revolutionary piece of legislation known as the Triennial Act. The **Triennial Act** guaranteed that Parliament would meet at least once every three years (with or without royal consent). A more radical wing of Parliament pushed for broader changes, such as the eventual elimination of bishops in the Church of England. In January 1642, an infuriated Charles I tried to arrest these radical members of Parliament, which further stoked the flames of a budding English Civil War. A furious mob of Londoners protested outside the king's palace, forcing Charles I to flee to northern England to raise an army. People loyal to the king (known as Royalists or Cavaliers) joined him in exile. Meanwhile, Parliament created its own troops, known as the **New Model Army**. The banishment of the king marked the official start date of the English Civil War, which lasted from 1642 to 1649.

Oliver Cromwell

The New Model Army was mostly composed of a faction of extreme Puritans, known as the **Independents**. The Independents believed their battle against the king was a religious war. They believed their army was fighting for their Lord. The Royalists or Cavaliers mockingly called these devout crusaders "Roundheads" (because they cut their hair short, just over their ears). Led by an impressive general known as **Oliver Cromwell**, the New Model Army successfully defeated the Cavaliers and captured King Charles I in 1646. By the end of 1646, this disciplined faction had already managed to create a schism in the rebelling forces. A more moderate group wanted to restore King Charles I with a new Presbyterian state church. In 1647, this moderate group marched on London in order to carry out negotiations with the former monarch of England. Capitalizing on this momentary lapse of moderation, King Charles I escaped and fled to Scotland to seek out help in his homeland. Cromwell, infuriated by these events, escalated the civil war in 1648, and once again captured the king. This time, however, Cromwell showed no mercy. In 1649, Cromwell and his radical army held a public trial, incriminated Charles I, and beheaded the king. This was an uncommon act in the seventeenth century, when kings in trouble were usually either imprisoned or murdered behind closed doors. The public execution of a monarch was, indeed, revolutionary in its own right. The Cromwellian revolution had triumphed in England, if only for a brief period, establishing a commonwealth in place of the old absolute monarchy.

Glorious Revolution

Outcome of the English Civil War

Under the leadership of Oliver Cromwell, the new Parliament—called "the Rump Parliament"—abolished both the House of Lords and the monarchy and established the **Commonwealth of England**. Cromwell's reign was immediately met with various controversies and resistances. He had to squash uprisings in Ireland and Scotland. He faced domestic opposition from a radical group known as the Levellers. The **Levellers** wanted annual Parliamentary sessions, equality for women, and democratic elections. The Rump Parliament also proved to be difficult to please. Cromwell had to eventually dissolve the Rump Parliament by force. Cromwell's military government enacted the Instrument of Government, a written constitution, which helped to reconstitute the legislative powers of Parliament, under the leadership of the Lord Protector (Cromwell's official title). The military government created more opposition by levying higher taxes, and, by the time Cromwell died in 1658, the country was longing for the restoration of the monarchy, which occurred when Charles II, heir of the Stuart monarchy, assumed the throne.

Restoration

Shortly after Oliver Cromwell's death in 1658, his Commonwealth government completely collapsed. The English people were longing for an end to military governance. Thus, in 1659, Parliament voted to restore the monarchy of England. They placed Charles II, son of Charles I, in power. As Charles II rode into London in 1660 as the new ruler of England, he was cheered and celebrated by the English people. Since Charles II officially restored the monarchy of England, his reign is referred to as "the **Restoration**." Charles II abolished all Puritan laws. He allowed the people to indulge in the arts just as they had prior to Cromwell's rule. Theater and sporting events were restored. Even dancing, which had been banned by Puritan laws, was restored. The arts flourished during Charles II's Restoration. Charles II also worked with Parliament to pass habeas corpus laws that protected the freedoms of English citizens. The Habeas Corpus Act of 1679 introduced laws that banned wrongful imprisonment and ensured the right to a fair trial. Charles II, a respected ruler in English history, ruled until his death in 1685. Since he did not have a child to inherit his throne, the monarchy passed into the hands of Charles II's brother, James II. There just happened to be one matter that proved to be extremely controversial about James II's rule—he was a Catholic. While a group known as the Tories supported his Catholic rule, another more powerful group known as the Whigs opposed his papist heritage. This schism in English politics culminated in an event known as the Glorious Revolution, the bloodless overthrow of the Catholic king.

Glorious Revolution

The **Glorious Revolution** stemmed from lingering Protestant animosities toward Catholic rule in England. James II made matters worse by appointing Catholic nobles to office and dissolving Parliament once they protested his disregard for English law. When James II's wife gave birth to a rightful Catholic

heir to the throne, English Protestants nearly revolted. They could not stomach the thought of more decades of Catholic rule. Instead of creating more turmoil and violence in England, they decided to search for a more diplomatic resolution. They encouraged James II's older daughter Mary (a Protestant married to William of Orange, ruler of the Netherlands) to take the throne, along with her husband, in a bloodless revolution in the name of Protestantism. William of Orange subsequently marched on England with his army, forcing James II to flee to France. With no blood shed, this moment in English history became known as the Glorious Revolution.

Continuities and Changes to Economic Practice and Development

Agricultural Revolution

Between 1648 and 1815, increases in labor and land productivity catapulted the world into a **Second Agricultural Revolution**. This increase in productivity was inspired by new agricultural techniques, one of which was known as the **Norfolk four-course crop rotation**. Developed in Norfolk, England, in the seventeenth century, the Norfolk four-course system replaced the medieval three-field system, which relied on a fallow year (a year in which the farmer let the soil "rest"). The Norfolk four-course system increased productivity by not relying on a fallow year. The Norfolk four-course system also relied heavily on fodder crops (crops used for animal feed). Norfolk-style crop rotation unfolded as follows:

- In the first year, wheat was grown.
- In the second year, turnips were grown (which were used to feed livestock in the winter).
- In the third year, barley was grown (with ryegrass and clover).
- In the fourth year, the ryegrass and clover were either grazed or cut for feed.

These fodder crops helped produce an excess of animal manure that could be used to increase the nitrate levels of the soil. The second and fourth years helped produce more fertilizer, which, in turn, helped produce heavier cereal yields in the first and third years of the cycle.

Another farming advancement that helped catalyze the Second Agricultural Revolution was the institution of enclosure systems. In England and Western Europe, governments began implementing new acts that replaced feudal open field systems (dominated by a medieval tenant system) with enclosures (dominated by new notions of private property and individual ownership). In the fourteenth century, the Black Death helped to accelerate the need for enclosures by encouraging the break-up of feudal lands. By the sixteenth and seventeenth centuries, Parliament (and other Western European governing bodies) was approving enclosures at an unprecedented pace, which allowed farmers to have more individual control over the land. This individual control proved to be quite fruitful, thanks to the introduction of the previously mentioned Norfolk four-course system, which approached crop rotation and production more strategically than in feudal times. The result was a large-scale land reform movement that helped individual farmers and landowners gain more control over tilling/grazing rights and practices.

Agricultural Products from the Americas

Agricultural products were an important part of the growing Columbian Exchange between the Americas and Europe. The global transfer of food, plants, and animals from the American colonies to Europe helped boost the food supply in Europe. Foods that had previously been confined to the American continents—such as turkeys, sweet potatoes, pumpkins, avocados, peppers, cassavas, pineapples, cacao beans, peanuts, beans, potatoes, tomatoes, vanilla beans, and corn—made their way to the European continent, much to the delight of residents there. In particular, corn and potatoes proved to be invaluable for European populations. Corn and potatoes were inexpensive to grow and nutritious enough to sustain the growing populations of Europe. They became cornerstones in European diets, allowing Europeans to live longer, healthier lives. These foods not only incited a population boom in Europe, but also in Asia (sweet potatoes were planted throughout China), increasing the overall world population.

Changes to Labor and Trade in Commodities

Labor and trade commodities were freed from traditional restrictions imposed by governments and corporate entities because mercantilist theory (which espoused these systems) faded in favor of new economic theories, such as those set forth by John Locke. These new economic theories placed a greater emphasis on "free trade" and the "free market." This type of economic liberalism helped capitalism take on its modern form, which, to a large extent, still influences global economic politics today.

Cottage Industry

Textile production was the predominant industry in Europe by the eighteenth century. Great Britain and France developed textile industries that accounted for almost 75 percent of all exports for each country. While Europe was beginning to industrialize in the eighteenth century, most textiles continued to be produced in traditional contexts, using traditional methods. Throughout the mid to late seventeenth century, in urban centers, such as London and Paris, master artisans continued to employ classic methods for textile production in their guild workshops. By the eighteenth century, however, as cities experienced overcrowding, textile production began to shift to rural sectors in the countryside. In these rural sectors, textiles were manufactured via a putting-out system (sometimes referred to simply as a "domestic" system). Merchants and entrepreneurs from the rising capitalist class would purchase raw textile materials, such as flax and wool. They would "put out" these raw materials to workers living in the countryside. These rural workers would spin these raw materials into cloth, using simple machines. The merchants and entrepreneurs would sell the cloth to customers in the city, making enough profit for continuous production. This "putting-out system" became known as the **cottage industry**. Weavers and spinners conducted their work in their own cottages. Entire families participated in this cottage industry, supplementing their low wages from farming. The urban merchant-entrepreneur class, however, gained more wealth through the "cottage industry," profiting off the labor of their rural counterparts.

Development of the Market Economy

By the end of the sixteenth century, traditional family banking firms were becoming increasingly obsolete with the expansion of mercantile capitalism. These traditional institutions were no longer able to provide the complex services needed to accommodate new commercial enterprises. As a result, new financial practices and banking institutions arose to take their place. Banking institutions sought to turn private savings into venture capital.

Fire insurance was widely issued following the Great Fire of London in 1666. This was the beginning of the popularization of insurance as an institution, and property and liability insurance became common around this time. Several important insurance companies were formed, including the London Assurance Corporation, the Royal Exchange Assurance Corporation, and Lloyd's of London, which first specialized in marine insurance.

The idea of the right to property and protections against confiscation of property arose following the English Civil War. Political movements like the Levellers argued that property earned through a person's labor should be protected. Property rights were an important issue since most voting rights were based on owning property.

The Bank of England was instituted by Parliament in 1694 primarily to help the English government raise funds for use in the war against France. A royal charter established the bank as a joint-stock bank. No other banks of this kind were allowed in England and Wales until 1826.

Economic Development and Mercantilism

The European-Dominated Worldwide Economic Network

The agricultural, industrial, and consumer revolutions in Europe—an era of rampant mercantile growth catalyzed by agricultural booms, colonial systems, technological advancements, and population increases—would not have been possible without the expansion of economic globalization. European exploration created global trade networks, which in turn helped create new agricultural techniques, which then created greater agricultural prosperity. These developments also helped launch new industrial capabilities, which further mechanized both farming and manufacturing. Lastly, a global supply-and-demand chain arose that forever changed European (and worldwide) consumer tastes.

Mercantilist Policies in Europe

During the sixteenth century, European countries adopted the economic policy of **mercantilism**, which uses government regulation to promote a positive trade balance as the key to increasing a country's wealth. Mercantilist policies developed national currencies, monetary reserves, and positive trade balances to ensure that imports exceeded exports. Mercantilist economic policies viewed the exploitation of colonies and slaves as a positive because it increased the wealth of the home country. Often European nations sought wealth in colonies, first through the possibility of finding areas rich in gold, then through agricultural endeavors. Colonies were a way for a country to import raw goods from their own colonies, becoming more self-sufficient and reducing their reliance on trade with rival powers. As the trade routes became more efficient and the colonies more stable, the transfer of slaves for plantation work in sugar cane and tobacco fields became an ever-increasing source of revenue.

Transatlantic Slave-Labor System

Slavery in the Americas was a hereditary phenomenon during the peak centuries of the Atlantic slave trade. This slave trade was mostly economic in origin: the sugar and tobacco plantations of the Americas demanded an excess of cheap or free labor. Initially, Europeans looked to Native Americans as their enslaved labor supply. Quickly, however, millions of Native Americans died because of the spread of unfamiliar diseases. As a result, the Atlantic slave trade reared its ugly head, and millions of Africans were uprooted to work the fields in the Thirteen Colonies, the Caribbean, and Brazil in place of Native Americans. The passage by sea of slaves from West Africa to the West Indies and the colonies became known as the **Middle Passage**.

Triangular transatlantic trade flourished in the seventeenth and eighteenth centuries. First, ships from Britain's North American colonies carried rum to Africa where it was traded for slaves and gold. Then, the ships took the slaves to French and Spanish colonies in the Caribbean and exchanged them for sugar or molasses. In the last part of the triangular trade system, merchants sailed back to North America where the sugar and molasses was used to make rum, and the cycle could start over again.

Consumer Culture in Europe

Overseas products and influences contributed to the development of a consumer culture in Europe. Products such as sugar, tobacco, rum, and coffee were cultivated in the American colonies and brought back to Europe. Spices, silk, and tea were only available from the East, and mercantilist policies in Europe enabled an increase in national wealth which allowed these items to be more easily traded.

Increase in European Food Supply

Many new crops and products were introduced in Europe that came from the Americas, such as potatoes from South America and tomatoes from North America. Other crops were able to grow more readily in the fertile soil of the new colonies including soybeans, oranges, cacao, and bananas. This importation and transplantation of agricultural products from the Americas contributed to an increase in the food supply and also led to more varied diets and improved nutrition in Europe.

Commercial and Industrial Enterprises in Europe

In addition to agricultural products, foreign lands provided raw materials, finished goods, laborers, and markets for the commercial and industrial enterprises in Europe. Raw materials such as lumber, iron, cotton, and wool were transported from the colonies to Europe to be manufactured into finished goods in European factories. The colonies in turn provided a market for European countries to export finished goods that were not readily available outside of Europe. These goods included cloth, furniture, kitchen utensils, guns, and knives. The production of raw materials and agricultural products in the New World required a large labor force. Along with slaves transported from Africa, indentured servants, usually from Europe, made up a large portion of the work force. Indentured servants could take passage to the Americas, and the cost of their passage was a contract to work for several years without wages.

Dutch Golden Age

Development of the Dutch Republic

Historians often refer to the seventeenth century as the golden age of the Dutch Republic. The Dutch Republic, along with England, successfully resisted monarchical power. During this golden age, the United Provinces of the Netherlands established itself as a dominant economic force in the transatlantic world. Along with France and England, the United Provinces of the Netherlands helped establish the Atlantic seaboard as the new economic epicenter of Europe. Formally recognized through the Peace of Westphalia (1648), seven northern provinces joined together to advance the interests of a new Protestant merchant class. They joined together in a Protestant revolt against the Hapsburg monarchy that lasted roughly from 1581 (initial union) to 1648 (official recognition). Once officially recognized as a state, the United Provinces of the Netherlands established Amsterdam as the financial and commercial capital of Europe.

During the **Dutch Golden Age**, Amsterdam wrested financial and commercial dominance from Antwerp (Belgium). Between 1570 and 1660, the population of Amsterdam doubled as refugees from foreign wars flocked to the new commercial powerhouse. The urbanization and expansion of Amsterdam—and the entire Dutch Republic—in the sixteenth and seventeenth centuries attracted merchants from all over Europe. In less than 100 years, Amsterdam's population mushroomed from 30,000 inhabitants to 200,000 inhabitants. As a result, a new oligarchy (rule by a small group of nobles) emerged, one that united the state's urban gentry with its rural landholders to help advance its commercial progress. Amsterdam merchants built vast fleets and state-of-the-art ports to strengthen their commercial activities. The newly invented shallow-draft ship—known as the Dutch *fluyt*—helped Amsterdam merchants ship large quantities of herring, timber, iron, and cereals. A new network of canals also helped transport goods such as glass, sugar, wool, tobacco, beer, books, and guns/munitions. A select number of shipyard owners, manufacturers, and merchants added to the blossoming Dutch oligarchy. This group, known collectively as the **Amsterdam burghers**, flourished as a result of the new wave of capital investments, which also helped found the Exchange Bank of Amsterdam and the Amsterdam Stock Exchange. These wealthy burghers, however, were inspired by a Calvinist-Protestant lifestyle that stressed simplicity. The burghers of the Dutch Golden Age wore dark clothes and lived in simply

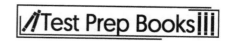

furnished homes. This simple style followed Dutch explorers traveling and settling throughout the Atlantic world, in places such as New Amsterdam (modern-day New York).

By the second half of the seventeenth century, the commercial prowess of the Dutch Republic began to wane in the wake of the meteoric expansion of the English and French empires. Internally, the Republic wavered as a result of a schism between the House of Orange (the supporters of traditional monarchy) and the States General (the purveyors of republic values). Burdened by foreign competition and wars, the Dutch Republic temporarily ceded power to the House of Orange between 1672 to 1702. Republican leaders regained power after the death of William III of the House of Orange in 1702. However, the damage had already been done. Around this time, wealthy burghers began rejecting their traditional Calvinist heritage. Likewise, foreign wars with England and France proved to be costly, which further undermined the financial success of the Dutch Republic. By 1715, the commercial supremacy of the United Provinces of the Netherlands was in full disarray. England, backed by a new industrial economy and an expansive empire, emerged as the region's economic leader by the mid-eighteenth century. The Dutch Golden Age was over before the Industrial Revolution was in full swing.

Balance of Power

Competitive State System

The **completive state system** simultaneously created new patterns of diplomacy—such as alliances and new treaty processes—while also creating new forms of mechanized naval and land-based warfare. Alliances sprouted as emerging nation-states vied for power in Europe. These alliances were ever-changing, making diplomatic relationships even more complicated. Likewise, new treaty processes emerged following the historic signing of the Peace of Westphalia. Treaties resulted from conversations between all nations involved. As diplomacy seemingly became more "civilized," warfare became more gruesome due to technological advances in canonry and firearms that made battlefields even more dangerous. Military forces also became more bureaucratic in this era, as governments began expanding military power through civil departments.

Decline of Religion as a Cause for War

The Peace of Westphalia (1648), which ended the Thirty Years' War, served as a turning point in European relations. Firstly, it marked the official beginning of the decline of the Hapsburg states of Spain and Austria. Secondly, it greatly strengthened France as a political power by ceding regions of Germany to the French kingdom. Thirdly, it also fractured the power of the German state by creating autonomous provinces that were not directly under the control of the Holy Roman Empire.

However, the most significant transition signaled by the Peace of Westphalia was the fact that, as the official end of the Thirty Years' War, it also ended the regional emphasis on religious wars. The Peace of Westphalia symbolically represented the end of the dream that a Roman Catholic empire would one day rule all of Europe. It also acknowledged that the future of balancing power in the region rested in a new modern state system that structured diplomatic and military objectives around sovereignty (rather than spirituality). A new method of peace negotiation emerged, one that had little to do with the power of the papacy. This new method of negotiation, which is still used today, was based upon the notion that sovereign states had the power to negotiate diplomacy on their own terms, without ecclesiastical intervention.

Partition of Poland

As Prussia, Austria, and Russia jockeyed for political prowess in eastern Europe, Poland, once a great kingdom, suffered a temporary but serious setback that eradicated its presence from the European map for the next several decades. Unlike Prussia, Austria, and Russia, Poland did not have a strong absolute monarch. The King of Poland, who was elected by nobles, struggled to exert control over his electors. Much like the case of the English Civil War, the King of Poland suffered at the hands of an aristocracy that wanted to severely limit his power. The nobles created conditions where the king became only a figurehead. These conditions eliminated any chance of monarchical absolutism or enlightened despotism. The king was limited by a delimited bureaucracy, restricted finances, and lean military (less than 20,000 men protected the kingdom). Hindered by these restrictions on absolutism, Poland became the prey of its imperial neighbors. Poland's powerful neighbors—Prussia, Austria, and Russia—began meddling in its affairs, which eventually led to the dissolution of the independent Polish state and the partitioning of its territory. In order to balance power in the region, the three surrounding imperial governments simply agreed to divide its territory equally. To avoid war, they split 30 percent of Polish lands and 50 percent of its population by 1772. When the Poles attempted to resurrect a strong monarchy within the remaining territory in 1791–1792, all three surrounding powers intervened. By 1793, Poland was being partitioned by its neighbors for a second time, and in 1795, it underwent a third and final partition that officially disbanded the Polish nation.

Diplomacy of European States

The year 1648 marked the official end of the violent Thirty Years' War, a conflict over ruling families, religious beliefs, and territorial boundaries that affected dozens of smaller Protestant and Catholic states in Germany and Central Europe. The Peace of Westphalia (1648) officially ended the war. The Peace of Westphalia is important for five reasons:

- It symbolized the end of religious wars in Europe.

- It weakened the once-powerful Hapsburg states of Spain and Austria.

- It allowed German princes to declare their independence from the political overreach of the Holy Roman Empire.

- It strengthened the expanding French nation-state by awarding it some German territories.

- It introduced a new method of peace negotiation that has pervaded modern European history, a method that ensures all nations involved in conflict come together for a resolution.

This historic shift was followed by the rise of the modern nation-state. This shift symbolized the end of the notion of a sweeping Catholic empire in Europe, and it created a modern, independent system of states.

Austrian Defeat of the Turks

Leopold I, ruler of Austria between 1658 and 1705, attempted to extend the Austrian Empire even farther south and east. This expansion, however, proved difficult because of the consistent attempts at westward expansion by the Ottoman Empire. Following their occupation of Transylvania, Ottoman military forces attempted to lay siege to Vienna in 1683. The Battle of Vienna that ensued proved to be a turning point in Austrian-Ottoman relations. The Austrian military, backed by other European national groups, laid waste to the Ottoman troops, decisively exiling them from the region by 1687. The ensuing **Treaty of Karlowitz** in 1699 officially allowed the Austrian Empire to secure former Ottoman enclaves in Slovenia, Croatia, Hungary, and Transylvania. The Ottoman Empire, once a threat to stability in the region, never fully regained its prominence.

Louis XIV's Nearly Continuous Wars

Louis XIV helped France become the most powerful country in Europe. He expanded the French military to 400,000 in wartime and 100,000 in peacetime. France's population exploded to twenty million people (four times England's population at the time). Unfortunately, Louis XIV, greedy for power and territory, forced the powerful French nation, which had superior military tactics and weaponry, into a series of continuous wars that eventually weakened its political prowess. The wars included:

- **Dutch War:** Louis XIV declared war on the Spanish Netherlands in 1667. He then invaded the Dutch Netherlands in 1672. The Dutch used the same tactic they used against the Spanish army years before—they opened up their dikes on the French troops, flooding the countryside. The war proved disastrous for both sides. They officially ended the war with the **Treaty of Nijmegen** in 1678. The damage wrought by the conflict severely weakened the French nation.

- **Nine Years' War:** Sometimes referred to as "the first global war," the Nine Years' War (1688–1697) witnessed Louis XIV's French military battle against a European coalition (consisting of the Dutch Republic, the Holy Roman Empire, Spain, Savoy, and England). The war was not only fought in Europe, but also in India and North America. Although the war ended officially through a series of treaties in the 1680s and 1690s, the war eventually fractured into newer, more-complicated conflicts. The Nine Years' War simply set the stage for another fruitless European conflict, the War of the Spanish Succession.

- **War of the Spanish Succession:** Louis XIV tried to increase his powers in ways other than war. For example, Charles II, King of Spain, remained childless throughout his reign. In order to expand the power of the Bourbon Dynasty, Louis XIV received permission to place his seventeen-year-old grandson, Philip of Anjou, on the Spanish throne once Charles II had died. Upon Charles II's death in 1701, Philip assumed the throne. This political maneuver unified Spain and France under Bourbon rule. Other countries believed this political maneuver was a threat to all of Europe. In 1701, Portugal, Austria, Great Britain, the Dutch Republic, and several smaller Italian and German states banded together to fight the growing power of Louis XIV's Dynasty. The ensuing conflict was known as the War of the Spanish Succession. It lasted from 1701 until 1713. Although Louis XIV's grandson was able to remain King of Spain in accordance to the **Treaty of Utrecht** (which officially ended the war), the war proved to be costly for France. It officially called for the separation of France and Spain into two nation-states, and it allowed Great Britain to grow in territory and power.

Advances in Military Technology

The early modern era was marked by a miniature "military revolution" that witnessed the expansion of military bureaucracies between the periods of 1648 and 1815. Governments began subsuming military operations in bureaucratic civil departments. These departments specialized in warfare, introducing new technologies and training techniques. The regimented nature of these expanding bureaucracies was backed by technological advancements in firearms, fortifications, and cannonry. Military advancements spawned new rivalries over military techniques and technologies. The balance of power leaned toward states that could marshal sufficient resources to compete in this new military environment.

Absolutist Approaches to Power

Limits of Absolute Monarchies

Absolute monarchs like Louis XIV tried to limit the power of the nobility by excluding it from government. However, absolute monarchs typically increased certain social powers by allowing certain individuals to collect taxes and administer justice on behalf of the monarchy. In France, Louis XIV expanded the power of a group known as intendants. This group helped maintain financial and judicial privileges in the kingdom. Other absolute monarchs also followed Louis XIV's lead by allowing nobles to be a part of royal palace life. Nobles upheld their social positions and legal privileges in the kingdom by catering to the king's interests in the royal court. Kings like Louis XIV opened up their ornate palaces to allow hundreds of nobles to live in apartments there. This reinforced the social position of the aristocracy while also increasing the power of the absolute monarch. By taking nobles away from their own homes, kings created their own cadre of tax collectors to send outside the palace walls. This made these nobles dependent upon the king's power.

Louis XIV and Jean-Baptiste Colbert

Louis XIV's reign would not have been as powerful without the support of his financial minister, **Jean Baptiste Colbert**. Colbert was a political supporter of mercantilist theory, which meant he believed the French nation should protect its own domestic industries by exporting more than it imported. Colbert, like Louis XIV, wanted wealth to stay within France. Both men wanted to make France self-sufficient by controlling and expanding domestic manufacturing. Colbert supported industry in France by extending government funds and tax benefits to domestic companies. He also boosted interest in colonization, recognizing the economic opportunities afforded by French settlers and trade in North America. In particular, Colbert tried to invigorate the fur trade in North America by offering incentives for colonization efforts. During Colbert's reign as minister of finance, Louis XIV also maintained military and religious control. Religious control was pursued through the **Edict of Nantes**, which protected the religious liberties of the French Huguenots. Colbert understood that these protections had economic benefits—they shifted the focus from religious conflict to economic competition. The Huguenots were a cornerstone of the emerging working classes in France. When Colbert died, Louis XIV revoked the Edict of Nantes, unravelling the work of Jean Baptiste Colbert and robbing France of many of its skilled workers.

Westernization of the Russian State and Society

Peter I, known by historians as **Peter the Great**, was part of the famous **Romanov Dynasty**, which helped restore order in Russia in the early seventeenth century. The Romanovs strengthened the early modern government of Russia by quelling rebellions and establishing an effective law code. Peter the Great, who became sole ruler of Russia in 1696 after his feeble-minded brother passed away, continued the Romanov tradition of strengthening the laws of the land. As **czar** (or lead ruler) of Russia, Peter the Great was revered for his Western reforms. As a young czar, he embarked on a "Grand Embassy" (or long visit) to Western Europe. There, with his identity disguised, Peter learned about the politics, economics, and social norms of the West. While in the Netherlands, he immersed himself in the trades to gain a better understanding of the manufacturing and mercantilism of Western Europe. Prior to his journey, most common landowners (called boyars) and peasant farmers (called serfs) did not understand the ways of the West. Serfdom (a kind of indentured farming) was a medieval practice still employed in Russia.

As part of his westernization efforts, Peter the Great strengthened the Russian military, using the Prussian model. He increased the number of troops to nearly 200,000 men. He also limited the power of

the boyars (landowners), imposed heavy taxes, introduced the potato into Russian farming, brought the Russian Orthodox Church under state control, began printing a national newspaper, raised women's status, and ordered nobles to wear Western clothing. Peter even moved the capital west, to St. Petersburg. All in all, Peter the Great made Russia stronger by transforming its political, religious, and cultural institutions. These westernization attempts were later expanded upon by **Catherine the Great**, an enlightened Russian despot who ruled from 1762 to 1796. Catherine sought to expand Russian territory in honor of Peter's Western reforms. She helped expand Russia westward into Poland, making her nation into a new international powerhouse. Using Enlightenment philosophers as a guiding light, she recommissioned the laws of Russia, strengthening the nation in the Western tradition. Together, Peter the Great and Catherine the Great are remembered as the enlightened, Eurocentric leaders who helped bring Russia into modernity.

Scientific, Philosophical, and Political Developments

Contextualizing the Scientific Revolution and the Enlightenment

Spread of Scientific Revolution Concepts and Practices

Prior to the 1500s, most scientific thinkers believed in a geocentric universe. Most scholars followed the abstract theories of Aristotle, and most medical practitioners believed that human bodies worked in the same ways as pig bodies. The **Scientific Revolution** dispelled all these archaic frameworks for thinking, which had been heralded as truths by the Roman Catholic Church. Indeed, the Scientific Revolution replaced all these abstract old assumptions by emphasizing mathematical logic and scientific reason. The **Enlightenment** simultaneously exposed the world to classical philosophers that had previously been forgotten in the archives and storehouses of Muslim universities and private collections. New political, social, and ethical theories emerged that honored the past—through neoclassical frameworks—but also challenged the present by paving the path to a previously unimagined future.

Put simply, the Scientific Revolution and the Enlightenment attacked the irrational nature of medieval science and philosophy. Reason, backed by new scientific tools and methods, became the new truth; it gradually displaced abstract theology as the primary way to understand the world. European culture underwent a distinct *rational* turn, one that was publicly challenged by the inquisitions of the Roman Catholic Church. The early modern world subsequently became a battleground between rationalism and traditionalism. Some historians, noting the wave of Enlightenment revolutions that followed, would say that rationalism won this battle (though tradition continued to exist, in open resistance and in isolation).

Enlightenment Thought

What was once considered reason in the Middle Ages proved to be entirely unreasonable by the time the Scientific Revolution was in full swing. Aristotle and Galen's influence on medieval thinking crumbled in the wake of new discoveries and ideas. The concepts and practices of the Scientific Revolution were applied to political, social, and ethical issues to create entirely new conceptions of reason in the early modern era. The Scientific Revolution's emphasis on systematic observation challenged the abstract notions of reason set forth by medieval scholars. As new discoveries, such as Galileo's telescopic validation of Copernicus's heliocentric theory, challenged the ecclesiastic canon of Roman Catholic Church, inevitably these discoveries challenged the Church itself. The Church, in turn, resisted. The result was a new wave of inquisition and censorship by the Roman Catholic Church that affected the scientists of the era. Galileo's theories were seen as a threat to the religious and political order of the time.

Both sides of the "heliocentric vs. geocentric" debate claimed to be inspired by reason. Nonetheless, the new emphasis on scientific—rather than theological—reason eventually won the favor of the masses. This paradigm shift created skeptics out of former believers, and the consequence of this new, widespread skepticism was revolutionary foment. By challenging theological ethics, scientists also challenged the Church. By challenging the Church, they ultimately challenged the political order of the time. These developments laid the foundation for future revolutions.

New Public Venues and Print Media

In the eighteenth century, an expansion of literacy was catalyzed by better print technologies. The number of publishers and literate members of the public skyrocketed in this era, enabling the popularization of Enlightenment ideas. Magazines and daily newspapers were created, with the goals of expanding the ideas of the salons and coffeehouses and creating a more educated citizenry. Books also were also more widely circulated in this period, which undermined old conceptions of literacy being an endeavor of high culture (the culture of the wealthy and powerful).

Additionally, new secondary schools and universities sprouted up all over Western and Central Europe. While these universities initially championed archaic Aristotelian values, they eventually embraced Enlightenment culture, especially in such revolutionary hubs as the University of Paris. While not quite a public venue, these universities became epicenters of advances in medicine and philosophy, which, in turn, benefitted the public. A strong interplay existed between universities and other Enlightenment social institutions, such as public coffeehouses, taverns, and salons.

New Political and Economic Theories

By the eighteenth century, most European nations continued to be ruled by monarchs. While many Enlightenment philosophers, such as Voltaire, argued that monarchy remained the most pure and sustainable form of governance, gradually the Enlightenment began to weaken old conceptions about the strength of absolute rule. Conceptions of the divine right of monarchs were quickly superseded by new secular visions for governance. As Europe became increasingly secularized, new political and economic theories emerged that challenged absolutism. These theories, to a large extent, also challenged mercantilism (which had long been a financial weapon of monarchy). These new theoretical frameworks, in some instances, morphed into enlightened absolutism, a fusion of old monarchical and new Enlightenment ideals. Yet, in other instances, the Enlightenment's emphasis on natural law and natural rights (which were believed to be inalienable, or naturally possessed by all humans) outright challenged monarchy and mercantilism as affronts to individualism. In these instances, the result was sometimes rebellion or revolution.

The American Revolution, the French Revolution, the Haitian Revolution, and the Latin American revolutions were all inspired by the Enlightenment values of equality before the law, freedom of religious expression, freedom of speech and expression, and freedom from the excessive taxation efforts of mercantile systems. Indeed, the American Revolution, launched by the Declaration of Independence, argued that life, liberty, and the pursuit of happiness (three Enlightenment-inspired ideals) were inalienable rights. This revolutionary wave of Enlightenment values helped topple monarchies, create new republics, and establish new economic ventures.

Rational Analysis of Religious Practices

Voltaire was one of the many Enlightenment philosophers to champion religious tolerance. Voltaire joined other philosophers in condemning religiously inspired tortures and executions. He famously condemned these barbaric acts in his *Treatise on Tolerance* (1763), one of his major works on religious

tolerance. Religiously backed torture was still commonplace in the eighteenth century. Voltaire argued that a more natural, more rational form of religion was needed to move society away from these barbaric institutional religious beliefs. Voltaire began championing **deism**, a natural religion built upon the belief that God created the universe but has no direct involvement in its workings. Following Newtonian theories, Voltaire conceptualized a Creator deity who did not extend grace or answer prayers but rather allowed the world to exist naturally, according to fundamental scientific tenets.

Experiences of Everyday Life

The daily lives of Europeans transformed dramatically as a result of the Columbian Exchange and the Scientific Revolution. These transformations took form in demographic, environmental, medical, and technological shifts.

Demographic Changes

Demographic changes occurred in three major forms: 1) growing populations, 2) longer life expectancies, and 3) urban migration. Growing populations and longer life expectancies were not only the result of environmental changes but also the consequence of the emerging Columbian Exchange between the Americas and Europe. New, inexpensively produced foods shipped from the Americas (such as potatoes, peanuts, cassava, sweet potatoes, and corn) enriched life in Europe. These foods were inexpensive and nutritious enough to sustain blossoming populations. Urban populations, in particular, blossomed as a result of trade and human migration. Rural migrants, hoping to better their lives by participating in the growing merchant manufacturing economies of Europe, moved to cities in droves. While the rural poor who moved to the cities did not always taste the fruits of their labor, cities expanded at an unprecedented rate, shifting the demographic makeup of Europe's budding nation-states.

Environmental Changes

Daily life changed dramatically in the eighteenth century as a result of unpredictable environmental changes. The Second Agricultural Revolution, and its coinciding increase in birthrates, benefitted from positive climate changes that increased food production. These climate changes put an end to the Little Ice Age of the seventeenth century. Moderate summers afforded eighteenth-century Europeans with better growing conditions, which, in turn, made basic survival more attainable. A more hospitable climate prepared early modern Europe for more revolutionary changes in society. With the emphasis shifting from basic personal sustenance to sustainable national and international crop production, Europeans began focusing their attention on more scientific ways to enhance agricultural production. Climate shifts created greater yields in vegetables and meat, which were reinforced by scientific experimentation. The hospitable environment, therefore, allowed the Scientific Revolution to blossom in the agricultural sectors of Europe.

Medical Changes

Medical changes also helped increase life expectancy. Better medicines and birthing methods decreased infant mortality rates and increased the average life expectancy for men and women. Many scientists and doctors attempted to improve medical tools and techniques. These scientists and doctors included:

Paracelsus

Born Philippus Aureolus Theophrastus Bombastus von Hohenheim, the Swiss-German physician known as **Paracelsus** revolutionized the medical industry by challenging medieval medical orthodoxy. While many of his theories are considered archaic by today's standards, Paracelsus is still considered "the father of modern toxicology." Paracelsus experimented with inorganic substances for medical purposes, which also led him to study the toxic nature of certain substances.

Andreas Vesalius

Flemish physician **Andreas Vesalius** famously published *De humani corporis fabrica* (On the Fabric of the Human Body), a scholarly tract that helped modern scientists have a more informed understanding of human anatomy. Dissecting human corpses, Andreas Vesalius created more accurate depictions of the human body. He consequently rejected the theories set forth by previous scientists, such as Galen, who had been heralded as experts during medieval times.

William Harvey

Searching for a better understanding of the circulatory system, **William Harvey** improved upon Andreas Vesalius' theories. He was one of the first scientists to recognize that the heart pumps blood throughout the rest of the body, and he published *On the Motion of the Heart and Blood in Animals* in 1628.

Edward Jenner

Working in Great Britain in the late 1700s, **Edward Jenner** discovered ways to inoculate people against disease through the creation of vaccines. He promoted vaccination using materials from individuals with cowpox to protect his patients and others against smallpox.

Robert Boyle

Robert Boyle is known for applying the scientific method to chemistry. In a book entitled *The Sceptical Chymist* (1661), Boyle challenged Aristotelian notions of "the four elements" (earth, air, fire, and water). He is known as the father of modern chemistry for his discovery of **Boyle's law**, which helps explain the interrelationship between the pressure, volume, and temperature of gas. Boyle also claimed that all chemical properties are made up of primary particles, which would later be described as atoms by future scientists.

Effects of the Commercial Revolution

The commercial revolution launched by American colonization in the sixteenth through eighteenth centuries altered the sociocultural landscape of European society by introducing new commercial interests into domestic and private life. The cottage industry—or putting-out system—changed family dynamics. Spinners and weavers were supplied with textiles from merchants to be spun to and woven. The merchants profited greatly from this system, which disrupted old feudal family structures. Rural workers began putting their entire households to work, which helped establish proto-industrial patterns that made women and children economic contributors. The family unit became central to the production of refined goods in the commercial revolution.

The Scientific Revolution

New Ideas and Methods in Astronomy

Emboldened by the theories of the Enlightenment and backed by the new tools and techniques of the Scientific Revolution, many astronomers began challenging the authority of ancient and medieval philosophers. Above all, the greatest challenge to traditional knowledge was the notion that the cosmos was heliocentric rather than geocentric. This concept was validated by the theories set forth by pathbreaking scientists such as Copernicus, Brahe, Kepler, Galileo, and Newton.

Nicolaus Copernicus

The notion of a heliocentric universe was not new by the time **Nicolaus Copernicus** began toying with it in the 1500s. In fact, some ancient Greek scientists and philosophers had believed that the sun—rather than the earth—was at the center of the universe. Copernicus validated this ancient Greek belief by studying the earth, the stars, and other celestial bodies for over twenty-five years. There was only one major problem with this Copernican theory—it went completely against the canonical laws and beliefs of the Roman Catholic Church. The Roman Catholic Church had long assumed that the universe revolved around the earth, and, more specifically, around humanity (God's creation). Copernicus believed the Roman Catholic Church was wrong quite some time before he published *On the Revolutions of the Heavenly Bodies*, which was not published until 1543, the last year of his life. He had not published the treatise earlier, fearing retaliation by the Roman Catholic Church. Copernicus was right about his fears; those who championed his heliocentric theory after his death faced ridicule by the Roman Catholic Church, and, in some cases, inquisition and exile.

Tycho Brahe

Copernicus's *On the Revolutions of the Heavenly Bodies* proved to be overwhelmingly uncontroversial (at least initially) in spite of its inherent heresies—that is, until a Danish astronomer named **Tycho Brahe** documented heaps of data that helped further validate Copernicus's heliocentric theory. While Brahe, living in Denmark, escaped punishment from the Roman Catholic Church, his mountains of mathematical data sparked a series of controversies for Brahe's scientific inheritors, namely his assistant, Johannes Kepler, and Kepler's intellectual contemporary, Galileo Galilei.

Johannes Kepler

Johannes Kepler worked as Tycho Brahe's assistant until Brahe died in 1601. Using Brahe's mountains of data, Kepler disproved the old Roman Catholic belief that stated that all celestial bodies orbited perfect circles. Kepler discovered that planets actually orbit in elliptical patterns rather than circles. Kepler created a series of laws that validated these orbiting patterns and planetary motions. These laws were used, in turn, to validate the heliocentric theory set forth in Copernicus's *On the Revolutions of the Heavenly Bodies*. Kepler became one of the first early modern scientists to mathematically prove that the planets revolved around the sun.

Galileo Galilei

It was the Italian scholar **Galileo Galilei** who ultimately thrust Copernican theory into full-blown heresy. First, at only seventeen years old, Galileo used scientific observation to disprove Aristotle's theory that claimed a pendulum swung at a slower rhythm before approaching its resting place. Galileo uncovered the true law of the pendulum by carefully timing the back-and-forth swings of a chandelier. He used math and science to disprove archaic theories. His discoveries proved to be influential for the young Galileo, who spent most of his life disproving other theories. Next, he went on to disprove Aristotle's theory that claimed that heavy objects fall to earth faster than lighter objects. These findings set the stage for future gravitational theory. Lastly, after building his own telescope (a new invention for the time), Galileo published his telescopic observations in a study entitled *Starry Messenger*. This study undermined canonical law more than any other scientific study to that point. It proved that celestial bodies (such as the moon) were not perfect (that is, not completely smooth). It argued that Jupiter had its own set of moons and the Sun had its own set of dark spots. Lastly, it supported Copernican theory by providing observations that backed Kepler's laws of motion.

The Catholic Church warned Galileo to stop publishing his findings in support of Copernican theory. Galileo ignored these warnings, publishing a pro-Copernican tract entitled *Concerning the Two Chief*

World Systems in 1632. Galileo was called to the Roman Catholic court to stand trial for his findings. Under the threat of inquisition and exile, Galileo had to deny his alleged heresy. He knelt before the cardinals of the Roman Catholic Church and denied his findings, a move that saved him from punishment or exile but somewhat tarnished his scientific contributions.

Sir Isaac Newton

Sir Isaac Newton spent a great deal of time studying objects, forces, and how an object's motion responds to forces. He went on to publicize his Theory of Universal Gravitation that proposed the idea that gravity is a force that acts on all objects on earth. Newton also made great advancements by using mathematics to describe the motion of objects and to predict future motions of objects by applying his mathematical models to situations. Through his extensive research, Newton is credited with summarizing the basic laws of motion for objects here on Earth.

Anatomical and Medical Discoveries

Throughout medieval times, most Europeans studying and practicing medicine cited the writings of **Galen**, an ancient Greek physician, as an expert on anatomy. However, Galen had only dissected animal cadavers; he had never dissected a human body. Most of his theories about human anatomy were purely speculative. Galen mistakenly assumed that human anatomy was similar to the animal anatomy he studied. By the sixteenth century, scientists began challenging Galen's speculative theories. In particular, a Flemish physician named Andreas Vesalius helped prove Galen's theories were inaccurate. Vesalius dissected human cadavers in spite of the taboo nature of this practice. He published his observations in a treatise entitled *On the Fabric of the Human Body* in 1543. His publication was filled with detailed drawings of his anatomical discoveries. William Harvey, an English physician, further challenged Galen's speculative theories by publishing *On the Motion of the Heart and Blood in Animals* in 1628.

Harvey had discovered that the heart acted much like a pump, circulating blood throughout the body. His new descriptions of the circulatory system challenged Galen's traditional humoral theory of the body and of disease, which assumed that imbalances in the body's humors (fluids such as blood, yellow bile, black bile, and phlegm) corresponded with a particular type of human temperament (sanguine, melancholic, choleric, and phlegmatic emotions, respectively). Physicians working in the 1700s, such as Edward Jenner, also challenged Galen's humoral theory by proving that certain diseases (such as smallpox) could be inoculated against through vaccinations.

Inductive and Deductive Reasoning

Scientific learning and investigation blossomed in the seventeenth century with the development of the scientific method. The **scientific method** provided scientists with the means to scrutinize the natural world. This method is carried out by establishing a problem or question, formulating a hypothesis (or unproved assumption), testing the hypothesis via an experiment, and confirming or disproving the hypothesis through data. Without the scientific method, scientific inquiry in the modern world would not have been able to evolve past its primitive, medieval pondering. Two men, in particular, were responsible for fashioning and advancing this method of investigation: Francis Bacon and René Descartes.

Francis Bacon

Often known as the father of the scientific method, **Francis Bacon** had few scientific credentials before he advanced his modern framework for logically gathering and testing ideas. A lawyer by trade, Bacon attacked medieval scholarship for its overreliance on the abstract nature of Aristotelian theory. He

argued that medieval scholars reasoned through abstractions rather than scientific objectivity. In his unfinished masterpiece, *The Great Instauration*, Bacon established the foundations of the modern scientific method by arguing that scientists should observe the world through concrete experimentation rather than abstract thinking. He argued that scientists should then draw conclusions from these experiments, thus laying the groundwork for modern empiricism (experimental methods). Bacon's emphasis on systematic observation and experiment sparked the interest of other thinkers in the Scientific Revolution, such as French mathematician René Descartes, who further refined Bacon's nascent scientific method.

René Descartes

René Descartes famously combined principles from algebra and geometry to formulate a new method for mathematics: analytical geometry. His new analytical approach to the universe helped strengthened the scientific method by emphasizing a rejection of abstract theories about the cosmos. Descartes approached the scientific method in a slightly different way than Bacon; he relied on mathematics and logic more than experimentation. He believed every assumption remained speculative unless proven to be true through mathematics and reason. He trained himself to take strict steps toward reasoning that allowed him to evaluate truths in the world.

Together, the perspectives set forth by Descartes and Bacon laid the groundwork of the modern scientific method, which is one part experimentation (Bacon) and one part mathematical reasoning (Descartes).

Alchemy and Astrology

As chemistry and astronomy challenged medieval scientific fallacies, many scientists still clung to the false promises of pseudo-sciences such as alchemy and astrology. Indeed, alchemy and astrology were the forerunners of chemistry and astronomy. Alchemists tried to convert substances into gold by using magic (which was usually accompanied with such property-changing materials as heat, salt, or acid). Many of the famous chemists of the Scientific Revolution actually began their careers as alchemists. The Swiss-German physician known as Paracelsus, who is known as the father of toxicology, actually began his career as an alchemist and continued to experiment with alchemy even as he made astute observations in chemistry. Likewise, many of the early astronomers were still tied to the pseudo-scientific trappings of astrology; they believed the position of the stars directly impacted human experiences and natural events. These early scientists believed that spirits and magic still controlled the universe. While alchemy and astronomy eventually waned as a result of the discoveries by the chemists and astronomers of the Scientific Revolution (Boyle, Copernicus, Brahe, Kepler, Galileo, and Newton), these old pseudo-sciences were slow to die out. Indeed, many of the early purveyors of scientific reason still clung to the promises of magic, the dark arts, and spirits behind closed doors.

The Enlightenment

Applying the Principles of the Scientific Revolution

Voltaire is a well-known philosopher of the Enlightenment. His *Philosophic Letters* and *Treatise of Tolerance* laid the foundation of Enlightenment values by espousing new notions of inalienable human rights and denouncing barbaric forms of punishment. Voltaire applied the principles of the Scientific Revolution to society and human institutions, attacking the Roman Catholic Church for its inaccurate abstractions and false understandings of the cosmos.

Beginning in 1751, **Diderot** famously published multiple volumes of his *Encyclopedia*, a compendium of books discussing Enlightenment values and scientific research. Diderot believed his *Encyclopedia* was the critical way to apply the principles of the Scientific Revolution to his own context. He wanted to expose everyone to the wonders of scientific objectivity. So, he circulated his *Encyclopedia* to educated people all over the globe in order to advance the principles of the Scientific Revolution and the Enlightenment. His efforts to disseminate his knowledge incited the ire of the French government and the Roman Catholic Church. They feared his book would provoke a revolt. Many of the aristocrats financing Diderot's project backed out once the authorities of church and state got involved. His backers feared they would be arrested. Fearless in his own right, Diderot continued to release new volumes until 1772, hoping that he could awaken the world to the supremacy of scientific reason.

French philosopher **Baron de Montesquieu** contributed to the Enlightenment by promoting Anglophile theories that honored classical philosophy and history—he believed that the British government, with its apparent separation of powers, represented the best political system in Europe. Montesquieu concluded that the division of power between the executive, legislative, and judicial powers of the British government afforded liberties to citizens that would otherwise be denied in an absolute monarchy. This analysis of British government, while undeniably oversimplified in nature, laid the foundation for his famous 1748 publication, *The Spirit of the Laws*. In this treatise, Montesquieu laid the foundation for a philosophy of government that would later be known as "checks and balances," the belief that the separate branches of government should balance power by occasionally opposing or checking one another's aims. This philosophy proved to be a powerful force in eighteenth-century political theory, paving the way for such foundational governing documents as the U.S. Constitution.

Italian philosopher **Cesare Bonesana Beccaria** used Enlightenment ideas to call for reforms in the criminal justice systems of Europe. Channeling the philosophical trends of the time, Beccaria claimed that European criminal justice systems were too focused on avenging crimes. He believed laws were meant for preserving order, not avenging criminal activities. Like many other Enlightenment philosophers, he railed against the excesses of European legal system, ridiculing the use of torture and cruel and unusual punishments. In 1764, he published his most famous work, *On Crimes and Punishments*. He favored the abolition of torture and capital punishment, and he argued that every human being deserved a just and speedy trial. He also argued that the degree of punishment should not exceed the crime. Like Locke, he believed the criminal justice system, as well as the rest of government, should serve the common good. These theories helped spark transformations in the criminal justice systems of North America and Europe throughout the late eighteenth and early nineteenth century.

New Political Models
John Locke and **Jean-Jacques Rousseau** were two of the most influential late Enlightenment philosophers. Together, they laid the foundations of modern political theory. John Locke laid this foundation by promoting the notion of **natural rights**—he believed humans were naturally capable of governing themselves and taking care of the well-being of their fellow men and women. Rousseau furthered this foundation by promoting the idea of a social contract. He believed governments had a duty to form (and protect) a social contract with citizens that helped protect their rights. These notions of natural rights and social contracts helped spawn later revolutions, such as the American Revolution and the French Revolution. These Enlightenment-era political beliefs still serve as cornerstones for modern republicanism and democracy.

Exclusion of Women from Political Life
While many Enlightenment thinkers, like Rousseau, believed in inalienable human rights, they often did not extend full human rights to women. Working in a distinctly patriarchal era, men like Rousseau argued that women should be segregated in society and excluded from political life. The power of the

Enlightenment, however, was that it espoused values that undermined these patriarchal ideas. Feminism, in many ways, has its roots in Enlightenment thought.

By espousing new notions of inalienable human rights, the Enlightenment inevitably helped advance women's rights in the form of an emerging kind of feminism. **Mary Wollstonecraft** was one of the earliest promoters of feminism. Her *Vindication of the Rights of Women* (1792) is considered one of the earliest feminist tracts. It argued that the subjugation of women by men was equally as appalling as the subjugation of citizens by monarchs.

Disseminating Enlightenment Culture

In major European cities such as Paris, Enlightenment values began to spread like wildfire thanks to the cultural and intellectual capital of young people. New ideas were consolidated and exchanged behind the walls of various popular social institutions, such as salons, coffeehouses, academies, lending libraries, and masonic lodges. These social institutions allowed the brightest young minds of Europe (and the Americas) to create Enlightenment circles. Salons, in particular, became the epicenter of many Enlightenment circles in Paris, where they were run by several influential women in the city. **Salon** initially referred to the large drawing rooms where social gatherings took place in the mansions of these influential women. Eventually the word "salon" referred to the gathering itself. As hostesses of salons, these wealthy women played an influential role in creating excitement around the Enlightenment. Salons were intense Enlightenment settings, where famous philosophers, scientists, artists, and leaders could come to discuss their ideas and enjoy artistic performances. Many famous historical figures from the Enlightenment era, such as Voltaire, frequented these female-hosted salons.

New Political Theories

In the 1600s, two English political theorists—Thomas Hobbes and John Locke—helped revolutionize the ways in which Europeans conceptualized government. Both political theorists emerged in England during the tumult of the civil war era, yet their views on the roles of those who governed and those who were governed differed greatly. Their views, at the core, resulted from very different analyses of human nature.

Thomas Hobbes' political theories were best captured in his 1651 publication, *Leviathan*. Hobbes believed human beings were ultimately selfish beasts who gravitated naturally toward wickedness. He believed the only way to tame the wickedness of the masses was through a strong ruler. Hobbes believed that every human being had a natural social contract with the ruling government, because, without the ruling government, they would suffer from the resultant social chaos. Hobbes believed society needed to be governed by absolute rulers in order to keep a naturally brutish citizenry under control. As the title of his publication implied, he believed that rulers had to be as strong as leviathans (sea monsters) to impose order on the unruly masses.

John Locke had a much different conception of human nature; he believed all humans were reasonable creatures who had the ability to improve as a result of experience. Locke believed humans were naturally capable of self-governing. Locke was highly critical of absolute monarchy, choosing instead to promote self-government. Locke—much like many other Enlightenment philosophers—believed in natural rights (i.e., life, liberty, and the pursuit of happiness). Every government, according to Locke, was responsible for protecting these natural rights of humanity. In the aftermath of the Glorious Revolution, Locke published one of his most notable works, *Two Treatises on Government* (1690). This publication was used to justify the overthrow of King James II. Locke's theories had a deep influence on other revolutions, including the American Revolution, and have been cited as the foundation of modern-day democracy.

New Economic Ideas

Adam Smith espoused political and economic theories that promoted free trade and free market ideals. Smith believed capitalist economic competition functioned best in societies that were not threatened by the looming hand of government. Smith believed businesses should have the right to compete, thrive, and perish freely in society without any government intervention. His ideals challenged old mercantilist theories and practices that promoted political intervention in economic affairs.

New Philosophies of Deism, Skepticism, and Atheism

Enlightened intellectuals such as Voltaire and Diderot cited scientific advancements in knowledge as a reason to question the authority of the Church in European society. While the major contributors to the Scientific Revolution—Kepler, Galileo, and Newton—saw science as a reflection of God's omnipresence and omnipotence, many Enlightenment philosophers were more critical of orthodox religious values. They believed traditional religion was the enemy of individual freedom and consciousness. Voltaire openly attacked organized religion. Diderot undermined its authority with the dissemination of his controversial *Encyclopedia*, which served as a compendium of Enlightenment values. Together, Voltaire and Diderot contributed to a growing tide of skepticism, which portrayed the dogmatic canon of the Church as the enemy of scientific progress. Scholars such as Pierre Bayle of France began publishing new, rational textual criticisms of the Bible. His most famous work, the *Historical and Critical Dictionary*, attacked traditional biblical exegesis by referring to the Israelite king of the Old Testament, David, as a treacherous man. Thus, the skepticism of the era extended into the work of theological exegetes like Bayle.

Skepticism also took form in entirely new theological worldviews, such as deism and atheism. **Deism** argued that God was a non-interventionist Creator who left the world to be controlled by humanity. This individualist theology was adopted by many of the Founding Fathers of the United States of America, who honored the Enlightenment through their religious beliefs. Some philosophers even went so far as to take an entirely atheistic stance, claiming that there was no greater supernatural power or God in the universe. Atheists chose instead to believe that science was the only beholder of truth in the universe, not some distant God. Atheism outright challenged the idea of theism, the belief that there is a higher being or entity in control of the universe and of one's fate.

Changes in Views on Religion

During the Enlightenment, secular, or worldly, belief systems challenged preconceived notions of religiosity. Secularization merged with individualism, pushing spirituality away from the public eye and into private life. As Enlightenment thinkers began to challenge institutional religion, religiosity was quickly repackaged as a "private matter," one that need not be displayed ostentatiously in society. Philosophers like Voltaire criticized the excesses of the traditional beliefs and practices of organized religion. Organized religion was seen as a barrier to religious purity. Many Enlightenment philosophers believed the surest way to understanding the mysteries of God was through private reflection, not public worship. More individualistic religious frameworks, such as Deism, emphasized a non-interventionist, distant Creator. These increasingly individualistic religious frameworks attempted to eradicate the "superstitious" and "fearmongering" characteristics of the monotheistic traditions of Western Civilization.

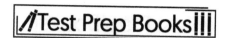

Eighteenth Century Society and Demographics

Changes in Population and Food Supply

Prior to the eighteenth century, European agriculture was confined to feudal fields, which were open to multiple parties instead of relegated to small landholdings. A short Ice Age in the seventeenth century created an inclement climate that proved to be disastrous for farmers. Poor transportation and primitive three-crop rotation only served to further disrupt and limit the food supply in Europe. Famine was common in this era of European history because seventeenth-century agricultural practices were still tied to the inefficiencies of medieval times.

The end of the mini Ice Age, the introduction of four-course crop rotation, the containment of crops to small (private) landholdings, and the implementation of new farming technologies (such as better plows) helped revolutionize agricultural practices in the eighteenth century. Likewise, the introduction of inexpensive and more sustainable crops (such as potatoes, peanuts, sweet potatoes, cassavas, and corn) helped create excess sources of food for the growing populations of Europe (and the European-American colonies). The stabilization of the food supply led to a population boom that many historians cite as a Second Agriculture Revolution (or simply as the Agricultural Revolution).

Second Agricultural Revolution

Often referred to as the **Second Agricultural Revolution**—or simply the Agricultural Revolution—the eighteenth century witnessed a series of technological advancements in trade, transportation, and agricultural production that increased the overall food supply in Europe. Indeed, the Agricultural Revolution of this era allowed populations to grow, both in cities and rural sectors, and in Europe and its colonies. The Second Agricultural Revolution was also fed by the emergence of a new Columbian Exchange between Europe, Africa, and the Americas. The Columbian Exchange brought new, more sustainable crops to Europe, which created more food for the growing masses in the cities and the countryside. Clement climate conditions ensured that more crops survived the forces of nature. A reduction in floods, droughts, and famines mitigated demographic crises, giving rise to more sustainable urban population booms.

Reduced Smallpox Mortality

Beginning in the fourteenth century, the **Black Plague** began terrorizing Europe, killing unprepared residents *en masse*. The plague continued to terrorize people throughout most of the late medieval era and into the early modern period. In fact, the plague became such a focus of European existence in this era that some scholars believe that the ubiquity of plague deaths opened people up to the human-centered values of the Renaissance, the Enlightenment, and the Scientific Revolution. The Black Plague also undermined faith in religious institutions, which failed to save millions of souls from the disease. Nonetheless, by the eighteenth century, the plague had been isolated to remote pockets in Europe, disappearing as a major epidemic threat to existence. Subsequently, scientists and physicians across the continent tried to ensure that another plague would never happen again in Europe. Medical advancements in this era focused on ways to eradicate disease and boost the life expectancy of average Europeans. In particular, Edward Jenner's discovery of inoculation techniques sent shockwaves across the medical community. Jenner discovered a vaccine that could be used to reduce smallpox mortality rates in Europe. Jenner's inoculation efforts paved the way to later advances in medicine that helped prevent mortality rates associated with common communicable diseases.

Limits on Population Growth

By the eighteenth century, throughout most of Europe, newly married couples began establishing independent households. These independent households were formed away from the newly married couples' parents. Unlike medieval times, in this era nuclear family households became more common. The nuclear family consisted of just two generations, parents and children. Men and women, particularly non-noble ones, began marrying later than they had in medieval times. Men married, on average, between the ages of twenty-seven and twenty-eight. Women, on average, married between the ages of twenty-five and twenty-seven. Late marriage became its own natural form of birth control, placing limitations on birth rates (though other forms of primitive birth control, such as glans condoms and coitus interruptus, existed). Population growth was limited by these marriage patterns, even as illegitimate birth rates skyrocketed to upward of 5 percent in some western and central European nations. There was an average of five births per family, but these births were delayed by late marriages and birth control, and they were spaced out in intervals of every two to three years. Additionally, close to 40 percent to 60 percent of women of childbearing age remained unmarried.

Decreasing Infant and Child Mortality

Child mortality rates declined during the early modern period thanks to advances in child-rearing and medicine. As a result, children, particularly infants, held a newfound importance in the family. Children became the living symbols of private life, private comfort, and public good. Early childhood education and schooling became integral extensions of Enlightenment ideals. New spaces in the home and new educational resources were spent on preparing children to become contributing members of society.

Increasing Migration to Cities

The mass migration of rural workers into European cities occurred at a time in history (roughly the fifteenth to eighteenth centuries) in which both life expectancy and the overall quality of life were on the rise. The result was the early stages of a process known as **urbanization**, a word used to describe the growth of population and infrastructure in cities. Urbanization would blossom further during the Industrial Revolution, but it began to gain momentum during the age of the Scientific Revolution and Enlightenment. The Columbian Exchange provided food and goods to Europe that could help sustain these growing populations. Poor workers from rural areas flocked to cities for new opportunities. In particular, they flocked there in order to try to take part in the growing manufacturing and merchant economies.

While the number of residents belonging to "the urban poor" increased, placing a social and environmental strain on European cities, this mass migration to city centers also helped create a new urban elite. New urbanites, rich or poor, were exposed to a new kind of European urbanism. On the one hand, social elites enjoyed new leisure, new entertainment, and new political/economic clout. On the other hand, the poor rural migrants were often forced into further destitution. This era saw an increase in social venues for the elites, such as coffee shops, universities, and salons, but it also saw an increase in vagrancy, infanticide, and prostitution among the poor.

Migration in Search of Work

The Agricultural Revolution of the eighteenth century increased food production as a result of an improved climate and higher yields per acreage. These higher yields benefitted from technological advances (such as the Rotherham swing plow) and new farming techniques (such as the Norfolk four-course system). These new technologies caused unemployment for many rural peasants because fewer workers were required to create higher farming yields. Many rural workers looked to the bustling industrial-capitalist infrastructures of European cities as a potential solution to their problem. Hundreds

of thousands of workers from rural areas migrated to European cities in search of work. This mass migration strained the urban infrastructures of Europe, as many rural migrants struggled to find enough work in their new urban homes. The result was the emergence of an entirely new urban underclass that struggled to survive in abject poverty and unsanitary conditions.

Growth of Cities

In cities, the problem of poverty eroded tradition communal values, forcing many lower-class city dwellers into professions of beggary and prostitution. High death rates, particularly among children, still plagued European cities, even years after the Black Death. Cities struggled to meet the demands of the urban underclasses; they struggled to provide protection and a healthy environment through infrastructure and governance. Open sewers flooded districts due to the strain of mass migration. Many people died as a result of unsanitary living conditions such as polluted water and open sewers. In western Europe, an estimated 10 percent of the entire population remained dependent on begging, prostitution, or charity for basic sustenance. As a result, a new Christian notion of the "idle poor" emerged, which eroded centuries of emphasis on Christian charity. Nonetheless, many charitable institutions sprouted in the churches, but these institutions also struggled to meet the demands caused by the dire circumstances in urban sectors.

Concentration of the Poor in Cities

Poverty became more prevalent in western and central European cities by the eighteenth century as a result of population booms and underdeveloped urban infrastructure. Overcrowding became a concern as rural migrants flocked to cities to find work as laborers. While a new industrial economy was beginning to develop, unskilled workers struggled to find employment opportunities in these urban hubs. Poverty became so visible that entirely new classes of licensed and unlicensed beggars formed in cities such as Venice, Bologna, Mainz, London, and Paris. In cities such as Mainz, over 30 percent of the city population belonged to this beggar class. By the end of the eighteenth century, around 10 percent of the total populations in Great Britain and France were part of the emerging beggar class.

Eighteenth Century Culture and Arts

Development of Public Opinion

Censorship continued to be a pressing issue during the Age of Enlightenment and Scientific Revolution. Scientists and philosophers were threatened by inquisition and imprisonment if they did not uphold the canonical values of the Roman Catholic Church. Likewise, many absolute monarchs threatened anyone who spoke out against the crown. Even revolutionary rulers, like Oliver Cromwell in England, threatened people with censorship. Scientists like Galileo Galilei were placed on trial for publishing controversial findings, such as the heliocentric theories set forth in *Concerning the Two Chief World Systems* (1632). Truth became confounded with heresy or treason as religious and political leaders tried to maintain control over an increasingly literate populace. However, the invention of the Gutenberg printing press, coupled with subsequent advances in printing technology, encouraged the growth of the literate masses. Printing materials became the ideological weapons of Enlightenment thinkers. Tracts like Thomas Paine's *Common Sense*, among others, helped ignite entire revolutions. A growing literate public ensured that public opinion would be known and heard (and, if necessary, printed for all eyes to see).

Challenges to Accepted Social Norms

By the eighteenth century, Enlightenment values became deeply embedded in all corners of European and American society. The natural sciences, literature (including travel literature), and popular culture, in particular, exposed literate populations to cultures that existed outside Europe. This exposure challenged the previously isolated social norms of people in European nations. New cultural tastes were acquired through the popularization of natural science, the dissemination of travel literature and novels, and the emergence of cultural relativism in popular culture.

Changes in Artistic Expression

The art created during the Enlightenment was influenced by humanism with its focus on the human instead of the divine; painters began shifting their energies away from religious themes. Religion, in general, was a fading institution, as the focus shifted to the inalienable rights of common citizens. Painters began depicting scenes that centered on private life and the public good, both of which were cornerstones of Enlightenment values. Royal power, which had been a common artistic theme of medieval times, also faded in the wake of Enlightenment values. Many painters sought to illustrate the ways in which Enlightenment ideals could influence all aspects of society and the political masses.

Baroque Art and Music

Throughout much of the seventeenth and early-mid eighteenth centuries, the arts—literature, architecture, paintings, and music—had been dominated by a Baroque style that catered to the luxurious tastes of absolute monarchs such as Louis XIV of France. The Baroque style was characterized by an obsession with the grand and the ornate. Elaborate palaces such as Louis XIV's Versailles were adorned with elegant, gold-leafed painting frames, opulent statues, and ornamental architectural features. Monarchs employed artists-in-residence to create opulent paintings that were rich in color and detail. The music of the time was dominated by dramatic organ and choral selections, such as those composed by Johann Sebastian Bach and George Frederick. All the arts were representations of the attempt of absolute monarchies to exert power over their states. It was not until the Enlightenment that these artistic styles began to change.

Neoclassicism

The Enlightenment also shifted the artistic tastes of the time. The opulence of the Baroque style faded in the wake of the Enlightenment's renewed emphasis on reason, order, and balance. **Neoclassicism** emerged as the new style of Enlightenment artists. Borrowing themes from classical Greek and Roman artwork and architecture, Neoclassical artists set out to imitate the simple and elegant structures of the classical world. Greek and Roman philosophy also influenced Neoclassicism, as painters tried to imitate nature and human anatomy in their artwork. The humanist tendencies of the Enlightenment era gave artists an interest in depicting the experience of living in a secular society. Novels emerged as the preferred literary construct of the era. In the 1700s, a flood of novels captured readers' attention by telling tales of extraordinary individuals. Examples of such novels include *Robinson Crusoe* by Daniel Defoe (1719), *The History of Tom Jones, A Foundling* by Henry Fielding (1749), and *The History of Sir Charles Grandison* by Samuel Richardson (1753). The humanist focus helped make novels more relatable to the growing literate classes of society. The entertaining stories were written in vernacular languages and reached a wider audience thanks to the technological advancements of the printing press.

Consumer Revolution

In feudal times, most farms and residences remained communal. Peasants contributed to agricultural production and manufacturing systems in large feudal landholdings that were owned by nobles. This system was transformed dramatically as a result of the consumer revolution, which increased the privatization of land, property, and labor. As a result of these privatization efforts, new venues for leisure activities emerged. These new venues included coffeehouses, taverns, and salons. Likewise, the

commercial revolution resulted in the widespread accumulation of foreign goods in private residences. New goods from Asia, Africa, and the Americas made their way into European homes.

Enlightened Absolutism and Other Approaches to Power

Enlightened Absolutism

The Enlightenment did not remain confined to the salons and art circles of Eastern and Central Europe for long; it also began infiltrating the ideological systems of the royal courts. Even with these ideas circulating, monarchy remained the predominant method of rule. Many Enlightenment philosophers, such as Voltaire, championed the prospects of monarchy. Yet these philosophers also encouraged monarchs to rule more justly and compassionately. This fusion between the new and the old created an entirely new framework for government: enlightened absolutism, or enlightened despotism. Referred to by some scholars as "enlightened despots," the kings and queens who embraced this new brand of absolutism promised to carry out reforms that embodied the spirit of the Enlightenment. Enlightened despots were contradictory figures—they wanted to support the Enlightenment, but they also wanted to maintain control and expand their influence as monarchs. The enlightened despots simultaneously honored and undermined Enlightenment values. King Frederick II of Prussia, known as Frederick the Great, is a prime example of this type of enlightened despot.

King Frederick II of Prussia, known as **Frederick the Great**, championed Enlightenment ideals by carrying out reforms that promoted improved educational standards, encouraged religious freedoms, reduced censorship practices, and abolished torture. His reforms only went so far, however. For instance, although Frederick the Great was against serfdom in theory, he never abolished the system of serfdom in practice. Frederick the Great, like leaders before him, was still reliant on the support of the Junkers (the landed nobility of Prussia), so he did not want to challenge them by abolishing a system that benefitted their socioeconomic interests. Nonetheless, Frederick the Great's efforts to instill Enlightenment values in his royal court should not be downplayed. He consulted regularly with Voltaire, and he even referred to himself as "first servant of the state." His efforts to become an enlightened despot appealed to the philosophers and his countrymen, and his reforms were quite radical for their time.

Toleration for Christian Minorities

Changing relationships between the ruler and the state encouraged enlightened despots of the late eighteenth century to extend religious tolerance to Christian minorities, and, in some particularly enlightened states, civil equality to Jews. Prior to the Enlightenment, the state and the citizen existed to serve the monarch. As a result of the Enlightenment, many monarchs claimed that it was their divine duty to serve the state and its citizens, as in the case of Frederick the Great, who considered himself "first servant of the state". This shift in mentality—combined with the renewed emphasis on secularization that followed the Peace of Westphalia (1648)—prepared the world for a new era of religious tolerance and freedom of worship. **Holy Roman Emperor Joseph II** of Austria reflects this shift in religious tolerance more than any other Enlightenment monarch of this era. As part of his radical reforms, Joseph II promoted freedom of worship for Protestants, Catholics, Orthodox Christians, and even Jews (who were historically marginalized by Christian rulers' policies). Other enlightened despots, such as Frederick the Great and Catherine the Great, also enacted policies that favored religious tolerance, but few monarchs were as radical as Joseph II when it came to religious freedom.

Rise of Prussia and Changes to Austrian Empire

The Peace of Westphalia (1648) ended the Thirty Years' War, enabling the states of the Holy Roman Empire to gain their autonomy and sovereignty. The German state fractured into hundreds of smaller sovereign states. Two of these sovereign states emerged as dominant European powers in the seventeenth and eighteenth centuries: Prussia and Austria.

Frederick William I came to power in Brandenburg-Prussia during the turmoil of the Thirty Years' War (c. 1640). Brandenburg-Prussia was an autonomous principality that united three disconnected regions in eastern, central, and western Germany. Realizing that Brandenburg-Prussia was a fractured territory without natural frontiers for defense, Frederick William I recruited an impressive standing army of close to 50,000 men to assist him with unifying and protecting the territory. To sustain the expensive military forces, Frederick William I created the **General War Commissariat**. This department allowed Frederick William I to levy taxes to sustain his military interests. The General War Commissariat quickly evolved into a government bureaucracy. Most members of the General War Commissariat were Junkers, landowning Brandenburg-Prussian aristocrats. These Junkers served as generals and soldiers for Frederick William I's growing army.

Frederick William I recruited the Junkers to his cause by promising them unlimited power over peasants in exchange for their loyalty to the expanding Prussian state. Frederick William I would promote Junkers to the highest ranks of his military as long as they promised not to challenge the authority of the emerging Prussian state. The peasant class did not benefit as much from the political power play—the Junkers appropriated their land, forcing them back into serfdom which had been previously banned. While serfdom was not new, it evolved into something new with Frederick William I's concessions to the Junkers. Frederick William I also built the economy by supporting local mercantile industries and constructing the Brandenburg-Prussian infrastructure (i.e., roads and canals). Additionally, Frederick William I enacted high tariffs, levied stiff taxes and subsidies, and manipulated industrial monopolies in his favor. All this benefitted the Junkers rather than the emerging working class and industrial middle class of Brandenburg-Prussia. By the time his son, Frederick II, assumed power in 1688, Brandenburg-Prussia had consolidated a tremendous amount of money and power. As a result of assisting the Holy Roman Empire in the War of the Spanish Succession, the Holy Roman Emperor Charles VI announced that Frederick II would officially be granted the title "King of Prussia." Frederick III transformed into King Frederick I, ruler of Prussia, and Prussia remained a dominant military force in the region for decades to come.

The Hapsburg Dynasty of Austria had long been a dominant force in European affairs by the time the Peace of Westphalia was enacted in 1648. Nevertheless, the Thirty Years' War shifted power away from the former Hapsburg stronghold in Germany. The Hapsburgs' dream of creating a strong empire in Germany was crushed by the Thirty Years' War—they were forced to pursue a new dream, one that focused on creating a new Austrian Empire in eastern and southeastern Europe. At the expense of the disintegrating Ottoman Empire, the Austrian Hapsburgs expanded primarily south and east into regions such as Hungary, Transylvania, Slovenia, and Croatia. These territories added to the empire's hereditary claims in Lower and Upper Austria, Tyrol, Styria, Carniola, and Carinthia. Following the War of the Spanish Succession, the ever-expanding Austrian Empire also gained possessions in Spanish Italy and the Spanish Netherlands. The Austrian Empire remained relatively decentralized, with various laws and various national groups. The Hapsburgs were technically emperors, but they were also the archdukes of Austria and the kings of Hungary and Bohemia. These decentralized territories remained unified through their common bureaucratic service to the House of Hapsburg. Military officers and government

bureaucrats joined together in a loose confederation of loyalty, which eventually evolved into a military juggernaut.

By the eighteenth century, the Austrian Empire was a force to be reckoned with. Yet the rise to military prowess was not without struggle. The diverse assortment of nationalities within the Austrian Empire—the Germans, Croatians, Hungarians, Czechs, and Italians—made it difficult for Charles VI of the Hapsburg Dynasty, who rose to power in 1711, to maintain control over his decentralized kingdoms. Throughout his reign, Charles VI reflected upon the future of his empire, which did not have a male heir to the throne. Without a son to lead the empire upon his death, Charles VI convinced leaders in Europe to recognize his eldest daughter, Maria Theresa (1717–1780) as the heir and future empress. Through these agreements, Maria Theresa was supposed to assume the throne peacefully upon her father's passing. The exact opposite occurred—Maria Theresa's reign was plagued with foreign wars, namely with the emerging state of Prussia to the north of Austria.

In 1740, Maria Theresa officially succeeded her father. Her succession as Empress of Austria occurred just a few months after King Frederick II assumed the throne in Prussia. The expansionist efforts of King Frederick II immediately placed him at odds with Empress Maria Theresa. Frederick II wanted to take over the Austrian land of Silesia, which was known for its agricultural production and industries. In typical patriarchal fashion, Frederick II labeled Maria Theresa an inept ruler just because she was a woman. He believed his army could overpower her authority in the land of Silesia. In 1740, his army occupied Silesia, launching the region into the War of the Austrian Succession.

Maria Theresa, a savvy politician in her own right, garnered the support of the Hungarian nobles in her empire. They helped her create a formidable army for the War of the Austrian Succession. Around this same time, Great Britain joined Austria in a war against France (which just happened to be an ally of Prussia). Maria Theresa eventually lost Silesia to Prussia via the **Treaty of Aix-la-Chapelle** (1748) but proved to be generally successful in stifling all other Prussian aggressions against her empire.

Maria Theresa, who famously gave birth to Marie Antoinette, future bride of King Louis XVI of France, eventually mended relations with the French kingdom, creating an alliance that can best be described as a diplomatic revolution. King Frederick II, a constant thorn in the Austrian empress's side, countered this alliance by signing a treaty with Great Britain (Austria's former ally). The result was political turmoil: Austria, France, and Russia joined arms against Prussia and Great Britain in a global conflict that became known as the **Seven Years' War**, known as the **French and Indian War** in the colonies of North America. The war lasted from 1756 to 1763, dramatically shifting global politics and economics in favor of Great Britain. Maria Theresa simultaneously strengthened and destabilized the Austrian Empire in her lifetime, making her reign one of mixed results in an age of perpetual Austrian-Prussian conflict.

Conflict, Crisis, and Reaction in the Late Eighteenth Century

Contextualizing Eighteenth Century States

Political and Military Conflicts

Europe experienced numerous crises and conflicts between 1648 and 1815. Some of the most significant military conflicts were the War of the Spanish Succession (1701–1714) and the Seven Years' War (1756–1763), largely because British victories paved the way for its rise as a global power. In addition, Britain's victories over the French resulted in colonial transfers and financial crises, and King Louis XVI of France struggled to beat back a revolutionary groundswell.

The **French Revolution** (1789–1799) was the defining political crisis of this period, and it sparked the beginning of a paradigm shift in European models of political sovereignty. Prior to the French Revolution, absolute monarchs reigned across Europe, with the exception of Britain's constitutional monarchy. A monarchy functioned as a country's sole sovereign authority, meaning it was the primary source of political authority. In contrast, the French Revolution was fought to make the people the true sovereign, and therefore, revolutionaries believed governments should reflect citizens' attitudes, values, and desires. Following a failed attempt at forming a constitutional monarchy, the French Revolution grew more lawless, violent, and chaotic. European monarchies rejected to popular sovereignty, formed broad international coalitions, and launched a prolonged war against France. Although France never succumbed to the European coalitions, the **Revolutionary Wars** (1792–1802) destabilized the government. In 1799, a supremely talented French general, **Napoleon Bonaparte**, overthrew France's republic government and eventually installed a military dictatorship.

Almost immediately after assuming authority, Napoleon launched a series of highly successful military campaigns against his European rivals in the early stages of the **Napoleonic Wars** (1803–1815). Napoleon's victories spread the French Revolution's ideals, political system, and legal code across much of Europe. The threat of French imperialism caused Europeans to embrace nationalism, mirroring the way that French revolutionaries used nationalism to implement popular sovereignty. Once the European coalition finally defeated Napoleon, they held the **Congress of Vienna** (1814–1815) to restore European monarchies, suppress revolutionary fervor, and promote peace.

Economic Developments

During the seventeenth and eighteenth centuries, the most important economic development was the growth of global markets. European colonization of territory in the Americas, Africa, the Indian subcontinent, and Southeast Asia boosted the frequency and intensity of international commercial exchanges. Europeans extracted raw products and natural resources from colonies, produced manufactured goods, and then exported those goods back to the colonies. While commercial rivalries strengthened the global market as European states competed to expand their networks, these rivalries also expanded the scope of warfare. For example, the Seven Years' War spread to European colonies in the Caribbean, North America, South America, the Indian subcontinent, and Southeast Asia. Therefore, European states often sought to avoid or end disruptive military conflicts through diplomacy. Colonial territories served as enticing bargaining chips in diplomatic negotiations, and European states regularly entered into agreements to expand foreign powers' access to their colonial markets. These agreements increased in the late eighteenth century after European governments adopted more liberal economic policies, such as limits on aristocratic privileges and legal protections for private businesses. The introduction of free markets, the free movement of labor, and free trade deals spurred the development of capitalism in Europe, which further intensified the development of global markets.

Intellectual Movements

The Enlightenment (1687–1800) and Romanticism (1790—1850) were this period's most influential intellectual movements. The Enlightenment promoted empiricism and rationality above all else. Empiricism was first developed during the Scientific Revolution (1543–1800) as a means of improving experimentation, and the Enlightenment greatly expanded the application of scientific concepts. For example, Enlightenment philosophers used empiricism to craft philosophical arguments for equality, civil liberties, and popular sovereignty. Although proposed political and social reforms weren't always implemented, the Enlightenment's emphasis on rationality transformed European culture. This transformation is perhaps most evident in the enhanced cultural value of education and scientific

innovation, which further spurred the spread of the Scientific Revolution and advancement of modern science in a virtuous cycle.

Romanticism was a movement grew in response to the Enlightenment's struggle to fulfill its lofty promises of progress. Reason couldn't fully express the horrors of the French Revolution, the terror of never-ending warfare, and the spontaneous eruption of nationalism. Romantic artists, musicians, and writers filled this void through a renewed focus on feelings and emotions. This subjectivity better reflected how people felt when experiencing irrational and traumatic events, particularly when those events were emotionally driven. As a result, Romanticism helped people understand disruptive political movements and dramatic societal changes.

Rise of Global Markets

Expansion of European Commerce

The development of **capitalism** represented a major breakthrough in the rise of global markets. During the mid-eighteenth century, British economists challenged mercantilist policies and their underlying assumptions about economic competition between states, namely, that economic growth could be achieved without harming rival states. In general, capitalism prioritized freedom in economic activities, and states implemented free trade policies to support the growth of international commerce. Rather than treating other states as economic competitors, states began specializing in economic sectors where they were the most efficient and trading their surplus for the goods they no longer produced. Free trade agreements also allowed states to trade with their rival's colonies, which further expanded the global marketplace. For indigenous populations in the colonies, capitalism strongly mirrored mercantilism in continuing to oppress them. The primary difference between the two systems was that under capitalism most state-owned enterprises were replaced with private industries.

Capitalism promoted the private accumulation of wealth and free markets. Economic freedom triggered a period of rapid industrialization with numerous social, political, and cultural effects. The most dramatic consequence was the creation of a middle class. As more merchants and industrialists joined the middle class, this social group challenged traditional political authorities such as monarchies. The middle class also had sufficient disposable income to purchase significant amounts of domestic and foreign consumer goods. A greater diversity of consumer goods had a deep cultural impact, especially in allowing individuals to be more selective about what they consumed. In effect, capitalism's emphasis on the individual placed further pressure on political and social systems to be more responsive and flexible.

Commercial Rivalries

European rivalries directly led to the growth of a global market during the late seventeenth century. To gain an advantage over rivals, European states sought to conquer and exploit colonial territories. Consequently, the Netherlands, Portugal, Spain, France, and Britain engaged in a fierce maritime competition to establish colonies and increase access to foreign markets.

European states especially valued Atlantic trade routes because they connected Europe with the Americas and West Africa. Britain and France had previously established West African colonies largely for the purpose of securing a steady supply of slaves, but a handful of European states had other economic interests in this region. In the Americas, several powers, including the Netherlands, Portugal, Spain, France, and Britain, controlled vast colonies. Therefore, these European states maintained large naval forces to protect and strengthen their overseas economic interests.

European Sea Powers

During the eighteenth century, Britain emerged as the preeminent naval power after its Royal Navy defeated Dutch forces in the Caribbean and thwarted French expansion in North America. Along with warfare, commercial rivalries had a heavy influence on diplomacy. Military conflicts often ended with states agreeing to expand or limit foreign access to its colonies. Given its disproportionate power and influence, Britain steadfastly refused to loosen its colonial monopoly and aggressively deployed diplomatic means to expand British merchants' access to foreign markets. Most infamously, Britain implemented a series of Navigation Acts, which prohibited foreign ships from entering British colonial ports or transporting British goods. By the end of the eighteenth century, Britain had emerged as the leading commercial power on the Atlantic Ocean.

Rivalries in Asia

European rivals similarly vied for control over lucrative territory in Southeast Asia and on the Indian subcontinent. In Southeast Asia, European states established colonies to consolidate control over the spice trade and gain access to the lucrative Chinese market. Spain, Portugal, and the Netherlands held numerous islands and archipelagos located in the present-day countries of Indonesia and the Philippines. French Indochina consisted of territory in present-day Cambodia, Laos, and Vietnam, while Britain controlled territory in present-day Borneo, Brunei, Myanmar, Malaysia, and Thailand. Of particular importance, the Netherlands' control of the East Indies funded its empire. Britain, in addition to holding vast territories in Southeast Asia, forced Danish, Dutch, French, and Portuguese merchants to abandon their trading posts on the Indian subcontinent.

Britain's Ascendancy

Rivalry Between Britain and France

During the late seventeenth and eighteenth centuries, Britain established a global empire so large that it was commonly referred to as "the empire on which the sun never sets." Since Britain industrialized before its European rivals, it could more efficiently transform raw resources into manufactured goods. Britain's sizable investment in its Royal Navy allowed the country to protect trade routes, transport goods, and project political and military power on a global scale. Furthermore, Britain benefited from an innovative government and civil institutions that were used to consolidate political power. In 1707, England, Scotland, and Wales united to establish Great Britain as a constitutional monarchy with a parliamentary system. Compared to other European states, Britain also allowed more representative government. Popular representation strengthened the political system's legitimacy and supported more responsive policymaking. Britain also deftly handled the administration of its vast colonies. British colonies enjoyed some limited right to self-government, which served to legitimize colonization. Similarly, Britain benefited from delegating political and economic power to the British East India Company, which reduced costs and increased commercial efficiency.

Britain successfully leveraged economic, political, and military advantages to best its chief rivals—the Dutch Republic, France, and Spain—in several global conflicts. From 1701 to 1714, Britain allied with the Dutch Republic, the Holy Roman Empire, Prussia, and Portugal in the War of the Spanish Succession to prevent the House of Bourbon from aligning the French and Spanish crowns. Britain emerged from this conflict as the undisputed victor. After wartime debts bankrupted the Dutch Republic, Britain supplanted the Dutch as the dominant commercial power in Asia. Under the Treaty of Utrecht (1713), Britain annexed strategically valuable island fortresses from Spain and received commercial rights within the Spanish Empire. Following the War of the Spanish Succession, the only country that could seriously threaten Britain's global empire was France.

Anglo-Franco competition culminated in the Seven Years' War (1756–1763). Britain primarily allied itself with Prussia, while French formed a grand coalition with Austria, the Holy Roman Empire, Spain, and Sweden. Due to these powers' extensive colonial holdings, fighting rapidly spread across Europe, North America, South America, India, and West Africa. The British Royal Navy played a decisive role in the conflict because it limited France's ability to coordinate between the disparate theaters of war. In the European theater, Britain relied on the King of Prussia Frederick the Great's brilliant military leadership, and Prussia repeatedly bogged down and defeated numerically superior armies. Britain also exploited its ability to raise enormous colonial armies, particularly in North America and India. Following a series of strategic victories, France sued for peace and signed the Treaty of 1763, which involved a colossal colonial transfer to the victors. Britain annexed all French possessions in present-day Canada as well as the Spanish colony of Florida, and France was further forced to cede its Louisiana territory to Spain.

Rather than licking its wounds and reevaluating its geopolitical ambitions, France doubled down on its opposition to Britain during the American Revolutionary War (1775–1783). France provided the American rebels with financial aid, weapons, logistical support, troops, and naval power. French support was indispensable for the Americans, but France was lending money it didn't have and couldn't reasonably repay. So, although the American Revolution was a notable setback for Britain, it triggered a catastrophic financial crisis in France.

Britain's global empire had significant economic, political, social, and cultural effects. Given its expansive territorial holdings and hegemonic naval power, Britain effectively dominated the international trade system. As a relatively liberal constitutional monarchy, Britain simultaneously served as a champion of representative government and defender of aristocratic privileges in society and government. Furthermore, Britain's superpower status facilitated the dissemination of English architecture, customs, food, language, legal system, and sports all over the world.

French Revolution

Causes of the French Revolution

The **French Revolution** (1789–1799) was an important event in modern history. Historians continue to debate the relative importance of its many short-term and long-term causes, but they can be broadly grouped into three interrelated categories.

First, the French government's attempts to compete with Britain had proven disastrous. Britain soundly defeated France in the Seven Years' War (1756–1763), resulting in an explosion of national debt and the forfeiture of valuable French colonies in North America. France then further overextended itself in lending financial and military support to the rebels in the American Revolutionary War (1775–1783). As a result, the French government experienced a crippling debt crisis and stunted economic growth throughout the 1780s.

Second, a number of material issues plagued the French economic system in the run-up to the French Revolution. France's antiquated tax system prevented the government from efficiently raising revenue, which compounded the economic consequences of a soaring national debt. Instead of reforming the taxation system, the government introduced even more regressive taxes on the bourgeoisie (middle class) and peasants. Unsurprisingly, these tax policies sent the public into an uproar. The French government also deregulated agricultural industries, exacerbating long-term environmental issues and underperforming harvests. As the famine and bread shortages worsened, French peasants faced starvation.

Third, the French political system was unstable and unable to fend off new ideological challenges. France historically had a rigid class system known as the **Estates General**. The Third Estate accounted for approximately 95 percent of the French population, but they were categorically denied a way to voice economic and political grievances. This hopelessness pushed citizens to embrace Enlightenment concepts such as human rights and popular sovereignty.

Constitutional Monarchy

The political situation eventually became untenable, and on May 5, 1789, **King Louis XVI** called for a meeting of the Estates General for the first time since 1614. Representatives presented "books of grievances" to highlight the country's most pressing problems, but the Estates General failed to make much progress. Soon afterward, the Third Estate held a separate meeting and formed the National Constituent Assembly, which declared itself to be the true representative of French citizens. On July 14, 1789, a citizen militia stormed the Bastille, a royal fortress, and seized its weapons. This symbolic victory legitimized the Assembly and triggered a mass rebellion against the monarchy.

After the storming of the Bastille, the Assembly abolished feudalism and special privileges enjoyed by the Catholic Church, including an elimination on a 10 percent income tax known as the tithe. On August 26, 1789, the Assembly issued the **Declaration of the Rights of Man and of the Citizen**. Drawing from Enlightenment ideas, the Declaration declared the existence of universal and inalienable universal rights, such as the rights to freedom, representative government, and equal protection under the law. However, at this point, the Assembly was merely calling for the establishment of a constitutional monarchy rather than an outright regime change.

The French Revolution took on a new dimension when women rioted over the price of bread in Paris on October 5, 1789. With the support of revolutionaries, women marched on the Palace of Versailles and successfully secured an audience with the king. The power of this protest forced King Louis XVI to accept that reform couldn't be avoided. The Catholic Church similarly failed to preserve its traditional rights and powers. After it abolished the tithe, the Assembly passed the **Civil Constitution of the Clergy** on July 12, 1790. The Civil Constitution essentially nationalized the Catholic Church, relegating clergy to the status of public servants. Additionally, the Assembly forced the clergy to either swear an oath of loyalty to the Civil Constitution or face expulsion from France.

In September 1791, the Assembly ratified a formal constitution, establishing a constitutional monarchy in France. The Constitution of 1791 created a unicameral Legislative Assembly, but voting rights were limited to men who paid a certain amount of taxes. The Constitution also replaced the traditional administrative departments with eighty-three departments of relatively equal size to promote popular representation. Additionally, the Constitution abolished all hereditary privileges and offices except for the King of France.

Despite its reforms, the constitutional monarchy failed in dramatic fashion. King Louis XVI worked to undermine his constitutional limitations, and the reforms didn't sufficiently address France's dire financial situation. The lower classes also rejected the Constitution, demanding the right to vote and more relief from the burdensome taxation system. Furthermore, the constitutional monarchy was forced to literally fight for its survival in the Revolutionary Wars (1792–1802) against a powerful coalition of European states that rejected republicanism. At various points, the successive coalitions included: Austria, Britain, the Dutch Republic, Italian states, the Holy Roman Empire, Portugal, Prussia, and Spain. With the French Revolution on the brink of collapse, the Legislative Assembly introduced universal male suffrage and held elections for its successor organization, the National Convention, in

1792. As its first act, the National Convention abolished the monarchy and established the French Republic.

Reign of Terror

The French Revolution escalated with the execution of King Louis XVI on January 21, 1793, for allegedly conspiring to support the armies invading France. Horrified by the King's execution, the European coalition increased its efforts to overthrow the National Convention. As the tides of war turned against France, radical revolutionaries known as the **Jacobins** consolidated power in the National Convention. The Jacobins were instrumental in convincing the National Convention to pass a measure known as *levée en masse* (mass conscription). Mass conscription of young men was used to create a national army. Although the policy was generally unpopular, mass conscription revived the French military and thwarted the European coalition's invasion of France. The Jacobins founded numerous institutions to protect the National Convention from alleged counter-revolutionary elements, such as monarchists, constitutional monarchists, and the bourgeoisie.

One of the most powerful political institutions was the **Committee of Public Safety**. The National Convention delegated broad emergency powers to the Committee, including oversight duties over the military, judiciary, and legislature. Two Jacobins, Georges Danton and Maximilien Robespierre, played an outsized role in using the Committee to suppress domestic opposition, including monarchists, constitutional monarchists, and the bourgeoisie. At times, the Committee even targeted other revolutionary factions. For example, when the Society of Revolutionary Republican Women challenged the disenfranchisement of women, the Committee denounced the group as counterrevolutionaries. Facing threats of further persecution, the Society of Revolutionary Republican Women was forced to dissolve in 1793.

Under Danton and Robespierre's leadership, the National Convention and the Committee of Public Safety implemented several policies designed to squash public unrest, such as wage increases and price fixing schemes to lower the price of bread. Additionally, Robespierre spearheaded the implementation of numerous de-Christianization policies. For example, the National Convention established the deist Cult of the Supreme Being as a state religion to undermine the Catholic Church. Jean-Paul Marat's journalism helped popularize many of the Jacobins' reform efforts. Throughout the early stages of the French Revolution, Marat passionately advocated for human rights, condemned the monarchy, and legitimized the Jacobins' revolutionary institutions. Following his assassination in 1793, the Jacobins publicly portrayed Marat as a revolutionary martyr, which further strengthened their credibility as the vanguard of the French Revolution.

In the spring of 1793, Danton and Robespierre leveraged their growing political influence to reestablish the Revolutionary Tribunal. The **Revolutionary Tribunal** oversaw approximately 300,000 arrests and 17,000 executions during its infamous Reign of Terror (1793–1794). Much of this persecution was focused on Robespierre's political rivals, such as the Girondist faction of the Jacobins. For example, the Revolutionary Tribunal executed the Girondist leader Olympe de Gouges after she challenged the National Convention to support gender equality. Eventually the leaders of the Reign of Terror became its final victims.

Revolutionary Armies

Following Robespierre's execution on July 28, 1794, the National Convention ratified a new constitution to create the **Directory**, a five-member committee. The Directory brought a halt to the mass executions, outlawed the Jacobins, and restored the rule of law. However, the Directory was unable to solve the country's financial issues, mostly due to the demands of waging war against the European coalition.

Despite its unsustainable costs, a series of decisive military victories allowed the Directory to export its revolution. Between 1797 and 1799, the Directory founded "sister republics" in the Netherlands, Switzerland, and Italy. On the Italian Peninsula, Napoleon Bonaparte established himself as a military hero by repeatedly defeating Austrian forces. Upon his return to France in late 1799, Napoleon orchestrated a coup and assumed the title of First Consul, marking the end of the French Revolution and beginning of a military dictatorship.

The French Revolution's Effects

The French Revolution's impact on Europe cannot be overstated; it had far-reaching effects on European economics, politics, culture, and society. Prior to the French Revolution, monarchies unilaterally governed European economic, political, and social systems, and full-fledged feudalism continued in some regions, particularly in Central Europe. The desire to preserve these traditional power structures united European states in their opposition to the new French Republic.

European middle and working classes were the chief beneficiaries of the French Revolution's dismantling of aristocratic privileges. Along with gaining political representation and civil liberties, the collapse of feudalism broadened citizens' professional opportunities. Consequently, the introduction of truly free labor markets laid the foundation for industrialization, spurring the transition toward capitalism. Similar changes occurred in European political systems. Facing the threat of a popular insurrection stoked by the French Revolution's emphasis on human rights and equality, European monarchies disavowed absolutism and accepted some limited political reforms, including an expansion of legal protections and civil rights. European monarchies also utilized nationalism to condemn French aggression and justify the need for continuous warfare as a matter of national defense.

Economic and political reforms naturally resulted in considerable social and cultural shifts. Secularism increased as the separation of church and state spread across Europe, and consumer culture grew as European economies and societies liberalized to varying degrees. The French Revolution also caused sweeping changes to class structure. As the power of European aristocracies declined, class structure became more closely related to wealth than to bloodlines. Furthermore, the French Revolution reconfigured the relationship between individuals, families, social groups, and the state. Compared to the state's prior dominance over society, individuals and social groups gained more ownership over the course of the state. Just like in the French Republic, European family units began to function as centers of patriotism and political learning.

Haitian Revolution

The French Revolution inspired a slave insurrection in one of its most valuable colonies, Saint-Domingue, which culminated in the stunning **Haitian Revolution** (1791–1804). From beginning to end, the Haitian Revolution was a brutal affair, costing the lives of approximately 200,000 Haitians and 150,000 Europeans.

After the National Constituent Assembly issued the Declaration of the Rights of Man (1789), African slaves began demanding the abolition of slavery on Saint-Domingue. Despite the French Revolution's professed commitment to equality, the slavery question was highly divisive. While French revolutionaries debated whether equality was more important than cheap labor, African slaves took destiny into their own hands. On August 21, 1791, thousands of slaves rebelled in brutal fashion, killing slave masters and their families en masse.

Under the leadership of former slave turned general **Toussaint Louverture**, rebel factions achieved several impressive early victories, but the conflict increased in complexity when Great Britain and Spain entered the fray in 1793. While Britain and Spain assisted the rebels to undermine France, neither country intended to abolish slavery, believing it would incite insurrections in their own slave colonies. At risk of losing France's most valuable colony to European rivals, the National Convention abolished slavery and extended political rights to the former slaves. The plan worked. Louverture switched sides, and his rebel forces played a decisive role in forcing a British and Spanish withdrawal. Afterward, Louverture consolidated political power on Saint-Domingue, issued a constitution, and declared himself Haiti's governor-for-life. However, Louverture's political situation changed when he drew the ire of Napoleon.

In 1802, French forces invaded Haiti, captured Louverture, and sent him to a French prison, where he died. Upon hearing of Napoleon's plans to reinstitute slavery, the island's black population preemptively rebelled, triggering a second bloody conflict. The rebels were again victorious, and the free republic of Haiti was officially established in 1804. The Haitian Revolution is considered a defining moment in world history because it was the first slave insurrection to successfully establish a free state, which challenged widely held assumptions about white superiority.

Criticism of the Chaos

Given the French Revolution's radical departure from the traditional status quo, it faced fierce criticism from the outset. Many European monarchies waged a propaganda war against the National Constituent Assembly's initial petition for liberal reforms out of self-interest. At the same time, millions of Europeans looked on with envy as the French revolutionaries abolished serfdom, rolled back the Church's abusive practices, and expanded political rights. Still, criticism mounted after the execution of King Louis XVI in 1793, one of the most shocking events in European history. The legendary British statesmen Edmund Burke, who had been a vocal supporter of the American Revolution, condemned the French Revolution as an unlawful power grab. When the French Revolution devolved into the Reign of Terror, public opinion outside France turned against the revolutionaries.

Napoleon's Rise, Dominance, and Defeat

Napoleon's Rule

Napoleon Bonaparte claimed the title of Emperor of France in 1804, transforming the French Republic into the French Empire. Shortly after his rise to power, Napoleon created the legendary **Grand Army**, which had an innovative command structure and organization.

Having risen from relative obscurity, Napoleon created a merit-based system of promotion in the army, and he opened elite leadership positions to anyone with sufficient talent. Therefore, the French army had a significantly more skilled leadership corps than other European armies, which continued to promote military leaders partially based on political connections. Napoleon leveraged the skill of his generals and delegated authority extensively. So, while Napoleon maintained direct control over battlefield strategy, he provided subordinates with considerable latitude in carrying out tasks. Furthermore, Napoleon reorganized the French military around corps, which contained multiple divisions. Prior to Napoleon, divisions were the largest army unit in European armies. Therefore, Napoleon's corps more efficiently integrated different types of units and optimized his preference for balancing the indirect and direct control of armies. Backed with Napoleon's nearly unparalleled tolerance for risk-taking and his mastery of military tactics, his restructured French military was devastating on the battlefield.

The **French Empire** dominated the first decade of the **Napoleonic Wars** (1803–1815). Although Britain maintained its status as a hegemonic naval power, it struggled to build a coalition capable of defeating the Grand Army. Unlike his contemporaries, Napoleon didn't seek to simply defeat opposing forces; instead, he took aggressive actions to completely dismantle armies for the explicit purpose of conquering entire states. As a result, Napoleon rapidly conquered nearly all of mainland Europe by 1812, and he governed his vast territories through the **Continental System**. Under this system, conquered territories were either directly incorporated into the French administrative system or forced to function as semi-independent client states. In either case, the Continental System forbade any contact with Britain, the lone power left standing in opposition to Napoleon.

Napoleonic Rule

Napoleonic rule had a profound impact on France and Europe. Napoleon was a highly capable political administrator, and he introduced several noteworthy reforms to consolidate political, economic, and social power. As he had done with the military, Napoleon created a merit-based system for civil services. This limited political corruption, and the bureaucracy became more centralized with a hierarchical command structure. To improve the effectiveness of his bureaucracy, Napoleon created Europe's first modern system of higher education with a standardized curriculum. The bureaucracy enacted numerous economic reforms, including a more equitable tax code, France's first central banking system, and the metric system to standardize commercial transactions.

Napoleon also sought to quell social unrest in two major ways. First, the **Concordat of 1801** reinstalled the Catholic Church as a civil institution, undercutting tensions between French Catholics and the regime. However, Napoleon retained the supervisory power over Church finances and ecclesiastical elections. Second, the publication of the Napoleonic Code standardized French civil law and promoted civil rights, including property rights, religious tolerance, and equal protection under the law. Napoleon enforced all these social, economic, and political reforms under the Continental System, and they had an enduring impact. The vast majority of contemporary European states continue to use the metric system and base their civil law systems on the Napoleonic Code.

Although Napoleon ushered in the modern era of political administration, his consolidation of power and his pursuit of domestic stability involved numerous oppressive policies. Napoleon heavily relied on propaganda, censorship, and manipulation to legitimize his power. More specifically, Napoleon forced the French press and artistic community to portray him as a magnanimous leader who simply desired peace and stability in Europe. Similarly, Napoleon engaged in rampant electoral engineering to create the illusion of unanimous support. Even when Napoleon was inarguably the most beloved public figure in France, he rigged elections so that he received more than 99 percent of the vote. Napoleon also regularly limited citizens' rights when it suited his interests. In direct violation of the Napoleonic code, Napoleon instituted a system of secret policing to enforce his manipulative schemes and suppress revolutionary fervor. The secret police especially targeted women who rejected Napoleon's patriarchal administrative system and called for gender equality. Under Napoleonic rule, men held legal authority over their families, and women were systematically denied property and electoral rights.

Nationalist Responses to Napoleon

The French Empire's domination and subjugation of Europe provoked fiery nationalistic reactions in several states. British nationalism surged throughout the Napoleonic Wars, especially as it became increasingly obvious that only Britain could save Europe from French rule. Nationalism also increased in Germany after Napoleon annihilated the Holy Roman Empire, triggering its dissolution. While French conquests and the Napoleonic Codes played an indispensable role in German unification, it also

cultivated nationalist opposition to Napoleonic rule. German student organizations (*Burschenschaften*) led the patriotic charge, holding large-scale protests to rally support for independence.

Spanish nationalism also increased after Napoleon stabbed his former ally in the back, coerced the abdication of King Ferdinand VII, and installed his brother Joseph Bonaparte as King of Spain in 1808. This betrayal resulted in the bloody **Peninsula War** (1808–1814). Spanish nationalists relied on guerilla tactics against the superior Grand Army. Although the Grand Army won practically all the battles until Britain intervened in 1812, the guerillas' persistence and resilience drained French resources and resolve. Similar to what occurred in Spain, Russian nationalist forces supported the implementation of extreme scorched-earth policies to defend against the Grand Army. When Napoleon broke the Russo-French alliance and invaded Russia in 1812, Tsar Alexander ordered his forces to avoid meeting the Grand Army on the battlefield; instead, the Russians conducted a strategic retreat in which they burned down cities and food stores to deny resources to Napoleon. As the conflict dragged out, the harsh Russian winter decimated the Grand Army. Consequently, Napoleon limped out of Russia with approximately 10 percent of his original forces, marking France's first disastrous defeat in the Napoleonic Wars.

Upon his return to France, Napoleon successfully revived the Grand Army and scored several victories against the British-led European coalition. However, this comeback ended less than a year later, when the Europeans decisively defeated the Grand Army at the **Battle of Leipzig** in October 1813. Soon afterward, the European coalition captured Paris, forced the French regime to unconditionally abdicate power, and exiled Napoleon to the Mediterranean island of Elba. Napoleon remained on Elba for less than a year before escaping and returning to France. During what is known as the **Hundred Days**, Napoleon rallied popular support and used it to depose the Bourbon monarchy. The return of Napoleon shocked the rest of Europe, which quickly re-mobilized the coalition. On June 18, 1815, the British General Arthur Wellesley and Prussian Prince Blücher dealt the deathblow to Napoleon's regime at the legendary **Battle of Waterloo**. Soon thereafter, British forces captured Napoleon, and he was exiled to Saint Helena, a remote island in the Atlantic Ocean, where he died in 1821.

The Napoleonic era had a profound impact on European economics, politics, society, culture, and identity. Napoleon's conquest of the European mainland spread the French Revolution across the continent, increasing support for popular sovereignty, nationalism, secularism, equality, and civil rights. Furthermore, the Napoleonic Code is widely credited with supporting the growth of the European middle classes and facilitating German unification. Under Napoleon's Confederation of the Rhine, German states replaced local feudal lords. Although these new governmental institutions functioned as French client states, the Confederation was nationalistic and united by shared language, culture, and ties to the land. Similar developments occurred in Italian states, laying the foundation for the establishment of the Kingdom of Italy in 1871. In addition to the advancement of national identities, Europe's united opposition to Napoleon increased regional solidarity, setting the stage for the future development of a European identity.

Congress of Vienna

Restoring Balance

In response to the chaos of Napoleonic rule, European states met at the **Congress of Vienna** (1814–1815) to establish a framework for an enduring peace in Europe. Five states headed the Congress of Vienna—Austria, Britain, France, Prussia, and Russia—but nearly all European states participated, usually through sending a delegation. Most European states initially hoped to limit France's role in the negotiations, but the French Foreign Minister forged an alliance with smaller states to elevate France's role in the proceedings.

After many rounds of contentious negotiations in a variety of formal and informal settings, European states passed a series of measures intended to restore a balance of power and prevent the spread of dangerous ideologies. To create a greater balance between European states, the Congress of Vienna redistributed territory Napoleon conquered to Austria, Prussia, and Russia. Austria received Italian territories; Prussia gained control over German and Swedish states; and Russia seized Poland and was permitted to retain control over Finnish territory. Furthermore, several states gained independence at the Congress of Vienna, including the German Confederation, the Netherlands, and smaller Italian states. Although the creation of a German Confederation conceded the importance of nationalism in state-building, the Congress of Vienna was incredibly conservative in its opposition to republicanism and revolutionary movements. The peace plan was predicated on restoring and solidifying the power of European monarchies, especially the House of Bourbon in France and Spain. This royal restoration was intended to stabilize European political systems, promote strong international relations between monarchies, and curb revolutionary fervor.

The Congress of Vienna functioned as a springboard for the creation of new political institutions used by European rulers to consolidate political power and enforce conservatism. Aside from domestic institutions designed to suppress revolutionary movements, European monarchies formed an international political alliance known as the **Conservative Order** to coordinate the containment of nationalism and revolution. On the one hand, the Conservative Order succeeded in reducing European military conflicts for nearly a century, and this period of peaceful relations is commonly referred to as the **Concert of Europe** (1815—1914). Stronger rule of law increased social stability, but its enforcement came at the expense of suppressing nationalism and freedom of expression. Traditional religious authorities, such as the Catholic Church, also regained some state-sanctioned influence due to monarchies' support for cultural conservatism. Peace and political stability stimulated economic growth, but wealth continued to be inequitably distributed. Colonialism and imperialism also accounted for a considerable portion of European economic gains during the nineteenth century, which ultimately contributed to the outbreak of World War I.

Romanticism

Rousseau
Beginning in the late seventeenth century, the Enlightenment swept across Europe. Enlightenment philosophers stressed the importance of rationality, logic, and empiricism. However, as the eighteenth century drew to a close, intellectuals began challenging the Enlightenment's application of rationality to all facets of life. **Jean-Jacques Rousseau**, a Genevan philosopher most famous for his contributions to social contract theory, argued that while reason was inextricably linked to progress, so too was emotion. Additionally, Rousseau believed methodical reasoning wasn't suited to artistic endeavors, and that emotional expression was a valuable part of the human experience. Rousseau's appeal to emotion inspired other philosophers to explore the limitations of rationality, and these efforts ultimately resulted in the movement called Romanticism (1790–1850).

Romanticism as a Challenge to Enlightenment Rationality
Romanticism produced numerous legendary artists, musicians, and writers, including Francisco Goya, Ludwig van Beethoven, and Victor Hugo. Romanticism emphasized aestheticism, which emphasizes the intrinsic value of art based on its beauty. The Romantics placed value on spontaneous expression and

evocative emotional experiences, including anxiety, fear, and love. Therefore, Romantic works closely mirrored people's emotional experiences, and they enabled insight into the emotional power of mass political movements and nationalism. While reason could explain how or why something like the French Revolution happened, feelings and emotions could express what living through that chaos felt like. Unsurprisingly, Romantic philosophers accelerated the evolution of nationalism by demonstrating how geography informed the evolution of national economies, culture, and society.

Religious Revival in Europe

Spiritualism also increased during this period. Religious revivals pursued a more personal connection to the divine. Religious revivals occurred in several Protestant movements, and they also led to the creation of new movements, most of which relied on preaching a universal message of love to large crowds in natural settings. For example, John Wesley's **Methodist movement** organized tours across Europe and the United States to encourage followers to forge a spiritual connection with Jesus Christ and express that love through good works. In practice, Methodism increased the spiritual independence of the working classes and created a base of support for progressive social causes, including abolitionism and women's suffrage. As a result, traditional secular and religious leaders feared and regularly persecuted Methodists for challenging the status quo.

Consequences of the Romantic Movement

Although Romanticism only lasted for fifty years or so, its lasting legacy shaped the modern world. In countering the Enlightenment and appealing to emotions, Romanticism popularized the concept of competing worldviews. Rather than pursuing an objective truth, Romantics believed that reality was multifaceted, with people's interpretations differing based on lived experiences and individual perspectives. While many intellectuals abhorred Romanticism's rejection of objective reality, the conflict created new intellectual movements, like modernism. Similarly, Romanticism's elevation of emotions invigorated artistic and cultural movements, such as realism, impressionism, and post-impressionism. Cultural, political, and social effects also occurred as knowledge increasingly spread directly to the masses through emotional appeals.

Nationalism also destabilized the Congress of Vienna's plans for balancing European power as more people questioned the legitimacy of their traditional rulers. This dissatisfaction peaked in 1848 when nationalist revolutions disrupted dozens of European states. While the Revolutions of 1848 didn't achieve their intended goal of regime change, these nationalist movements weakened absolute monarchies, abolished the last vestiges of feudalism, and legitimized the concept of representative government. The Revolutions of 1848 also laid the groundwork for the creation of new nationalist states, including Germany, Italy, and Poland.

Practice Questions

Questions 1–2 refer to the passage below.

It was the more necessary to keep the army in hand, as there was renewed fighting in prospect. The eldest son of the late King, now claiming the title of Charles II, was about to make an effort to seat himself on his father's throne, and hoped, as his father had hoped before him, to have on his side the forces of Scotland and Ireland. For many years the problem of the relations between the three countries had been inviting a solution. Both Scotland and Ireland had social and political interests of their own, and the natural reluctance of the inhabitants of either country to see these merged in those of the wealthier and more numerous people of England would in any case have called for delicate handling. The rise for the first time of a powerful army in England made her relations with the two other countries even more difficult than before, and had contributed fully as much as zeal for Presbyterianism to the ridiculous scheme of re-establishing Charles I as a covenanting King. After the defeat of Hamilton, indeed, Argyle and the Scottish clergy had welcomed Cromwell's support in the overthrow of the power of the nobility, but the dread of English predominance had not been entirely dispelled, and the King's execution added a sentimental grievance to other causes of alarm.

Excerpt from <u>Oliver Cromwell</u> by Samuel Rawson Gardiner, 1899

1. Based on the passage, which military conflicts is the passage most likely describing?
   a. English Civil War
   b. Glorious Revolution
   c. Seven Years' War
   d. War of the Roses

2. Which statement most accurately describes the aftermath of the execution of King Charles I?
   a. The execution marked the beginning of the Long Parliament.
   b. The execution resulted in the steep decline of Oliver Cromwell as a powerful force in English politics.
   c. The execution of King Charles I led his son to rally support, consolidate power, and conquer Cromwell's forces to establish himself as King of England.
   d. The execution eventually led to the establishment of the Commonwealth of England.

Questions 3–5 refer to the passage below.

Peter now made arrangements for changing the system entirely. He established a central office at the capital for the transaction of all business connected with the collecting of the revenues, and then appointed collectors for all the provinces of the empire, who were to receive their instructions from the minister who presided over this central office, and make their returns directly to him. Thus the whole system was remodeled, and made far more efficient than it ever had been before. Of course, the old governors, who, in consequence of this reform, lost the power of enriching themselves by their oppressions and frauds, complained bitterly of the change, and mourned, like good Conservatives, the ruin which this radicalism was bringing upon the country, but they were forced to submit.

Excerpt from <u>Makers of History: Peter the Great</u> by Jacob Abbott, 1887

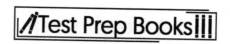

3. Which statement explains why the governors objected to Peter the Great's reforms?
   a. The governors wanted to elect the minister who presided over the new central office.
   b. The governors feared a reduction of tax revenues, which would weaken the central government.
   c. The governors favored a decentralized system, featuring a broad delegation of political authority.
   d. The governors believed increased bureaucratic red tape would strengthen radical political movements.

4. Peter the Great was most likely seeking to establish which political system?
   a. Absolute monarchy
   b. Feudal confederation
   c. Hereditary oligarchy
   d. Soviet democracy

5. Which statement best describes the impact of Peter the Great's reforms on Russia?
   a. The reforms replaced feudalism with capitalist economic policies.
   b. The reforms modernized Russia, supporting its rise as a European power.
   c. The reforms liberalized Russian society, expanding citizens' civil liberties and protections.
   d. The reforms empowered an advisory council of boyars to lead a stronger central government.

Questions 6–7 refer to the passage below.

My third observation on this head is, that superstition is an enemy to civil liberty, and enthusiasm a friend to it. As superstition groans under the dominion of priests, and enthusiasm is destructive of all ecclesiastical power, this sufficiently accounts for the present observation. Not to mention that enthusiasm, being the infirmity of bold and ambitious tempers, is naturally accompanied with a spirit of liberty, as superstition, on the contrary, renders men tame and abject, and fits them for slavery. We learn from English history, that, during the civil wars, the Independents and Deists, though the most opposite in their religious principles, yet were united in their political ones, and were alike passionate for a commonwealth. And since the origin of Whig and Tory, the leaders of the Whigs have either been Deists or professed Latitudinarians in their principles; that is, friends to toleration, and indifferent to any particular sect of Christians: while the sectaries, who have all a strong tincture of enthusiasm, have always, without exception, concurred with that party in defence of civil liberty. The resemblance in their superstitions long united the High-Church Tories and the Roman Catholics, in support of prerogative and kingly power, though experience of the tolerating spirit of the Whigs seems of late to have reconciled the Catholics to that party.

Excerpt from "Of Superstition and Enthusiasm," by David Hume, 1758

6. Which statement best expresses Hume's primary claim in the passage?
   a. Superstition united the High-Church Tories and Roman Catholics.
   b. Superstition and enthusiasm both undermine humanity's natural spirit of liberty.
   c. Enthusiasm has the ability to destroy all ecclesiastical power.
   d. Enthusiasm is superior to superstition in regard to the promotion of civil liberty.

7. The passage is most strongly associated with which of the following movements?
   a. The Enlightenment
   b. Mercantilism
   c. Romanticism
   d. Scientific Revolution

Questions 8–9 refer to the passage below.

> In his defense Galileo urged that he had already been acquitted in 1616 by Cardinal Bellarmine, when a charge of heresy was brought against him, and he contended that anything he might now have done, was no more than he had done on the preceding occasion, when the orthodoxy of his doctrines received solemn confirmation. The Inquisition seemed certainly inclined to clemency, but the Pope was not satisfied. Galileo was accordingly summoned again on June 21. He was to be threatened with torture if he did not forthwith give satisfactory explanations as to the reasons which led him to write the Dialogue. In this proceeding the Pope assured the Tuscan ambassador that he was treating Galileo with the utmost consideration possible in consequence of his esteem and regard for the Grand Duke, whose servant Galileo was. It was, however, necessary that some exemplary punishment be meted out to the astronomer, inasmuch as by the publication of the Dialogue he had distinctly disobeyed the injunction of silence laid upon him by the decree of 1616.

Excerpt from <u>Great Astronomers</u> by Sir Robert Stawell Ball, 1895

8. Based on the passage, which of the following most accurately articulates the Pope's dissatisfaction with Galileo?
   a. Galileo refused to follow the Pope's directive to revise certain scientific theories.
   b. Galileo's theories challenged the Church's doctrine and traditional authority.
   c. Galileo's theories undermined the Pope's relationship with the Grand Duke.
   d. Galileo disobeyed the Inquisition's injunction and obstructed their investigation.

9. Which statement best summarizes Galileo's most controversial contribution to the Scientific Revolution?
   a. Galileo advanced the theories of Nicolaus Copernicus, especially his heliocentric theory.
   b. Galileo first confirmed the existence of Saturn's rings, Jupiter's satellites, and Venus' phases.
   c. Galileo developed the theory of classical mechanics, including the laws of motion.
   d. Galileo first applied empiricism, inductive reasoning, and a methodological approach to science.

Questions 10–11 refer to the passage below.

> This monopoly has necessarily contributed to keep up the rate of profit, in all the different branches of British trade, higher than it naturally would have been, had all nations been allowed a free trade to the British colonies.
>
> The monopoly of the colony trade, as it necessarily drew toward that trade a greater proportion of the capital of Great Britain than what would have gone to it of its own accord, so, by the expulsion of all foreign capitals, it necessarily reduced the whole quantity of capital employed in that trade below what it naturally would have been in the case of a free trade. But, by lessening the competition of capitals in that branch of trade, it necessarily raised the rate of profit in that branch. By lessening, too, the competition of British capitals in all other branches of trade, it necessarily raised the rate of British profit in all those other branches. Whatever may have been, at any particular period since the establishment of the act of navigation, the state or extent of the mercantile capital of Great Britain, the monopoly of the colony trade must, during the continuance of that state, have raised the ordinary rate of British profit higher than it otherwise would have been, both in that and in all the other branches of British trade....

But whatever raises, in any country, the ordinary rate of profit higher than it otherwise would be, necessarily subjects that country both to an absolute, and to a relative disadvantage in every branch of trade of which she has not the monopoly.

Excerpt from The Wealth of Nations by Adam Smith, 1776

10. The author's statement in the third paragraph about monopolies' relative disadvantages to trade directly influenced which economic development?
   a. Increase of mercantilism
   b. Decrease of colonization
   c. Rise of capitalism
   d. Decline of British manufacturing

11. Which statement provides the correct definition for the acts of navigation mentioned in the second paragraph?
   a. The acts of navigation facilitated Britain's colonization of the Americas through the creation of highly detailed naval map.
   b. The acts of navigation restricted British merchants from competing with the colonial shipping industry.
   c. The acts of navigation included a range of policies intended to strengthen British colonial monopolies and dominance in international trade.
   d. The acts of navigation established a framework for free trade agreements and supported the growth of a global economic network.

Questions 12–14 refer to the passage below.

The second campaign, to which Napoleon alleged they so eagerly looked forward, speedily ensued, and hostilities were carried on with a degree of vigour which fired the enthusiasm of the army. Heaven knows what accounts were circulated of the Russians, who, as Bonaparte solemnly stated in his proclamation, had come from the extremity of the world. They were represented as half-naked savages, pillaging, destroying and burning wherever they went. It was even asserted that they were cannibals, and had been seen to eat children. In short, at that period was introduced the denomination of northern barbarians which has since been so generally applied to the Russians. Two days after the capitulation of Ulm Murat obtained the capitulation of Trochtelfingen from General Yarneck, and made 10,000 prisoners, so that, without counting killed and wounded, the Austrian army had sustained a diminution of 50,000 men after a campaign of twenty days. On the 27th of October the French army crossed the Inn, and thus penetrated into the Austrian territory. Salzburg and Brannan were immediately taken. The army of Italy, under the command of Massena, was also obtaining great advantages. On the 30th of October, that is to say, the very day on which the Grand Army took the above-mentioned fortresses, the army of Italy, having crossed the Adige, fought a sanguinary battle at Caldiero, and took 5000 Austrian prisoners.

Excerpt from Memoirs of Napoleon Bonaparte by Louis Antoine Fauvelet de Bourrienne, 1831

12. Why did Napoleon refer to Russians as savages?

a. Napoleon distrusted the Russians after they deployed scorched-earth tactics against his Grand Army.

b. Napoleon believed in the supremacy of European culture, and he didn't consider Russians to be Europeans.

c. Napoleon didn't believe the Grand Army could defeat the Russians, so he sought to motivate his troops out of desperation.

d. Napoleon routinely disseminated and exploited propaganda to gain an advantage when it served his interests.

13. Based on the historical context of the passage, which of the following most accurately describes Napoleon's military campaigns effects on the French Revolution?

a. Napoleon's military campaigns protected the French Revolution from European republican states.

b. Napoleon's military campaigns ultimately spread French ideals across the entire European continent.

c. Napoleon's military campaigns destroyed European monarchies, which culminated in a wave of democratic revolutions at the end of the conflict.

d. Napoleon's military campaigns demonstrated how the French Revolution rejected popular sovereignty.

14. The Grand Army did NOT feature which of the following characteristics?

a. Merit-based promotion

b. Flexible command structures

c. Large corps of troops

d. Orthodox battlefield strategies

Short Answer Question

1. Use the passage below to answer all parts of the question that follows.

> Herein, perhaps, may be found the secret of its complexity, of its seeming contradictions. The authors of the Revolution pursued an ideal, an ideal expressed in three words, Liberty, Equality, Fraternity. That they might win their quest, they had both to destroy and to construct. They had to sweep away the past, and from the resultant chaos to construct a new order. Alike in destruction and construction, they committed errors; they fell far below their high ideals. The altruistic enthusiasts of the National Assembly gave place to the practical politicians of the Convention, the diplomatists of the Directory, the generals of the Consulate. The Empire was far from realising that bright vision of a regenerate nation which had dazzled the eyes of Frenchmen in the first hours of the States-General. Liberty was sacrificed to efficiency; equality to man's love for titles of honour; fraternity to desire of glory. So it has been with all human effort. Man is imperfect, and his imperfection mars his fairest achievements. Whatever great movement may be considered, its ultimate attainment has fallen far short of its initial promise. The authors of the Revolution were but men; they were no more able than their fellows to discover and to hold fast to the true way of happiness. They wavered between the two extremes of despotism and anarchy; they declined from the path of grace. And their task remained unfulfilled. Many of their dreams were far from attaining realisation; they inaugurated no era of perfect bliss; they produced no Utopia. But their labour was not in vain. Despite its disappointments, despite all its crimes and blunders, the French Revolution was a great, a wonderful event. It did contribute to the uplifting of humanity, and the world is the better for its occurrence.

Excerpt from <u>History of the French Revolution from 1789 to 1814</u> by François Auguste Marie Mignet, 1824

a) Describe the intellectual history of the ideals that influenced the French Revolution.

b) Provide one historical example of a contradiction in the French Revolution.

c) Explain the historical context related to the author's claim that the French Revolution positively impacted the world.

a) The intellectual history of the ideals that influenced the French Revolution includes the Enlightenment and the Scientific Revolution. This can be seen when the passage mentions Utopia, a concept that was talked about during the Enlightenment. During the Scientific Revolution, humanism gradually became more influential among people, shown when the passage mentions the uplifting of humanity

Answer Explanations

1. A: The passage refers to Oliver Cromwell's efforts to overthrow the English nobility, the execution of King Charles I, and Charles II's plans to avenge his father's death by seizing the throne that was once occupied by his father. All three events were pivotal moments in the English Civil War, which ultimately resulted in the temporary dissolution of the English monarchy. Thus, Choice A is the correct answer. While the Glorious Revolution also involved a political conflict between the English monarchy and parliamentary factions in which Parliament triumphed, it ended peacefully. In addition, the Glorious Revolution took place several decades after the English Civil War, so Choice B is incorrect. The Seven Years' War was a global conflict over colonization fought between British-led and French-led coalitions during the eighteenth century. Therefore, Choice C is incorrect. Although the War of the Roses was an English civil war, it was mainly about rival aristocratic families competing for the throne in the fifteenth century, so Choice D is incorrect.

2. D: Regicide is always controversial, and the execution of King Charles I was no exception. Following a prolonged power struggle, parliamentary factions formally brought charges against King Charles for alleged tyrannical abuses of power, and he was executed on January 30, 1649. In the immediate aftermath of the king's execution, Oliver Cromwell consolidated political power, led parliamentary forces to a decisive victory over Charles I, and established the Commonwealth of England. Cromwell's outsized role in the Commonwealth effectively squashed the elected government's lofty ambitions of parliamentary rule. Thus, Choice D is the correct answer. Choice A is incorrect because the Long Parliament had already been in session for years before the execution of King Charles I. Choice B is incorrect because Oliver Cromwell's political power and military might reached new heights under the Commonwealth, especially after he seized the autocratic title of Lord Protector. Choice C is incorrect because although Charles II consolidated royal support in Scotland, he didn't defeat Cromwell on the battlefield. Instead, Charles I reclaimed his father's throne when Parliament restored the monarchy in 1660, nearly a decade after the English Civil War.

3. C: The passage is describing the creation of a centralized bureaucracy, one of the many reforms Peter the Great instituted to consolidate political power under his rule. Prior to the introduction of a central office, the Russian monarchy had delegated broad powers in setting and collecting taxes to the governors (aristocrats) under a decentralized system. According to the passage, the governors exploited their independence and enriched themselves through fraudulent and oppressive policies. In terms of the governors' self-interest, the more decentralized system was significantly more favorable. Thus, Choice C is the correct answer. The passage doesn't mention an election for the minister, and Peter the Great generally restricted civil liberties. Additionally, the governors would've been far more likely to support the repeal of the reforms than risk legitimizing it through their nominal participation. For these reasons, Choice A is incorrect. Based on the passage, the governors seem to care about their own share of tax revenue above all else, and they would almost certainly support a weaker central government. So Choice B is incorrect. Although the passage describes how the governors characterized the reform as radical, the passage never mentions bureaucratic red tape or radical political movements. Therefore, Choice D is incorrect.

4. A: The passage describes how and why Peter the Great implemented a policy to consolidate power under his regime at the expense of his political rivals. Of all the answer choices, this most closely aligns with the actions of an absolute monarchy. Aside from the passage's context clues, Peter the Great did

ultimately cultivate autocratic powers and establish an absolute monarchy. Thus, Choice *A* is the correct answer. Choice *B* is incorrect because a feudal confederation is characterized by a weak central government and decentralized political power. Choice *C* is incorrect because Peter the Great never intentionally sought to share political and economic power with the aristocracy. Choice *D* is incorrect because soviets (workers' councils) didn't secure meaningful political power until the Russian Revolution in the twentieth century.

5. B: Peter the Great is most fondly remembered for his modernization policies. These policies involved: centralizing the political bureaucracy, developing a manufacturing industry, building a navy, marrying his children to influential European families, and forcing public officials to adopt the latest European fashion styles. These modernization policies were mostly successful, which greatly improved Russia's standing in the European political order. Thus, Choice *B* is the correct answer. Peter the Great's policies somewhat modernized the Russian economy by increasing the production of manufactured goods; however, some aspects of feudalism persisted in Russia until the Russian Revolution. So Choice *A* is incorrect. Peter the Great ruled as an autocrat, regularly suppressing and persecuting political dissent in all forms. Since citizens held extremely few civil liberties under this regime, Choice *C* is incorrect. Peter the Great's reforms often targeted the boyars (member of the old aristocracy) to reduce their influence and power, so Choice *D* is incorrect.

6. D: The first sentence asserts that superstition decreases civil liberty while enthusiasm increases it, and the rest of the paragraph is spent supporting this claim. For example, Hume refers to the English Civil Wars to illustrate how enthusiastic parliamentary factions supported civil liberties and more superstitious groups backed the royalists. Given Hume's repeated emphasis on how enthusiasm promotes civil liberties more than superstition, this must be his primary claim. Thus, Choice *D* is the correct answer. Hume offers the example of how superstition united the High-Church Tories and Roman Catholics to strengthen his larger claim about the fundamental distinction between superstition and enthusiasm. So Choice *A* must be incorrect. Hume explicitly argues that enthusiasm leads to greater support of civil liberties, so Choice *B* is incorrect. Similar to Choice *A*, Choice *C* accurately states one of Hume's claims, but Hume describes how enthusiasm can destroy ecclesiastical power to strengthen his larger claim about how enthusiasm promotes civil liberty. Therefore, Choice *C* is incorrect.

7. A: The passage reflects Hume's support for civil liberties, tolerance, and secularism. Compared to the other answer choices, the development of these political values is most strongly associated with the Enlightenment. In addition, the passage strongly resembles a logical argument, and the Enlightenment applied the Scientific Revolution's empiricism and rationality to social sciences, including politics. Furthermore, Hume was a famous Enlightenment philosopher. Thus, Choice *A* is the correct answer. Mercantilism promoted protectionist economic policies, such as tariffs and trade restrictions. Since mercantilism doesn't directly relate to civil liberties, political tolerance, or secularism, Choice *B* must be incorrect. Choice *C* is incorrect because Romanticism focused on emotions and feelings, which often led to outbreaks of religious revivalism. While the Scientific Revolution influenced the Enlightenment, the Scientific Revolution rarely intentionally involved itself in political arguments. So Choice *D* is incorrect.

8. B: Based on the passage, the Pope was deeply dissatisfied with Galileo and even considered torturing the legendary astronomer. The source of the Pope's dissatisfaction was Galileo's publication of the *Dialogue*. According to the Pope, the publication of this book violated an injunction of silence. Given the historical context of the Church's suppression of scientific theories, the Pope likely viewed the publication of the *Dialogue* as a challenge to the Church's traditional authority and doctrines. Thus, Choice *B* is the correct answer. Galileo disobeyed an injunction of silence, not a request for revisions, so

Choice *A* is incorrect. The Pope claimed he refrained from torturing Galileo out of respect for the Grand Duke, so their relationship is still relatively intact at this point. Therefore, Choice *C* is incorrect. Galileo seemingly disobeyed an injunction, but the passage doesn't mention any obstruction of an investigation. So Choice *D* is incorrect.

9. A: Galileo's advocacy of Nicolaus Copernicus's theories played a significant role in the Scientific Revolution, and it also ignited a heated controversy. Galileo used his observations of celestial bodies and tidal theories to advance Copernicus' heliocentric theory, which placed the Sun at the center of the solar system. The Catholic Church viewed the heliocentric theory as heretical because the geocentric theory had previously been declared as official religious doctrine. Under the geocentric theory, the Earth was located at the center of the solar system. So when Galileo published the *Dialogue* to popularize the heliocentric theory with the broader public, the Church condemned, arrested, and imprisoned him. Thus, Choice *A* is the correct answer. Galileo made several groundbreaking discoveries about Saturn, Jupiter, and Venus; however, those discoveries were only controversial when applied to the heliocentric theory. So Choice *B* is incorrect. Isaac Newton developed the theory of classical mechanics based on his formulas about the laws of motion, so Choice *C* is incorrect. Likewise, Francis Bacon is widely viewed as the father of empiricism and methodological experimentation. Therefore, Choice *D* is incorrect.

10. C: In the third paragraph, Adam Smith argues that the colonial monopoly's advantages for related industries comes at the cost of creating an absolute and relative disadvantage for all non-monopolized economic sectors. Smith is essentially arguing for more free trade because it would expand the global network, generating greater levels of profit for more industries in more countries. This economic theory eventually convinced European governments to adopt free trade and free market policies, which contributed to the rise of capitalism in the late eighteenth century. Thus, Choice *C* is the correct answer. Smith is criticizing colonial monopolies, and mercantilism declined during the late eighteenth and early nineteenth centuries. So, Choice *A* is incorrect. European colonization continued for more than a century after the decline of mercantilism, so Choice *B* is incorrect. Similarly, Britain sustained consistently high levels of manufacturing after transitioning from mercantilist to capitalist trade policies. Therefore, Choice *D* is incorrect.

11. C: The passage refers to the Navigation Acts to mark the beginning of British mercantilism. Britain initially implemented a series of navigations acts to undercut European rivals as they engaged in a fierce maritime competition during the seventeenth and eighteenth centuries. For example, the Navigation Acts prohibited foreign ships from entering British colonial ports and transporting British goods. Thus, Choice *C* is the correct answer. British colonization of the Americas occurred before the introduction of the Navigation Acts, and these acts weren't related to mapmaking, so Choice *A* is incorrect. The Navigation Acts benefited British merchants at the expense of foreign competitors, so Choice *B* is incorrect. Since they were quintessentially a mercantilist economic policy, the Navigation Acts undermined the development of free trade agreements. Therefore, Choice *D* is incorrect.

12. D: In an official proclamation, Napoleon described the Russians as a people originating from the extremity of the world. Following this proclamation, Napoleon's troops circulated rumors about the Russians' supposed savagery, including allegations of cannibalism. This characterization of Russian troops illustrates how Napoleon used propaganda to manipulate public opinion. In this case, Napoleon was attempting to motivate his troops to fight harder by slandering his enemies. Thus, Choice *D* is the correct answer. Russians relied on scorched-earth tactics to fend off the Grand Army in 1812, but it's unclear whether Napoleon delivered the proclamation after he invaded Russia. Furthermore, Napoleon was a connoisseur of propaganda, so it's more likely he was merely seeking to gain an advantage. So

Choice *A* is incorrect. Napoleon believed in the supremacy of French culture, not European culture, so Choice *B* is incorrect. Napoleon led the Grand Army with such extreme confidence that it bordered on recklessness. Therefore, it's highly unlikely that Napoleon thought the Grand Army would lose to the Russians under any circumstances. Therefore, Choice *C* is incorrect.

13. B: As expressed in the passage, Napoleon initially crushed European armies, and he ultimately conquered nearly all of mainland Europe. As a result of these conquests, the French Revolution spread across Europe. For example, the Napoleonic Code has influenced the vast majority of contemporary European legal codes. Thus, Choice *B* is the correct answer. Napoleon's conquests arguably preserved some aspects of the French Revolution, but he was primarily fighting against European monarchies, not republics. So Choice *A* is incorrect. The Napoleonic Wars severely challenged European monarchies, but they survived and reclaimed their authority at the Congress of Vienna. Therefore, Choice *C* is incorrect. The French Revolution embraced and popularized the concept of popular sovereignty, so Choice *D* is incorrect.

14. D: The Grand Army held several critical advantages over rival European forces. Napoleon instituted a merit-based system of promotion, so the Grand Army had a more skilled leadership corps than most European armies. Therefore, Choice *A* is incorrect. Napoleon was a master delegator, and he installed flexible command structures to maximize the talent of his staff without relinquishing direct control over the Grand Army. So Choice *B* is incorrect. Napoleon also invented a larger army unit called corps, and it contained multiple divisions, which were the largest units in European armies. Therefore, Choice *C* is incorrect. Napoleon's battlefield strategies were far from orthodox; in fact, he was almost always more aggressive and innovative than his enemies. Thus, Choice *D* is the correct answer.

Short Answer Response

1.

a) The French Revolution's ideals can be traced back to the Scientific Revolution, the Enlightenment, and Romanticism. After the Scientific Revolution began to emphasize empiricism, rationality, and methodological experimentation, the Enlightenment applied those concepts to politics. Enlightenment philosophers challenged the assumption that society and government should be organized hierarchically with a select class of aristocrats having all the power. In contrast, Enlightenment philosophers developed the model of popular sovereignty, which vested sovereign authority in the people. Consequently, French revolutionaries used Enlightenment arguments for popular sovereignty to demand reforms, such as the right to political representation, civil liberties, and equal protection under the law. Unlike the other two intellectual movements, Romanticism developed alongside the French Revolution. Romanticism stoked the flames of nationalism as French citizens became more emotionally connected to their shared culture, experiences, and ties to the land. In effect, nationalism gave shape to the ideal of a nation that embodies the people. Along with fueling the French Revolution, Romanticism also facilitated the spread of revolutionary doctrine across Europe by adding an emotional appeal to mass political movements.

b) The passage repeatedly refers to the French Revolution's contradictory nature, and one of its most glaring contradictions relates to how the revolutionaries failed to apply the revolution's egalitarian ideals across gender lines. Women played a crucial role in the protests and bread riots that first forced Louis XVI to consider his people's grievances. However, once in power, the revolutionaries disenfranchised women, limited their civil liberties, and upheld patriarchal control in France. When female revolutionaries pointed out this contradiction, they were often persecuted as if they were monarchists. Examples include leaders of the French Republic persecuting the Society of Revolutionary Republican Women until it disbanded, and the execution of Olympe de Gouges for supporting gender equality in a state allegedly committed to equality. Despite this inequitable application of the principle of equality, the revolutionaries did make significant progress, particularly through the empowerment of commoners. However, the French Revolution's pervasive gender inequality stands as a stark reminder of how a generally positive event can nonetheless be imperfect.

c) The author views the French Revolution as a positive event, based on the horrors of what came before. Prior to the French Revolution, absolute monarchs ruled nearly all European states. As a result, commoners were systematically disenfranchised and subjected to an arbitrary legal system in which they had limited protections. Furthermore, absolute monarchs typically oversaw a feudal socioeconomic system, empowering aristocrats at the expense of everyone else. The lower classes especially suffered because they were forced to provide free labor and/or pay exorbitant taxes to aristocrats in exchange for the right to farm small parcels of land. So although the French Revolution fell short of delivering a utopia, it triggered dramatic changes in France and across Europe after it was spread through Napoleon's conquests. Monarchs and aristocrats no longer held disproportionate and unilateral power over society. Furthermore, popular sovereignty and universal male suffrage ensured that governments better reflected the will of the people. As a result, citizens enjoyed more economic freedoms, civil liberties, and equal protection under the law. In effect, the French Revolution paved the way for the development of modern-day European democracies, which unquestionably represents a positive development when compared to absolute monarchies and feudalism.

Period 3: 1815–1914

Industrialization and Its Effects

Contextualizing Industrialization and its Origins and Effects

European Demographic Changes

The process of **industrialization** is inextricably linked to the processes of urbanization, migration, and immigration. As factories blossomed in and around cities, these industrial sectors swiftly began to urbanize in terms of population density. The outgrowth of economic opportunity encouraged more workers, particularly those from marginalized rural sectors, to immigrate or migrate to industrial hubs. These industrial hubs became more diverse and populous as a result. Demographic shifts concentrated different nationalities in cities like London, increasing social tensions between groups. Overall, however, urbanization, immigration, and migration provided industrial cities with the cheap, exploited, and expendable workforce that was necessary to sustain economic efficiency and consumer culture. It also planted the seeds of socio-political division between a largely poor immigrant and migrant class and a wealthier corporate class.

Urbanization

Urbanization was responsible for an increase in poverty, class tensions, and social reform efforts in Europe. Cities expanded rapidly but were not able to sustain the rapid population increases. As a result, many European cities, such as Manchester, as well as American cities, such as New York and Chicago, created ramshackle tenement buildings to house their burgeoning working classes. Tenement houses became hubs of urban poverty. Immigrant and migrant families crammed into these tight spaces with poor conditions. As a result, crime, illness, and infant mortality rates increased in these destitute spaces. While the overall global life expectancy rates increased as a result of the Industrial Revolution and its coinciding advancements in medicine and technology, the living conditions of the working poor remained mostly dire. As a result, many European cities witnessed an explosion of reform movements that attempted to address the "social ills" associated with poverty and urbanization. In Europe and the United States, urbanization spawned the rise of Progressive reformers, activists, and politicians such as John Riis and Upton Sinclair who tried to combat the negative consequences of progress with philanthropy and social services.

Improved Agricultural Productivity

Agricultural productivity improved as a result of the mechanization of farm labor. New machines, such as the seed drill, allowed agricultural productivity to increase in a variety of farming activities. For instance, the cotton gin, invented by Eli Whitney, helped efficiently separate cotton fibers from seeds, which normally consumes a lot of time when carried out by hand. The cotton gin streamlined agricultural productivity so much that the total export of cotton in 1793 was less than ten thousand bales, even with the rise of slave labor in the American South. By 1860, thanks to the invention of the cotton gin, the total export of cotton reached four million bales. Ironically, however, as cotton became king of the American South, slavery increased as well. The rise of the Industrial Revolution in the agricultural sector became synonymous with the cries for and against slavery and abolition. Slave labor shifted from a purely manual process to one that focused on specialization. Much like the textile factories in the North, the cotton plantations of the South trended toward specialized labor roles.

Aside from slavery and cotton production, the Industrial Revolution impacted almost every sector of agriculture. Machines harvested produce at a faster rate. Fruits and vegetables were able to be refrigerated and shipped longer distances thanks to advancements in technology. Rail cars, and eventually automobiles, also increased agricultural sales. Meatpacking plants and urban stockyards arose in Midwestern cities like Milwaukee and Chicago. The industrialization of farming helped to increase agricultural production to a point where it was able to sustain growing urban populations and increase the overall life expectancy rates of industrial nations in the United States and Western Europe.

Legal Protection of Private Property

The Industrial Revolution transformed the ways in which businesses and common citizens conceptualized private property and its legal protection. John Locke's *Two Treatises of Government* (1689) helped establish the Western precedents for the legal protection of **private property** that would later be adopted by United States and European governments. Locke contended that every person has property, and every person has the right to safeguard that property in order to protect one's liberties from the overreaching hand of government. Locke argued that property rights, or the right to purchase or claim natural resources, were inextricably linked to natural rights. The Industrial Revolution helped extend these protections not only to natural resources, but also to intellectual property. During the Industrial Revolution, corporations battled over the rights to certain properties, particularly those that were unclaimed by U.S. and Western European authorities. This led corporations to carve the land up for their own business needs, and consequently protecting those lands through the law.

Intellectual property, or copyrights, were claimed in a similar fashion, allowing the "manufacturers and owners" of these ideas to profit from them. Battles over private property became even more complicated during the Industrial Revolution as socialists and communists such as Karl Marx argued in favor of public rights to property. The emergence of socialist and communist ideologies was, in many ways, a direct consequence of the rise of capitalist conceptions of private property during the Industrial Revolution, which valued individual rights over public rights in terms of both business and law. In the end, some might claim that the capitalist conceptions of private property eventually overshadowed socialist and communist arguments for a more communal stance on property rights: today, both individuals and businesses have the legal right to claim ownership over both land and ides. This victory for capitalism began long before the Industrial Revolution but was catalyzed by the Industrial Revolution's corporate values.

Abundance of Rivers and Canals

Rivers and canals became the first primary modes of industrialized production, trade, and transportation. These bodies of water provided a necessary element of industrialized production: steam power. **Steam power**, which emanated from water use, became the first great form of power during the Industrial Revolution. The water provided by rivers and canals could be converted into steam, which could then power the new machines of the Industrial Revolution. Likewise, the steamboats of the early industrial era utilized the same rivers and canals from which they obtained their water for transportation and trade. The riverways and canals of the United States and Europe were much like the highways of today—they allowed natural resources, people, and manufactured goods to reach their industrial destinations in the most efficient means possible for the era. The abundance of rivers and canals in Western Europe and North America allowed these regions to become the leaders of industrialization.

Access to Foreign Resources

While industrialization in the United States was largely built from a vast base of domestic resources, industrialization in Europe, particularly in Great Britain, relied largely on foreign resources. Industrialization was an outgrowth of European colonialism, in this sense. While Great Britain's colonized territories industrialized at a slower rate than the mother country, Great Britain itself was able to reap the benefits of its global empire. These benefits were largely the resources and labor forces of foreign territories. British strongholds in Africa, Asia, and the Caribbean provided British industrialism with the goods and workers it needed to refine and manufacture products for the transatlantic world. For example, prior to the rise of cotton in the American South, Great Britain relied heavily on its ties to colonized cotton sectors in Egypt and India. Colonization was originally an outgrowth of mercantilism, but it eventually became the progenitor of industrialism: it was the consequence of the need to buy and sell goods and expand markets, but it was well established as a historical trend well before the beginning of the Industrial Revolution. As the United States expanded into its own imperial powerhouse, it also annexed territories, such as Hawaii, rapidly for its own industrial uses. For example, westward expansion in the United States, annexation outside the contiguous states, and territories that comprised the main land mass sandwiched between the Pacific and Atlantic in the late nineteenth and early twentieth centuries allowed the United States to claim foreign resources as its own for the sake of further industrialization.

Accumulation of Capital

During the Industrial Revolution, a large amount of global capital was accumulated by emerging industrial nations such as the United States and Great Britain. These nations industrialized at a faster rate than other nations, for various reasons, and, as a result, became two of the wealthiest nations in the world. Wealth, therefore, was inequitably accumulated and dispersed throughout the globe. This, in turn, forced many nations into positions of economic submission or marginalization, such as African and Asian countries that were colonized. The gap between rich nations and poor nations grew as a result of this rapid wealth accumulation.

Development of the Factory System

The mercantile structures of colonialism had already set the stage for this new means of factory production. Indentured servitude and slave labor had set the precedent for the concentration of labor into single locations. The European powers were sequestering labor for as long as there had been colonies in the New World. The growing demand of the Columbian Exchange increased the need for the repetitious specialization of labor, whether it be in the silver mines of Mexico or the sugarcane plantations of Cuba. The rise of transatlantic capitalism shattered the world's previous reliance on subsistence farming and manufacturing as the seeds for globalization were planted in colonization. The "rise of the machine" only served to further mechanize the human condition, relegating millions of workers to rote forms of labor in newer, more complex systems of capitalist exchange. As the global system became more complex, the role of the worker became more simplified in the factory. This revolution in factory specialization is captured by Adam Smith in his famous tract *An Inquiry into the Nature and Causes of the Wealth of Nations* (1776), who noted that the division of labor resulted in acute specialization in the workplace. In 1776, Smith was already beginning to observe the increased reliance on specialized trade within a growing industrial system. Industrialization waged on this specialization would be concentrated further, particularly in the Waltham-Lowell factory system of New England.

The **Waltham-Lowell factory system** relied heavily on a vertically integrated supply chain. The Waltham-Lowell system attempted to house the specialized trades of spinning, weaving, dyeing, and shaping into one consolidated factory system. All of these specialized trades were housed "under one roof," so to speak.

The Lowell system even attempted to offer room and board to single women in apartments near the factories in order to concentrate labor even further. This concentration of labor had wide-reaching consequences on domestic life, social relations, and consumer culture. It put small manufacturers out of business. It changed family dynamics by bringing more women and children into the workforce. And it made the American economy one founded upon mass production. The concentration of labor made humans even more reliant upon machines, as millions of workers were forced to carry out specialized tasks in production and repair.

Prior to the factory era, most textiles were created in the household. The mill and the factory not only helped concentrate labor into one single location in textile towns like Lowell, but it also encouraged a specialization in labor. As men and women adapted their labor to accommodate new machines, they became specialists in their factory crafts. The woman pictured below, for instance, specialized in drawing each thread from the warp through a reed so that it could be placed on the loom. Her entire shift at the textile factory would be dedicated to ensuring that this task would be carried out repetitiously and with fidelity.

Girl Drawing Each Thread of Warp Through the Reed and Harness Ready to be Paced on Loom

In William H. Dooley's Textiles (1910)

This rote, specialized repetition in the workplace not only revolutionized the structure and function of labor, but it also transformed consumer tastes. Consumer culture in the United States and Europe, which had previously been dictated by subsistence, was gradually supplanted by popular fashion and

disposability as the industrial giants of the Western world increased their wealth through the specialized functions of the factory system.

Spread of Industry Throughout Europe

Spread of Industrial Production in Continental Europe

Industrialization could not be contained at its source in Great Britain. By the nineteenth century industrialization rapidly expanded to other shores, including continental Europe, the United States, Russia, and Japan.

The expansion of industrialization into continental Europe expanded unevenly by region in the 1800s. Pockets of industrialization emerged sporadically, and with different emphases. The Napoleonic Wars (1789–1815) disrupted much of the industrialization efforts in the region, particularly in France itself. Thus, other European countries quickly looked to close the industrial gap by replicating the technological advances of the "British industrial miracles." Belgium, an unlikely candidate, led Europe in mimicking the Industrial Revolution in Great Britain. **William Cockerill**, a Lancashire native, emigrated to Belgium with trade secrets in 1799. Cockerill's family led the charge in industrialization in continental Europe; his son, **John Cockerill**, engineered and ran one of the biggest industrial complexes in Belgium. John Cockerill's industrial complex manufactured railway locomotives, machines, and steam engines. Other British expatriates followed his lead, establishing new industries in rapidly-industrializing Belgium.

Germany was second only to Belgium in terms of European industrialization. Industrialization emerged in Germany in the early 1800s, but really started to gain momentum in 1835, when German engineers started mimicking British machine blueprints. German citizens sent their children to British industrial schools to learn the ins-and-outs of industrialization. Its ability to replicate British methods allowed Germany to emerge as one of the strongest military powers in continental Europe in the nineteenth century.

Places like Northern Italy, Bohemia, and France eventually industrialized with specific industries in mind. Northern Italy focused on textile production. Bohemia revolutionized its spinning industry. And France eventually caught up to its neighbors in the 1850s by expanding its railroad systems. However, many other European nations struggled. Spain and Austria-Hungary could not keep pace due to various limitations in geography and resources.

Steam-Powered Industrial Production

The inequalities of the new global economy become even more evident when analyzing the influence of steam-powered industrialization. Steam-powered technologies spread across the globe unevenly and were mostly restricted to Western Europe and the United States. Steam power was a crucial component of the first wave of industrialization between the early eighteenth and early nineteenth centuries. The power to create, maintain, and employ steam power put Western Europe and the United States at an advantage in the global economy. Steam power not only fueled the machines for production, but also powered the means for shipping and transportation. While Middle Eastern countries (such as the Ottoman Empire and Mameluke Egypt) and East Asian countries (such as Japan) tried to modernize at the same rate as Western powers, they failed to do so because they did not control steam power in the same way. The Middle East and Asia, therefore, did not maintain the same global share of manufacturing as Western Europe and the United States. As a result, their economies became increasingly marginalized by the turn of the twentieth century.

Second Wave Industrialization and its Effects

The **Second Industrial Revolution** refers to the technological innovations of the 1860s–1920s. This wave of industrialization witnessed the emergence of the steel, chemical, and oil industries. This era, sometimes referred to as the **Gilded Age**, witnessed the completion of transcontinental railroads in the United States and Russia. It also witnessed the invention of the light bulb and electricity, which helped quicken the pace of industrialization. Gasoline-fueled engines and automobiles eventually replaced steam-powered engines and trains in this era. Chemical production helped strengthen both the manufacturing and agricultural industries by creating new materials and pesticides. Precision machinery aided the production of highly-intricate mechanisms and consumer goods. This is the era that launched the United States into the position of an industrial-imperial world leader.

Reactions and Revolutions

Development of Machines and Fossil Fuels Revolution

Throughout the late eighteenth century and early nineteenth century, Great Britain and the United States experienced a wide-reaching mechanical revolution that dramatically altered the human experience. The inventions of the **mechanical revolution**, such as steam-powered engines, catalyzed a broader industrial revolution that had already started to change the social, political, economic, and technological conditions of the world. The factory method of the industrial revolution, defined by an acute specialization of skilled and unskilled labor concentrated in one place, actually came *before* the power and machinery; a new "division of labor" emerged in the age of colonization, creating factories long before the world became dependent upon fossil fuels and combustible engines. Workers were laboring in the factories of London and Massachusetts, creating millinery, cardboard boxes, clothing, and furniture long before the steam engine became applicable to transportation and production. New inventions, such as the combustible engine, and fossil fuel discoveries only intensified these industrial trends, creating entirely new means of economic production and social interaction. The result was a drastically different industrialized paradigm.

Steam Engine

Experimentation with steam power had been going on for several decades before **James Watt**, a British inventor, entered the field in 1763. Nevertheless, Watt is credited with creating a brilliant invention that harnessed steam power and made it a universal servant in manifold industries, revolutionizing the manufacturing and trade systems of the industrial world. Watt created a more efficient steam engine that capitalized on the expansive force of steam to drive ordinary machines with double-acting pistons and cylinders. Watt's steam engine encouraged more investors, such as Matthew Boulton, a manufacturer in Birmingham, to fund experiments with steam navigation on the rivers and canals of the Western world.

Coal and the Fossil Fuel Revolution

James Watt's steam engine was created to help cater to Great Britain's newfound love for a fossil fuel known as coal. **Coal** had become the primary fuel for heating homes in England by the sixteenth century, well before Watt ever attempted to build his steam engine. The reign of Elizabeth, coupled with the rapid increase in the demand for house coal, resulted in the rapid expansion of coalmining industries throughout the country. In fact, some historians believe this **fossil fuel revolution** helped bring England out of its medieval epoch. By the eighteenth century, in the years leading up to Watt's paradigm-shifting ingenuity, the men and women of Great Britain's coal communities struggled to mine enough coal to fuel the rapidly urbanizing households of England and Scotland. As small mines were used up, and as

coal tunnels deepened, the miners struggled to raise the coal in their small baskets. The solution: a machine that could mine coal at a more efficient pace. That solution turned out to be the steam engine. James Watt, eager to capitalize on this great need as Great Britain marched further toward industrial progress, took the blueprints of previous steam engines and made a steam-and-piston machine that utilized coal as a fuel. Thus, it was the fusion of Watt's dreams with Britain's needs that allowed the mechanical revolution and fossil fuel revolution to coalesce in the ever-expanding pathway toward industrialization. As the mines employed mechanical, steam-powered drills and water pumps, eventually inventors began looking to dominate the riverways, canals, and seas of this new industrial world.

Steamboat

With the mechanical revolution in full swing, a new inventor emerged. His name was **Robert Fulton**, a man who was both an artist and civil engineer. Assisted by the American Minister to France, R. Livingston, Fulton built and launched his first steamboat on the Seine River in 1803. Returning to the United States in 1806, Fulton and Livingston began experimenting with a steamboat named the *Clermont* on the Hudson River in New York. The boat made its first trip from New York City to Albany in 1807, making regular trips in the months and years that followed. Using machinery made by Watt in England, Fulton's steamboat became the first commercially successful vessel of its kind, launching the Western world into a new era of travel along the canals and rivers of England and America. The steamboat became a symbol of these emerging industrial giants; it also garnered interest in the potential for transatlantic travel, which, by 1819, was fully realized as the *Savannah* made the journey from Savannah, Georgia to Liverpool, England. The entire trip only took twenty-two days, revolutionizing transatlantic trade and international relations forever.

Petroleum and the Fossil Fuel Revolution

With these advancements in mining, production, and transportation, citizens in Great Britain and the United States began looking for newer, more efficient fuel sources. The discovery and consequential development of oil wells in the United States around 1860 gave the world exactly the fuel source that it needed to launch a second wave of industrialization, one that would witness the emergence of gas lamps, electricity, and automobiles. Crude petroleum further revolutionized the Industrial Revolution. It served as a source for machine power as well as light. By 1873, a United States citizen by the name of **G. H. Brayton** had developed a more efficient petroleum engine that mixed the vapor of petroleum with air constituted by the fuel. The application of petroleum engines to households, factories, and new modes of transportation paved the way to new furnace heating systems, gas lamps, and automotive transportation. In particular, the discovery of oil wells by George Bissell and Edwin L. Drake in Titusville, Pennsylvania in 1859 revolutionized the ways in which cities were illuminated. New gas lamps, in which the wicks were not discarded, were installed across cities in Europe and the United States. Eventually electric light bulbs replaced these gas lamps, but the gas lamps became the first great source of illumination for urbanization.

Ideologies of Change and Reform Movements

The ways in which people organized themselves into societies also underwent significant transformations in industrialized states due to the fundamental restructuring of the global economy. In the United States and Great Britain, in particular, the excesses, complexities, and social ills associated with global capitalism encouraged citizens to gravitate toward a Progressive ethos of reform. The Progressive ethos of reform emerged as a political platform between the 1870s and 1920s. **Progressivism** was directed by the belief that progress in technologies must also be balanced by progress of social welfare and justice. Progressive reformers in the United States and Great Britain, largely driven by a Christian sense of social welfare and justice, attempted to eradicate the social ills associated with urban life through philanthropic, political, and legal measures. The Progressive mindset gripped all levels of society; it influenced government, business, and the common masses.

Nineteenth Century Social Reform

In the nineteenth century, muckraking journalists also unveiled the excesses of capitalism. Absorbing socialist tendencies, these muckraking journalists wrote about and photographed the devastating effects of industrial urban poverty. **William Booth** was a British muckraker who founded The Salvation Army, a Christian movement that assisted with humanitarian aid. Booth's book, *In Darkest England and the Way Out*, lambasted British politicians for allowing England to fall in backward disrepair. He argued that poverty could be combatted with social welfare programs, and that the Industrial Revolution could be reined in through Christian sympathies.

Yet not all Progressive reforms were *good* in the universal modern sense. Progressivism also gave birth to xenophobic reforms in the United States and Great Britain. This xenophobic sentiment coalesced with **Social Darwinism**—a system of belief that applied Darwinian theories of "survival of the fittest" to nations and races—to form, perhaps, the most derogatory form of Progressivism: eugenics. **Eugenics** is a term that refers to the notion that society can create the fittest race through targeted breeding and sterilizing efforts. The eugenics movement, often believed to be a Nazi concept, was actually an outgrowth of American and British Progressive ideals during the Victorian period.

American and British eugenicists attempted to create a superior nation/race by systematically sterilizing people with disabilities. Eugenics also reinforced institutional racism in both countries, forbidding miscegenation, or the consummation of two separate races. Interracial marriages were forbidden, or, at the very least, frowned upon in the United States and Great Britain well into the civil rights era of the 1960s. Eugenics and xenophobia, on a global level, also reinforced imperialist and colonial tendencies that looked down upon other countries or races as being inferior to the American and British industrial empires. This was all defined by the notion of Progress on a global scale and speaks to the darker side of Progressive reform in world history.

The Industrial Revolution placed a greater strain on laborers by exposing them to dangerous working conditions, longer hours of work, and low wages. These industrial conditions and cultural constructs consequently gave rise to worker resistance, which typically took form as trade unions. **Trade unions** are voluntary workers' organizations that press businesses and governments for industrial reform. Unions were created for all workers in particular trades, and engaged in collective bargaining efforts, a form of negotiation between unions and businesses. Skilled trade unions typically led the way in these reform efforts, and, in some cases, when big businesses did not meet the collective bargaining demands of the employees, workers would strike. In other cases, workers would boycott company products to send a message. Many trade unions were largely motivated by the socialist and communist visions established by **Karl Marx**, author of *Das Kapital* and *The Communist Manifesto*. Marx argued that workers should rise up against their capitalist exploiters and lead a class-based revolution. While not many of these revolutions actually took form, Marxist ideology did encourage many workers to form unions and strike.

Roles of Women in the Industrial Age

Industrialization allowed women and children to take on new responsibilities in the household and the workplace. Previously, women's roles were limited in the household by the daily presence of men, who typically controlled the pace of homestead labor. Likewise, child labor was confined to family farms and

trades. All of this changed with the Industrial Revolution. The factory system, rather than the farm, became the epicenter of the family. Everything revolved around factory work, factory life, and factory time. This inevitably changed the dynamics of family and gender. Women gained more power within the household and society in the absence of men. Children and teenagers gained more responsibilities as workers who contributed to family subsistence through waged labor, such as working in coal mines as breaker boys. There were not any laws to restrict child labor at this time. Women also gained more economic rights: although men still greatly dominated factory work, women began entering the workforce at an unprecedented pace. Some single women even joined factory boarding homes that allowed for a relative amount of independence. Overall, the Industrial Revolution changed family dynamics by granting more rights to women, providing more economic opportunities to families, and making the factory the center of everyone's lives. The nuclear family, previously centered around a farming calendar and schedule, adapted to new conceptions of time, which were based on factory shifts.

Demographics also naturally shifted as previously-isolated cultures (such as rural villages and isolated nations) were concentrated in rapidly-urbanizing cities. Cultures mixed and matched through interethnic marriages in spite of the relative amount of ethnic segregation in cities. Immigrant population booms established intergenerational working-class lifestyles. Overall, cities became more diversified as a result of migration and immigration trends. Nationalization movements, therefore, responded to these demographic trends in two ways: at times nationalization was built on unity through diversity, and, at other times, it was built on the premise of eugenic homogeneity in the wake of diversity.

Rapid Urbanization

Prior to the Industrial Revolution, most citizens in Western Europe lived in rural areas. The local economies there were focused on agricultural production, typically only for the subsistence of families or towns. As a result of the Industrial Revolution and the rise of global capitalism, the Western industrial world rapidly urbanized, which meant that more residents flocked to cities. **Urbanization**—city building and the migration to cities—was the direct consequence of industrialization. Factory systems provided residents of cities with more food for sustenance and more jobs for survival. Places like Manchester, England, a textile production center in Great Britain, experienced rapid growth, shifting from fewer than 50,000 residents in 1750 to more than 300,000 residents by 1850. The cities urbanized so rapidly that the infrastructure at the time could not accommodate the population booms.

The result was the creation of a new urban working class, but this class often had to live in residential and working conditions that were less than ideal. Workers and their families crammed into dark, dirty tenement houses and apartments. Factory owners exploited these populations even further with dangerous conditions in urban factories. Business was not yet regulated by government, and the result was longer workdays for lower wages in dangerous conditions. Some of the most dangerous conditions were found in the coal mines that fueled the factories. Miners would work for long hours in harsh conditions without any rest or reprieve from the coal dust. Mining towns in Pennsylvania and Wales rapidly urbanized, creating dire conditions. The result of this rapid urbanization was more people living in squalor, and more people being exposed to rapidly-spreading diseases, such as Cholera and Spanish flu.

Nineteenth Century Perspectives and Political Developments

Contextualizing Nineteenth Century Perspectives and Political Developments

Industrialization of States and Expansion

Europe industrialized during the late eighteenth and nineteenth centuries. As such, European powers sought to expand their overseas empires and international trading opportunities to support industrialization. Imperialism benefited industrialization in three major ways. First, imperial powers imported cheap agricultural products and raw resources, such as timber, cotton, and precious metals. Second, colonized territory provided imperial powers with cheap labor. Third, colonized territory functioned as a proprietary market for the imperial powers' manufactured goods. Transoceanic trade relationships offered opportunities for imperial powers to export manufactured goods in exchange for capital, resources, and goods they didn't already produce. During the eighteenth and nineteenth centuries, Britain extended its empire to every continent except for Antarctica. To compete with Great Britain, a number of European powers, including Belgium, France, Germany, Italy, Portugal, and Spain annexed African territory. In addition, imperial powers used a combination of military force and economic coercion to secure "spheres of influences" in China that provided the powers with exclusive political and economic rights. In the late nineteenth and twentieth centuries, Britain, France, Germany, Japan, Russia, and the United States all established spheres of influence in China. During the late nineteenth century, Japan conquered the Korean Peninsula, and France established French Indochina in present-day Vietnam, Cambodia, and Laos.

Changes in Migration Patterns

Transoceanic empires and global capitalism severely altered immigration patterns during the nineteenth century. Overall, the number of migrants reached a then-unprecedented high due to the creation of two new paths of migration. First, business owners, investors, and entrepreneurs from imperial powers migrated to conquered territories. The conquered territories represented an opportunity to monopolize raw resources and utilize cheap labor. Second, people from colonized peoples migrated to the imperial power in the pursuit of greater economic opportunities. Many of these immigrants settled in large cities. In general, cities had more economic populations and large immigrant communities. For example, British cities attracted substantial numbers of immigrants from India and Kenya during the nineteenth century. Immigration again increased in the twentieth century due to nationalist revolutions, mass atrocities, and the continued expansion of global capitalism.

New Systems of Industrial Control over Colonies

Industrialization allowed some of the original empires of the global economy, namely the British empire, to exert new systems of industrial control over their colonies. Great Britain, which had endured the American Revolution and other global conflicts, reinvigorated its colonial efforts through industrialization. In fact, the British empire, once shrinking, expanded rapidly into Asia and Africa—with colonies such as British Somaliland and British India—because of its industrial successes. It allowed the British to exert more authority over both its old and new colonies due to its ability to militarize and create munitions at a much more rapid pace than its competitors. As more money entered the British system through industrial efforts, the more power the British empire had over its colonial holdings. Industrialization allowed Britain to exert both force and dollar diplomacy over its colonies. The British empire clearly strengthened and expanded during this period.

Expansion of Empires in Africa by European States

European colonization of Africa had been occurring long before the Industrial Revolution. The French had been mining for diamonds along the West African coast for decades before the scramble for Africa in the 1880s. Nevertheless, industrialization helped militarize many European nation states, making it easier to scramble to carve up Africa through colonization. The Maxim gun, invented in 1889, assisted with these efforts, providing European powers with a superior, modern weapon that made colonization easier. Originally, Europeans had hoped to separate Africa into colonies diplomatically. The **Berlin Conference** of 1884–1885 established rules for colonization. European attendees at the conference agreed that Africa could be colonized through simple claims. Not a single African nation had the opportunity to participate in the Berlin Conference of 1884–1885. Ultimately, European colonies decided that African resistance and imperial competition would have to be settled through war. Wars like the **Boer War** of 1899–1902 pitted the Dutch Boer and British settlers of South Africa and the African Zulu against one another. Because of their industrial strength, Britain ultimately won the war, establishing the Union of South Africa in 1902.

Settler Colonies

The **Union of South Africa** (1902) is an example of a settler colony being established in Africa by a European power. The British had no claims to the land previously, but after the Boer War of 1899–1902, Britain began sending British nationalists to rule the land. The British did the same in Somaliland, India, China, and Australia/New Zealand. Settler colonies sprouted up all over Africa. France took over Morocco and Algeria. Belgium claimed the Congo in 1908. By 1914, only Ethiopia and Liberia remained outside of European control on the African continent.

Anticolonial Movements

By the nineteenth century, many colonial enclaves had had enough with Western European influences. Anticolonial campaigns took place in Qing China, South Africa, Algeria, West Africa, German East Africa, and Ethiopia. Anticolonial campaigns in China coalesced in the great **Boxer Rebellion** of 1900, which attempted to eradicated foreign influence in the Middle Kingdom. In Africa, anticolonial campaigns suffered mixed fates. The Zulus expanded their influence in South Africa much to the chagrin of colonial forces. However, their resistance against the British and Boers ultimately came to an end in 1887, as their weapons and munitions were unable to match those of Western Europeans. The Zulus found themselves in the heart of a conflict between the Boers and the British, and they ultimately failed to defeat either. Native North Africans eventually lost a nearly fifty-year resistance campaign against the French. Likewise, African villagers in German East Africa and French West Africa could not resist colonization in the early 1900s. The only major successful resistance occurred when **Menelik II of Ethiopia** defeated the invading Italian forces at the **Battle of Adowa** in 1896. Nonetheless, most decolonization efforts in that era were unsuccessful: residents of Africa and Asia challenged colonial rule vehemently, but often imperialism was the ultimate victor.

Anti-Imperial Resistance

New imperialist ideologies, motivated by notions of racial and national superiority, created tensions with local populations, which ultimately led to anti-imperialist resistance efforts that birthed entirely new periphery states. One of the greatest examples of this historical phenomenon was the creation of various Balkans states in 1912 and 1913 as a culmination of resistance against the waning power of the Ottoman Empire. The **Balkans Wars** of 1912–1913, which served as a prelude to World War I, were inaugurated by the Balkan League, a coalition between Bulgaria, Greece, Montenegro, and Serbia. The two wars set the precedent for independence for the Balkans nations, who defeated the crumbling

Ottoman Empire. Other periphery states to emerge included the Zulu nation, near South Africa, which had been empowered by British military forces during the Boer War.

Rebellions Over Imperial Rule

Religious uprisings occurred in destabilized empires such as the Qing Dynasty in China, in response to British missionary influence. Two of the most famous religiously-inspired movements in these spheres were the Taiping Rebellion and the Boxer Rebellion.

The **Taiping Rebellion** was led by Hong Xiuquan after the Treaty of Nanjing afforded Christian missionaries from Great Britain and the United States with more latitude in China. Hong Xiuquan spent a lot of time with Christian missionaries, and he was inspired to convert to their religion. Xiuquan dreamed of a Christian China, one that would allow a "Heavenly Kingdom of Great Peace" to exert its influence in the Qing Dynasty. He believed the only way the Heavenly Kingdom of Great Peace would manifest itself in this world was through a Christian revolt. This revolt became known as the Taiping Rebellion. Beginning in 1840, it lasted over a decade, witnessed the conquest of large amounts of Qing territory, and was eventually quashed through military alliances between Chinese, British, and French troops.

The **Boxer Rebellion** was much different than the Taiping Rebellion because it was not motivated by Christian ideas but rather anti-Christian ideas. The Boxer Rebellion attacked Chinese Christians as part of its xenophobic campaigns against Western missionaries. The Boxers campaigned against the Dowager Empress's rule, which was sympathetic toward foreigner influence. By August of 1900, a multinational force that included United States, British, Chinese, Japanese, German, Italian, and Austrian soldiers quelled the rebellion.

Nationalism

The Enlightenment and rise of nationalism heavily contributed to the revolutions that took place between 1750 and 1900, and those revolutions resulted in the dissolution of empires and creation of new nation-states. First, Enlightenment philosophers popularized the concept of a social contract, which created an intellectual justification for self-government. For example, French and American political leaders both claimed violations of the social contract as the basis for their revolutions. Second, nationalism became a popular ideology, especially when communities shared language, religion, social customs, and territory. For example, German and Italian nationalist movements led unification efforts in their respective countries, and both movements succeeded in 1871. The revolutions had a dramatic effect on several empires as they lost control over their overseas territory. For example, the Spanish Empire and Ottoman Empire were both on the brink of collapse by the beginning of the twentieth century. Another major effect of those revolutions was the creation of dozens of new nation-states governed by constitutional monarchies or representative governments. For example, Romania and Serbia both gained independence from the Ottoman Empire and formed constitutional monarchies during the nineteenth century.

Commonality Based on Language, Religion, Social Customs, and Territory

The development of nation-states was facilitated through people gaining a greater sense of community based on common characteristics, such as language, religion, social customs, and territory. For example, Christianity provided the foundation for nationalist movements in Serbia and Greece that revolted against the Ottoman Empire in 1804 and 1821, respectively. Oftentimes, governments enacted policies intended to emphasize these shared characteristics to create a unifying national identity. For example, after the French Revolution, the new nationalist government formed the Committee for Public

Instruction to enlist teachers who instructed communities about the French language and social customs. This initiative was considered an essential part of crafting a national identity that bound the country together. Similarly, governments often sought to establish a national identity by fighting a common enemy, especially when the state's territorial integrity was threatened. For example, in the **Franco-Prussian War** (1870–1871), Prussian forces turned back a French invasion of German territory. This paved the way for the unification of Germany in 1871 under the King of Prussia's leadership.

Italian Nationalism

Nationalism destroyed many empires; however, in the case of Italy, it helped build one. **Italian nationalism** emerged from the tumult of the Austrian Empire that had ruled the territory in the early nineteenth century. However, between 1815 and 1848, hundreds of thousands of Italian residents were growing increasingly discontent with Austrian rule; they wanted their own Italian nation, one that would reflect the values of the Italian locals. As a result of this discontent, several Italian nationalist leaders emerged: Giuseppe Mazzini, Camillo di Cavour, and Giuseppe Garibaldi. These men would help lead revolts that would eventually lead to Italian unification.

New Imperialism: Motivations and Methods

Motivations for European Imperialism

States used a variety of rationales to justify **imperialism** between 1750 and 1900. European powers justified the colonization of the Americas and Africa based on the need to spread Christianity. This served two purposes. First, Catholic and Protestant powers believed they were in a competition to establish their denomination as the most influential denomination. So, they each favored colonization to grow their constituencies. Second, Christianity made colonization more palatable to domestic audiences because religious conversions were seen as saving Amerindians from eternal damnation. Religious conversions were also linked to European powers' rationale about their mission to civilize "savage" indigenous populations in the Americas and Africa, which was commonly referred to as the "white man's burden." Many Europeans believed they had a superior culture, so imperialism actually benefited colonized peoples under this view. During the late eighteenth century, Europeans developed **Social Darwinism** based on Charles Darwin's theory of evolutions to claim that only strong states would survive in global politics. Accordingly, European powers argued that imperialism was merely part of natural selection because they were the stronger states. Similarly, European and Japanese imperial powers also used nationalism to claim they had a right to extend their territory based on their inherent superiority.

Technological Advances Enabling European Imperialism

Colonial holdings reached well beyond the transatlantic world thanks to the innovative transportation technologies of the Industrial Revolution. With ships that could travel greater distances in a shorter amount of time, imperial powers—namely the United States, Western Europe, and Japan—were able to better dominate the Asian-Pacific region, which was previously a crucial trade sector of the early Spanish and Portuguese empires. Spain and Portugal, ravaged by revolutions and wars in the Americas, could no longer exert their authority over places like India, China, and the Philippines. These regions became the new targets of the new imperialist nation states, such as industrial Britain, the United States, and Japan. Great Britain exerted new authority over India and China (through the Opium Wars and Taiping Rebellion). The United States conquered Spain in the Spanish-American War, which allowed it to acquire Guam and the Philippines. It also annexed Hawaii (from Sandford B. Dole, the American-led republican president who overthrew the kingdom there) as part of its new imperial campaigns. Japan had forced a foothold in the Chinese mainland (Manchuria) and Korea. These new imperialist powers established lasting Asian-Pacific empires that would prove to be quite strategic in the earliest years of the twentieth century.

Imperialism's Global Effects

Imperialism, which had long been a British and Western European phenomenon, had spread to rapidly industrializing non-European nation-states by the end of the nineteenth century and beginning of the twentieth century. The United States, Russia, and Japan became the leaders of this "new imperialism," which extended throughout the globe.

The United States had gradually expanded from the Atlantic to the Pacific coast from 1776 to the 1860s. By the late nineteenth and early twentieth centuries, however, the United States was poised to expand its borders beyond its contiguous states and territories, and it did exactly that, first with the purchase of Alaska (1867), later with the annexation of Hawaii (1898), and with the Spanish-American War (1898). Through these endeavors, the United States quickly became an imperial power, ruling land in Alaska, Puerto Rico, Guam, Hawaii, and the Philippines.

Russia territorial expansion spanned several centuries, beginning in the sixteenth century and continuing well into the twentieth century. The nineteenth century, however, witnessed some of the most fervent expansionist efforts by the Russian empire, which was rapidly industrializing. The Russian empire eventually expanded from the Black Sea in the West to Manchuria/Korea in the East. Its imperial expansionist efforts resulted in multiple wars, including the **Crimean War** (1812–1815) and the **Russo-Japanese War** (1904–1905). In the process, Russia came to blows with powers in both Europe, Eurasia, and East Asia.

Japan began its expansionist efforts in the late nineteenth century, annexing territories in Manchuria (China) and Korea. These aggressive campaigns brought the Japanese Empire in direct blows with the Russians during the Russo-Japanese War of 1904–1905, which ultimately ended in a Japanese victory. Japanese imperialism set the precedent for future global conflicts in World War I and World War II.

Nineteenth Century Culture and Arts

European Artistic Expression
Romanticism in Art
As European thought evolved during this time period, so did European expression in the arts. A new form of art called **Romanticism** became popular. Romanticism emphasized emotion over reason, focusing on human senses, passions, and faith. Nature was given priority, with focus on nature's beauty. It also moved away from the Enlightenment view of nature as precise and always in harmony, instead opting to show its more unpredictable nature. Romanticism focused on personal freedom and feeling, tapping into humanitarian movements against slavery, poverty, and industry. Ideals like honor and chivalry were celebrated again, with a focus on community. Human nature was at the forefront of artistic expression, as it mirrored European thought at the time.

Artists captured this spirit of the time in their artwork. **Francisco Goya** of Spain used paintings to depict the atrocities committed against the Spaniards by the French during the occupation. **Caspar David Friedrich** painted nature as mystical and powerful. **John Constable** depicted rural English landscapes that showed humans being at peace with their environment. **J. M. W. Turner** used his artwork to show nature's power and terror, with images of storms and sinking ships, as well as landscapes and sunsets.

Eugène Delacroix, a French painter, painted exotic and bright pictures of the Revolution in France, showing war and destruction. These themes overlapped in much of the art of the time.

Romanticism in Music

Romanticism in music often touched on emotion and nationalism, using folk songs and emotion to conjure feelings in its listeners. **Ludwig van Beethoven**, a German composer, used his work to tap into human emotion. He was also the first to use vocal music in symphony. **Frédéric Chopin** wrote Polish folk songs and dances in his numerous piano works. **Richard Wagner**, through opera, developed a music-drama emphasizing Germanic myths and legends, which led to the popularization of the opera. **Pyotr Tchaikovsky**, a Russian composer, created melodies and Russian ballets. He has numerous productions still famous today, such as *The Nutcracker* and *Swan Lake*.

Romanticism in Writing

Romantic writers also used the themes of the time to influence their works. **Johann Wolfgang von Goethe** used *Sorrows of the Young Werther* to tell the story of a young hero who was misunderstood but stayed true to his feelings. After being rejected by a young woman, he committed suicide. This particular work influenced many tragic dramas of the time. His piece *Faust* told the tale of a man selling his soul to the devil in return for all knowledge, a critique on Enlightenment ideals.

Victor Hugo was a French romantic writer, creating timeless stories like *Hunchback of Notre Dame* and *Les Misérables*. **William Wordsworth** of England was a romantic poet who focused on nature. He used poetic conventions, advanced language, and majestic descriptors for basic subjects. **Lord Byron** was another English poet who had a melancholic writing style. **Percy Shelley, husband to Mary Shelley,** was also an influential English writer. He wrote *Prometheus Unbound*, which details the revolution of humans against their oppressors. **Mary Shelley** wrote the classic work *Frankenstein*, considered by many to be the first-ever work within the science fiction genre. **John Keats** wrote poetry early in his life that reflected on death, solitude, and love. He died at the age of twenty-five.

Realist and Materialist Themes

Realism, a belief that literature and art should show life as it really is, was a counter to Romanticism. This style of art caught on particularly toward the end of the nineteenth century and carried over into the beginning of the twentieth century.

The realist movement originated in France. **Honoré de Balzac** developed *The Human Comedy*, a work that showed urban society as amoral and brutal, representing a truly Darwinian outlook. **Émile Zola** depicted hard and brutal working conditions in her works about the French working class. In England, **George Eliot** (Mary Ann Evans) wrote about ways in which people are changed and maneuvered by their social class, and how it aligns with who they are as a person. **Thomas Hardy** wrote *Tess of d'Urbervilles*, a story about a woman who was ostracized from society for engaging in pre-marital sex, a critique of Catholic culture.

Charles Dickens wrote literature that criticized industrialization and urbanization. He illustrated issues of the poor and the need for reforms in many of his works, such as *Oliver Twist* and *A Christmas Carol*, which are still seen as masterpieces today. Russia's **Leo Tolstoy** is one of the most well-known realists, writing *War and Peace*, a story of Russian society during the Napoleonic Wars that is still highly regarded today. **Fyodor Dostoevsky** is another still-famous realist, writing about human suffering and strife in *Crime and Punishment*.

Practice Questions

Questions 1–3 refer to the passage below.

> I believe that this was the first moving line ever installed. The idea came in a general way from the overhead trolley that the Chicago packers use in dressing beef. We had previously assembled the fly-wheel magneto in the usual method. With one workman doing a complete job he could turn out from thirty-five to forty pieces in a nine-hour day, or about twenty minutes to an assembly. What he did alone was then spread into twenty-nine operations; that cut down the assembly time to thirteen minutes, ten seconds. Then we raised the height of the line eight inches—this was in 1914—and cut the time to seven minutes. Further experimenting with the speed that the work should move at cut the time down to five minutes. In short, the result is this: by the aid of scientific study one man is now able to do somewhat more than four did only a comparatively few years ago. That line established the efficiency of the method and we now use it everywhere. The assembling of the motor, formerly done by one man, is now divided into eighty-four operations—those men do the work that three times their number formerly did. In a short time we tried out the plan on the chassis.

Excerpt from *My Life and My Work* by Henry Ford, 1922

1. According to the passage, which one of the following best describes the primary economic benefit of this innovation?
   a. The innovation increased workers' ability to multi-task.
   b. The innovation decreased labor costs per worker.
   c. The innovation increased productivity in terms of both speed and quantity.
   d. The innovation decreased the size of the industrial workforce.

2. Which one of the following is the name for this type of production?
   a. Assembly line
   b. Assembly trolley
   c. Automated assembly
   d. Elevated assembly

3. According to the passage, how did this new method of production improve over time?
   a. The method improved by adopting the exact practices of other industries.
   b. The method improved after it was applied to the chassis.
   c. The method improved by continually increasing the number of operations per product.
   d. The method improved progressively through experimentation.

4. Which of the following nations saw their standing during the nineteenth century fall as other powers were rising?
   a. Ottoman Empire
   b. England
   c. Germany
   d. Russia

Questions 5–6 refer to the passage below.

"Take up the White Man's burden,

Send forth the best ye breed

Go bind your sons to exile,

to serve your captives' need;

To wait in heavy harness,   5

On fluttered folk and wild—

Your new caught, sullen peoples,

Half-devil and half-child.

Take up the White Man's burden—

The savage wars of peace—   10

Fill full the mouth of Famine

And bid the sickness cease;

And when your goal is nearest

The end for others sought,

Watch sloth and heathen Folly   15

Bring all your hopes to naught."

Excerpt from "The White Man's Burden" by Rudyard Kipling, 1899

5. Which of the following movements was this passage used to justify?
   a. Communism
   b. Nationalism
   c. Imperialism
   d. Liberalism

6. Of the following leaders, who would be the LEAST likely to agree with the sentiments of the passage?
   a. Bismarck
   b. John Stuart Mill
   c. Louis Napoleon III
   d. Edmund Burke

Questions 7–10 refer to the passage below:

What is dangerous for Japan is, not the imitation of the outer features of the West, but the acceptance of the motive force of the Western nationalism as her own. Her social ideals are already showing signs of defeat at the hands of politics. I can see her motto, taken from science, "Survival of the Fittest," writ large at the entrance of her present-day history—the motto whose meaning is, "Help yourself, and never heed what it costs to others"; the motto of the blind man who only believes in what he can touch, because he cannot see. But those who can see know that men are so closely knit that when you strike others the blow comes back to yourself. The moral law, which is the greatest discovery of man, is the discovery of this wonderful truth, that man becomes all the truer the more he realizes himself in others. This truth has not only a subjective value but is manifested in every department of our life. And nations who sedulously cultivate moral blindness as the cult of patriotism will end their existence in a sudden and violent death.

Excerpt from the essay "Nationalism in Japan" by Rabindranath Tagore, 1917

7. According to the passage, why is nationalism so dangerous?
    a. Nationalism promotes the imitation of Western political structures.
    b. Nationalism encourages countries to pursue imperialism.
    c. Nationalism strengthens Japanese social ideals.
    d. Nationalism undermines Japan's traditional religious traditions.

8. Which of the following BEST summarizes the "outer features of the West" that Japan adopted in the nineteenth century?
    a. Japan enacted a written constitution and modernized its military in the nineteenth century.
    b. Japan outlawed Shintoism and orchestrated mass conversions to Christianity.
    c. Japan encouraged nationalism to strengthen the Shogun.
    d. Japan adopted European moral laws and other positive social ideals.

9. Nationalism had the LEAST influence on which one of the following world events?
    a. German unification
    b. Latin American wars of independence
    c. Russo-Turkish War
    d. War of the Spanish Succession

10. Which of the following political theories is "Survival of the Fittest" most commonly associated with?
    a. Individualism
    b. National liberalism
    c. Social Darwinism
    d. Totalitarianism

11. The Zollverein was created to achieve which goal?
    a. Unify Germany under one government
    b. Grow the German army
    c. Defend against French and British invasions
    d. Set up a union for free trade

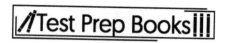

12. The Dreyfus Affair and the subsequent Emile Zola "J'Accuse" letter that helped bring an end to the crisis were centered around denouncing:
    a. Nationalism
    b. Anti-Semitism
    c. Socialism
    d. Marxism

13. The Triple Alliance was made up of which countries?
    a. United States, Britain, and France
    b. France, Britain, and Russia
    c. Austria-Hungary, Germany, and Russia
    d. Italy, Germany, and Austria-Hungary

14. Which of the following is part of the makeup of Romanticism?
    a. Individualism
    b. Grounded in the teachings of the Enlightenment
    c. A rejection of history
    d. A focus on order and symmetry

Short Answer Question

1. Answer all parts of the question that follows.

> The discovery of diamonds in South Africa, in 1867, exercised by degrees an enormous influence upon the attitude of the natives throughout Southern Africa. When the success of the dry diggings at the New Rush caused the formation of Kimberley, that town became the centre of an enormous gun trade. From north and east, thousands of Kafirs of various tribes flocked to a place where they could obtain, for the reward of their labour, the means of exterminating the hated white man in South Africa. The Gealekas under Kreli, the Gaikas of Sandilli, as well as the Zulus beyond Natal, were not slow to seize such an opportunity. For years the trade continued, and the weapons purchased were soon used against the Government which permitted their sale. Wars were waged upon the eastern and northern borders of the Cape Colony during 1877, 1878, and 1879. Sir Benjamin Pine, with some fancy and a great deal of truth, styles the diamond of the Kimberley mines the bloodstone of South Africa. As the Zulu system makes war a necessity constantly thirsted for by the army, advantage was taken of the easy opportunity of getting firearms afforded by the inconceivable blindness and fatuity of the British Government. In the year 1877, Cetywayo had quite made up his mind for a deadly conflict with the white man. Guns were purchased, preparations were made, and the army crouched like a tiger in its lair, ready to spring.

Excerpt from <u>History of the Zulu War</u> by A. Wilmot, 1880

a) Identify ONE specific historical example of the influence of British imperialism in Africa.

b) For the period of 1860–1914, identify ONE development that changed colonialism in the region of South Africa.

c) Explain the broader historical impacts of the Boer Wars (1899–1902).

Answer Explanations

1. C: The innovation's primary economic benefit was to increase productivity in terms of both speed and quality. The passage contains several examples of how the assembly increased the production of fly-wheel magnetos and motors. For example, at the end of the passage, Ford claims that the assembly line tripled the productivity for motors. Thus, Choice *C* is the correct answer. The innovation is that each worker is assigned one single operation to be completed on every product, which is the opposite of multi-tasking. So, Choice *A* is incorrect. Although the innovation might have decreased labor costs by standardizing tasks, the passage doesn't reference labor costs. Therefore, Choice *B* is incorrect. Choice *D* is the second best answer choice. Ford mentions that men can perform three times the amount of work, but it's unclear whether this means the workforce decreased. In other words, the workforce could've remained the same or even increased to support mass production. As such, Choice *D* is incorrect.

2. A: The passage is describing an assembly line, which Henry Ford used to mass produce his famous Model T cars. An assembly line is a method of production where workers are each assigned a single task, and the products are progressively built as they slide down the assembling line. The passage mentions how the assembly was divided into operations, and the product was assembled along a line. Thus, Choice *A* is the correct answer. Although Ford mentions how his assembly line has aspects of an overhead trolley, this method of production was not called the assembly trolley. So, Choice *B* is incorrect. The assembly line did use more automation than previous methods of industrial production, but the method of assembly wasn't referred to as automated assembly. Therefore, Choice *C* is incorrect. Choice *D* is incorrect because this method also wasn't called elevated assembly, though Ford did raise the height of the assembly line to increase the speed of production.

3. D: The method improved progressively through experimentation. Ford describes how he first got the idea from the overhead trolley used by Chicago beef packers and then they later elevated the height of the assembly line. In addition, the passage explicitly references "experimenting with the speed" of line and making use of "scientific study." Thus, Choice *D* is the correct answer. Choice *A* is the second best answer choice because the Chicago beef packing industry influenced Ford. However, Ford claims it was only loosely based on the beef industry's overhead trolley, and he repeatedly describes experimenting with the height and speed. So, Choice *A* is incorrect. The passage ends with Ford stating his intention to test the new method on a chassis, which is the automobile's frame. As such, the chassis didn't improve the method as described in the passage, so Choice *B* is incorrect. Choice *C* is incorrect because the increased number of operations was a consequence of Ford's experimentation; the method didn't improve simply because the number of operations increased. So, Choice *C* is incorrect.

4. A: Throughout the nineteenth century, most European nations grew through trade and expansion. Germany saw unification and expansion as their trade power grew. England saw the largest growth, becoming the dominant European power by the end of the nineteenth century. Russia also grew, expanding through military might and trading alliances in the region. The Ottoman Empire, however, once a proud nation, saw war and trade deficits end their reign as a major European power.

5. C: The "White Man's Burden" spoke to many of the feelings that Europeans had during the late 1800s about the rest of the world. Liberalism and communism had their roots in more social movements. The rhetoric of the nationalist movement, while definitely feeling superiority to outside nations, still did not desire to incorporate "outsiders," as the passage is talking about. This piece was used to justify imperialism, as nations sought to expand outward and help the perceived "uncivilized" of Africa and Asia.

6. B: John Stuart Mill was a liberal who believed that all humans were equal and would not have justified slavery or coerced labor; he certainly wouldn't agree with this passage. Bismarck's Germany used this text as part of a justification for expanding the German nation throughout the beginning of the 1900s, so Choice *A* is incorrect. Napoleon agreed that the French had a duty to civilize outsiders and would certainly echo the sentiments, making Choice *C* incorrect. Edmund Burke (Choice *D*) would have agreed with the text as well because his Whig beliefs centered on a stronger Britain that sought to expand.

7. B: The passage references the selfish nature of nationalism and how its violation of moral law leads to violent death. During the eighteenth and nineteenth centuries, nationalism motivated many bloody imperial conquests. Thus, Choice *B* is the correct answer. The passage mentions how Japan has imitated the "outer features of the West," which would include political structures. However, the passage draws a distinction between those features and nationalism because Tagore is urging Japan not to adopt nationalism. This wouldn't be possible if nationalism was an inherent part of the outer features. So, Choice *A* is incorrect. Choice *C* is incorrect because the passage asserts that nationalism is corrupting Japan's social ideals, not strengthening them. Tagore claims that nationalism violates moral law, but Japan's traditional religious practices are never specifically mentioned. So, Choice *D* is incorrect.

8. A: The passage mentions that Japan has already imitated the "outer features of the West" before issuing a warning against nationalism. During the late nineteenth century, Japan followed the example of great European powers by modernizing its navy and adopting the Meiji Constitution in writing. Both of these reforms fall under the category of "outer features of the West" as the phrase is used in the passage. Nationalism is defined in spiritual terms throughout the passage, so it would be an "inner feature of the West." Thus, Choice *A* is the correct answer. Shintoism is a traditional Japanese religion, and it's not mentioned in the passage. Japan also didn't orchestrate mass conversions to Christianity, so Choice *B* is incorrect. The Shogun was a Japanese military dictatorship that held power between 1185 and 1868. Japanese modernization efforts dissolved the Shogun, and nationalism was adopted under the new imperial Japanese regime. So, Choice *C* is incorrect. Choice *D* is incorrect because Japan didn't adopt European moral laws or social ideals; rather, Japan embraced nationalism in the late-eighteenth and early-nineteenth centuries.

9. D: The Prussian political leader Otto von Bismarck leveraged nationalism to rally support for German unification, which occurred in 1871. So, Choice *A* is incorrect. Mexican nationalists defeated Spanish colonizers in the Mexican Revolution, and Simon Bolivar led nationalist revolts across South America during the early nineteenth century. So, Choice *B* is incorrect. The Russo-Turkish War was largely caused by nationalist revolts in Bulgaria, Montenegro, and Romania against the Ottoman Empire, so Choice *C* is incorrect. The War of the Spanish Succession was fought in the early eighteenth century, which predates the rise of nationalism in continental Europe. Thus, Choice *D* is the correct answer.

10. C: "Survival of the Fittest" is most closely associated with social Darwinism, which applied Charles Darwin's theory of evolution to the global competition between nation-states. Social Darwinists believed only the strongest states would survive, which was used as a justification for imperial conquests. Thus, Choice *C* is the correct answer. Individualism is a moral philosophy that's most associated with democracy and capitalism, so Choice *A* is incorrect. National liberalism was a popular political ideology during German unification, and its proponents generally combine elements of capitalism, liberalism, and nationalism. So, Choice *B* is incorrect. Totalitarianism is a form of government that consolidates all political power under an authoritarian and autocratic dictator. So, Choice *D* is incorrect.

11. D: By the late nineteenth century, many had tried to unify the German states to form one nation; Germany was still not altogether under one rule. With many different ideologies, it was hard to maintain

113

113

one system of government. Still, trade was a desired outcome for many of the states and territories. The Zollverein sought to establish a network to grow Germany and protect the states against other European powers from dominating the trade in the region.

12. B: The Dreyfus Affair centered around the accusation against a French captain in the army of sending secrets to the Germans. The subsequent trial brought rage against French leaders for outing and accusing the soldier for being Jewish. Emile Zola's famous article, "J'Accuse," brought attention to the story, eventually leading to the reversal of Dreyfus's conviction, a stand against anti-Semitism.

13. D: The Triple Alliance was formed to create a counterbalance to the growing power of Britain and Russia by concerned nations in Eastern Europe. The alliance, which angered Britain, comprised Italy, Germany, and Austria-Hungary.

14. A: The elements of Romanticism allowed its steady rise in the late nineteenth century throughout Europe. Above all, Romanticism focused on rejecting the ideas behind the Enlightenment and embracing creativity. Enamored with unpredictability, the most discerning characteristic of the movement was its focus on individualism.

Short Answer Response

1.

a) One specific historical example of the influence of British imperialism in South Africa is the Cape Frontier Wars. In this series of conflicts, British forces worked with local allies to drive indigenous tribes, such as the Xhosas, Gealekas, Gaikas, and Zulus, off their lands. Following this annexation, the British colonial government constructed a rigid socioeconomic system that limited the political and economic rights of native populations. All of these actions were done to support imperialist policies. The primary purpose of imperialism was to extract resources from foreign lands for the benefit of the home country. Many European powers adhered to imperialist foreign policies during what's known as the **Scramble for Africa**. In the case of South Africa, British imperialists seized local lands to maximize the extraction of gold and diamonds, which fueled the British Empire's overseas ambitions.

b) Colonialism changed in the region of South Africa due to the development of gold and diamond extraction. Prior to this period, Britain's South African colony enjoyed a relatively independent parliamentary government, and it extended the franchise to black South Africans, which resulted in considerable assimilation and a reduction in racial tensions. However, the discovery of diamonds near the town of Kimberley in 1867, as well as the rapidly expanding gold-mining industry, led to Britain altering its colonial policies. Specifically, Britain publicly backed more imperialist politicians, such as Cecil Rhodes, to increase the extraction of gold and diamonds. Rhodes was an ardent white supremacist, and he believed South Africa's natural resources should be exclusively held and enjoyed by British citizens. Rhodes's tenure as the prime minister of Britain's South African colony laid the foundation for the Second Boer War. During this war, Britain used industrialized weaponry to subjugate black South Africans and consolidate control over valuable natural resources, such as diamonds and gold.

c) During the 1890s, Britain fought several conflicts called the **Boer Wars** against the descendants of Dutch colonial settler states, such as the Orange Free State and South African Republic. In the Second Boer War (1899–1902), Britain decisively defeated the Boers' guerilla fighters, triggering the collapse of the Orange Free State and South African Republic. This victory had two long-lasting consequences for South Africa. First, the defeated Boers were driven out of South Africa, leaving Britain as the region's undisputed power. Britain used its newfound authority to maximize the extraction of gold and

diamonds. Additionally, Britain transformed its holdings into the Union of South Africa, which remained a loyal dominion of the British Empire until gaining its full independence in 1961. Second, indigenous African tribes endured immense suffering during the Boer Wars. British forces regularly accused tribes of aiding and abetting the Boers, and they responded by driving entire tribes out of the region, including the Zulus. Furthermore, Britain implemented a scorched earth counterinsurgency policy against the Boers and African tribes during the Second Boer War. The Union of South Africa maintained many of these counterinsurgency policies, such as mass incarceration, containment of populations, and systematic harassment of targeted individuals. These policies would later help establish and enforce apartheid in South Africa.

Period 4: 1914–Present

Twentieth Century Global Conflicts

Contextualizing Twentieth Century Global Conflicts

Causes of Military Conflicts
The twentieth century was defined by successive global military conflicts: World War I, World War II, and the Cold War. World War I escalated into a global conflict due to long-term sources of tension, such as imperial competition, militarization, military alliances, and the rise of nationalism. The assassination of an Austro-Hungarian aristocrat by a Bosnian Serb nationalist triggered interconnected military alliances and drew the most heavily militarized European states into the war. Following the devastation of World War I, the Versailles Peace Conference failed to reach a sustainable agreement for peace in Europe. The Allied powers were divided between a desire to punish Germany and more idealist pursuits, like empowering the League of Nations to maintain international peace. The Treaty of Versailles' punitive measures contributed to Germany's economic and political destabilization, opening the door for a fascist takeover.

The Great Depression further accelerated political destabilization in Europe, and fascist parties in Italy and Germany exploited the situation in their rise to power. Fascism rejected communism's egalitarianism and democracy's pluralism in favor of creating a militarized state designed to promote ultranationalist preferences. Western Europe failed to prevent the rise of fascism in Italy and Germany for a variety of reasons, including economic and political turmoil, American isolationism, and ideological differences with the Soviet Union. Britain and France attempted to appease Adolf Hitler until Germany invaded Poland in 1939. Like its predecessor, World War II featured the deployment of total war military strategies, and Europe nearly drowned in the bloodbath. The conflict was the deadliest in human history because communism, democracy, and fascism were all fighting for survival. Following the Allied powers' victory in World War II, the Soviet Union and the United States achieved the status of global superpowers, and they competed for supremacy in the Cold War. As such, Europe functioned as a crucial ideological and geopolitical battleground from the end of World War II until the Soviet Union collapsed in 1991.

Technological Advancements, Intellectual Movements, and Cultural Movements
Scientific and technological advancements spurred both economic growth and cataclysmic destruction in the twentieth century. Advancements in biology, chemistry, and human anatomy created the field of modern medicine. Technological advancements boosted industrial output, expanded the variety of consumer goods, created new methods of transportation, and provided new forms of entertainment and communication, such as radio, film, television, computers, and telephones. As a result, Europeans lived longer lives, benefited from a much higher standard of living, and enjoyed myriad material benefits. At the same time, scientific and technological advancements facilitated industrial warfare and the production of new deadly weapons, like automatic rifles, chemical weapons, combat aircraft, ballistic missiles, and nuclear warheads. European states leveraged these advances to deploy total war military strategies, which caused unprecedented societal disruptions. In addition to the two world wars' unimaginable death toll, the conflict caused large-scale forced migrations and produced dramatic demographic changes.

In response to science and technology's role in the rise of violence, intellectual movements challenged the existence of objective knowledge. Existentialism emphasized the importance of subjective feelings over rational thought and questioned whether society's moral standards should be based on religion. Structuralism also challenged mainstream understandings of truth and knowledge, arguing that any analysis of an object must include that object's relationship to the broader culture, system, or structure. In addition, diverse twentieth-century cultural movements disrupted traditional aspects of European society, such as the women's rights movement. European culture also changed due to increased immigration in the 1960s and 1970s. After decolonization, millions of former colonial subjects immigrated to Europe for security and greater economic opportunity.

World War I

Interrelated Causes of World War I

World War I (1914–1918) began as a regional conflict in the Balkan region, but it quickly escalated into a world war due to a number of interrelated factors, such as imperialism, nationalism, the alliance system, and military planning. Imperialism ratcheted up tensions between global powers in the run-up to World War I. Beginning in the late nineteenth century, European powers—Belgium, Britain, France, Germany, Italy, Spain, and Portugal—engaged in an imperial competition known as the "Scramble for Africa." Between 1870 and 1914, the amount of African territory controlled by European imperial powers increased from approximately 10 percent to 90 percent.

Europe's and Japan's conquests required a heavy investment in militarization and colonization, so imperial powers often relied on nationalism to rally domestic support for those policies. Nationalism created a shared sense of inherent superiority, which provided a justification for invading and conquering foreign territories. Additionally, during the early twentieth century, nationalist movements in territories controlled by imperial powers increasingly vied for the right to self-govern. For example, the Bosnian Serb nationalist Gavrilo Princip assassinated the Archduke Franz Ferdinand of Austria-Hungary on June 28, 1914, to support Balkan nationalist movements in Bosnia and Herzegovina. This assassination triggered a regional conflict between Serbia and Austria-Hungary, and the conflict expanded due to the European powers' alliance systems and military planning.

Along with militarization, European powers entered into military alliances to protect their homelands and maintain control over imperial territories. During the late nineteenth and early twentieth centuries, military alliances were formed between Germany and Austria-Hungary, Britain and France, France and Russia, and Russia and Serbia. So, after Austria-Hungary declared war on Serbia one month after the **Archduke's assassination**, Russia mobilized its military and prepared military plans to protect Serbia. On August 1, 1914, Germany declared war on Russia to defend its ally Austria-Hungary. Fearing a French intervention on behalf of its ally Russia, Germany executed its military plans to invade France through Belgium on August 3, 1914. To defend France, Britain declared war on Germany the next day. As a result, alliance systems and military plans drew eight of the most powerful European countries into an armed conflict, setting the stage for what would become a global war.

Technological Impact on World War I

The traditional military strategy of trench warfare was extremely common during World War I, especially on the Western Front located between France and Germany. **Trench warfare** involved the digging of defensive trench lines and underground tunnel systems. Initially, trench warfare created a bloody stalemate because the trench lines were protected with new military technologies, such as barbed wire and machine guns. As such, frontal attacks on trench lines led to staggering casualty rates.

For example, more than 3.5 million soldiers died in trench warfare on the Western Front. Eventually, the widespread adoption of armored cars and tanks in 1917 rendered trench warfare obsolete because they could safely carry troops across the barbed wire and machine gun fire. Troop loss was also escalated by the introduction of airplanes, modern artillery, and chemical warfare. Airplanes were used for reconnaissance and strategic bombing campaigns, while long-distance artillery and poison gas increased the casualty rate in trench warfare. Naval warfare was also revolutionized during World War I through the large-scale deployment of submarines. Germany used submarines to bypass British blockades and restrict American aid to the Allied powers; however, Germany's policy of unrestricted submarine warfare contributed to the United States' decision to enter World War I.

Changing Political and Diplomatic Interactions

Resistance to World War I

World War I proved intensely unpopular in many nations for two reasons. First, countries deployed a military strategy known as total war. The goal of total war was to mobilize all the nation's resources for the war effort, so civilians were heavily impacted by military drafts and food rations. Second, trench warfare produced a military stalemate. For both the public and the troops, the conflict felt like it would last forever since little progress was made despite the then-unprecedented human cost. Consequently, a number of nations faced domestic protests and military mutinies. Irish nationalists capitalized on opposition to Britain's total war strategy, and they staged the **Easter Rebellion** in April 1916. Britain suppressed the rebellion within a week by the use of overwhelming force. Communists organized mass protests against the Russian Tsar over the country's food shortages, lack of military supplies, and astronomical casualty rate. The protests led to the **Russian Revolution**, which successfully overthrew the government in 1917. The Russian Revolution altered the global balance of power after the communists instituted a policy of rapid industrialization, turning the Soviet Union into a world power. European powers also faced domestic communist movements inspired by the Russian Revolution. During World War I, communist activists inspired a series of mutinies in the British, French, and German armies.

Fighting Spreads to Non-European Theaters

The involvement of imperial powers immediately spread the conflict into non-European theaters. In particular, Germany and Britain raised local military forces in their African colonies, and fighting was intense throughout Africa during World War I. Similarly, Britain succeeded in mobilizing local forces in India. Indian political leaders mostly supported the Allied powers because they believed Britain would reward their loyalty with the right to self-govern. India supplied more than 1 million soldiers to the war effort, and they primarily fought in Africa and the Middle East. Non-European countries' entrance into World War I further deepened the global nature of the conflict. Japan allied itself with the Allied powers on August 23, 1914, and they fought German forces in China and across Southeast Asia. Consequently, Japan gained control over a number of Pacific islands and territory in mainland China. The Ottoman Empire entered the war on the side of the Central Powers in November 1914, which escalated fighting in the Middle Eastern theater. In 1917, Britain promised Arab nationalists' independence if they revolted against the Ottoman Empire. With British and French military support, the ensuing **Arab Revolt** (1916–1918) successfully drove Ottoman forces out of territories located in present-day Saudi Arabia, Israel, Jordan, and Syria. The Ottoman Empire was also weakened by Christian nationalist movements, and it responded by rounding up and systematically killing Christians during the **Armenian Genocide** (1914–1923). More than one million civilians died in the Armenian Genocide.

Consequences of World War I

World War I caused the loss of an immense number of human lives, essentially wiping out a generation of Europeans. Austria-Hungary, Britain, France, Germany, and Russia each suffered more than one million military deaths, and there were more than 20 million soldiers wounded in combat. An additional 7.7 million civilians died as a result of the conflict. Aside from the human cost, World War I proved wildly disruptive for both the victorious Allied powers and vanquished Central Powers due to a number of reasons.

First, several European empires were dissolved or overthrown. The Austro-Hungarian Empire dissolved into a handful of independent states shortly before its military signed an armistice on November 3, 1918. The Russian Empire was overthrown in the Russian Revolution, and most of its territories were later absorbed by its successor state, the Soviet Union. The Allied powers partitioned the Ottoman Empire's territories, which triggered the **Turkish War of Independence** (1919–1922). The Turkish nationalists' uprising was successful, and they established the Republic of Turkey. Second, the conflict significantly increased globalization, particularly by consolidating European influence over Africa and the Middle East. Rather than granting African and Middle Eastern colonies their independence, the League of Nations created a mandate system that transferred the Central Powers' colonies to the Allied powers. Third, the United States became an undisputed world power for the first time. While World War I destroyed European populations and infrastructure, the United States was left relatively unscathed. Additionally, the United States bankrolled the Allied powers' war effort, so they benefited from their status as Western Europe's primary creditor during the interwar period.

Russian Revolution and Its Effects

Causes of the Russian Revolution
Long-Term Problems in Russia
World War I aggravated long-term systemic issues in Russian society, which ultimately led to the Russian Revolution. The Enlightenment had led to increased democratic representation in Western Europe during the late nineteenth century, but the Russian government was mired in political stagnation. Russian tsars continued to exercise top-down autocratic control over the government, essentially functioning like sixteenth century absolute monarchs. Although the Russian government officially abolished serfdom in 1861, peasants still primarily worked as tenant farmers and paid onerous taxes. Wealthy landowners called kulaks accounted for 1.5 percent of the population, but they owned 25 percent of the land. Inefficiencies created from unequal land distribution routinely exacerbated food shortages. Additionally, the Russian economy faced serious issues with its industrialization program. The mass relocation of peasants to cities led to housing shortages, sanitation issues, and intense social inequality. The Russian government also failed to protect workers from long hours, dangerous conditions, and minimal pay.

Given its weak industrial base and incompetent government, Russia was wildly unprepared for World War I. Germany repeatedly steamrolled the undertrained and ill-equipped Russian army. By the end of 1916, approximately 1.7 million Russian soldiers had been killed, 2 million captured, and one million were missing. Aside from causing national humiliation and tragedy, the war effort further deteriorated Russia's socioeconomic conditions. Rations resulted in food shortages, and working conditions plummeted as Russia struggled to supply its military. Overall, the vast majority of Russians were impoverished, starving, and tired of fighting an unpopular and costly war. As a result, protests and strikes increased in size and frequency, paving the way for the Russian Revolution.

Bolsheviks Rise to Power

The Russian Revolution occurred in two phases: the February Revolution and October Revolution. The **Petrograd Soviet**—"soviet" means workers' council—organized a series of protests and strikes on March 7, 1917. Those protests quickly progressed into a general strike, grinding Petrograd's industrial production to a halt. When Tsar Nicholas II called in the army, the soldiers refused to fire into crowds of protestors. Facing a military mutiny, Tsar Nicholas abdicated his throne on March 15, 1917. The February Revolution resulted in a split power structure, split between the Provisional Government and Petrograd Soviet. The Provisional Government held official state power, and it was composed of liberal aristocrats and intellectuals. The Petrograd Soviet helped organize similar Soviets across Russia, and these workers' councils advocated for a socialist system of government.

Public unrest continued as the Provisional Government struggled to enact political reforms, prevent food shortages, or withdraw Russia from World War I. Dissatisfied with the liberal Provisional Government's ineffectiveness, the Soviets organized mass strikes and military mutinies to foment more revolutionary changes in government. Tensions were heightened after **Vladimir Lenin** returned from exile and assumed leadership over the communist Bolshevik Party. Lenin's and the Bolsheviks' popularity skyrocketed as he advocated for peace, bread, and land reform. Under Lenin's and Leon Trotsky's leadership, the Bolsheviks staged the **October Revolution** on November 7, 1917. Bolshevik forces surrounded government buildings and the Winter Palace. As a result, the Provisional Government collapsed, and the Bolsheviks began instituting their plans to eliminate rival socialist parties and form a communist state.

Russian Civil War

The Bolshevik coup d'état started the **Russian Civil War** (1917–1922), during which the communist **Red Army** fought a variety of forces. Capitalists joined the Tsar loyalists to form the White Army, and both the Allied and Central Powers attempted to intervene on its behalf. After Germany successfully invaded the former Russian Empire's territory in Eastern Europe, the Soviets agreed to cede much of that territory under the **Treaty of Brest-Litovsk** in March 1918. All throughout the Russian Civil War, the Allied powers provided funding, weapons, and manpower to the White Army because they feared the spread of communism. Rival socialist political organizations opposed both the Red Army and White Army, but their Green Army militias lacked the military and financial resources to be a major player in the conflict. The Red Army eventually wore down the White Army, and the Soviet Union was officially established in October 1922. Civilians suffered immensely as a result of the conflict. The prolonged fighting destroyed infrastructure, decimated industrial and agricultural production, exacerbated famines, and spread disease. Overall, an estimated 8 million people died during the Russian Civil War.

Lenin's New Economic Policy

The Bolsheviks sought to revolutionize Russia through **Marxist-Leninist theory**. This theory was based on Vladimir Lenin's interpretation of Marxism. Marxism argued that the working class (the proletariat) would eventually revolt against the ruling class (the bourgeoisie) based on their inherent class conflict. Accordingly, a communist revolution would transfer ownership of the means of production (infrastructure and resources) from the bourgeoisie to the proletariat. Marxist-Leninist theory believed that this transition was only possible if a vanguard party, the Bolsheviks, practiced democratic centralism, meaning the establishment of a dictatorship theoretically under the proletariat's control. In practice, this meant the Bolsheviks centralized control over all economic decisions related to production and distribution. However, the Russian Civil War posed serious obstacles to this centralized transition from capitalism to communism, particularly in terms of food shortages, labor shortages, and the destruction of infrastructure. So, Vladimir Lenin proposed the **New Economic Policy** (NEP) in 1921 to

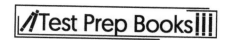

facilitate a more gradual transition from capitalism to communism. The NEP overturned some of the Soviet Union's nationalization policies, and it incorporated some limited free-market principles, such as allowing private ownership of small businesses and farms. Historians credit the NEP with stimulating a remarkable economic recovery, but Joseph Stalin reinstituted agricultural collectivism and centralized planning in 1928.

Versailles Conference and Peace Settlement

Conflicts at the Versailles Conference

Conflicting Goals

The Treaty of Versailles officially ended World War I, but the negotiators' conflicting goals resulted in a generally unsatisfactory peace settlement. While all the Allied powers participated in the negotiations except for Russia, the "Big Four" of Britain, France, Italy, and the United States made all the major decisions. Britain primarily wanted to secure reparations from Germany and establish a sustainable balance of power in Europe. France had suffered the most severe damage to its economic infrastructure, so it sought reparations, a French occupation of the Rhineland, and the annexation of valuable German territory. Italy desired reparations as well as the annexation of Austria-Hungarian seaports located in present-day Croatia. In contrast to the European powers that had suffered the vast bulk of the conflict's casualties and economic damage, the United States pursued an idealist agenda. U.S. President Woodrow Wilson advocated for rebuilding Europe, granting colonies the right to self-determination, and creating a **League of Nations** focused on peaceful relations.

Nonparticipation of Major Powers

Following a series of negotiations, the final peace settlement was viewed as a disappointment by many parties. Dismayed over not receiving the Croatian territories, the Italian public immediately removed its prime minister. British foreign policy officials believed the peace was unsustainable because it was too harsh on Germany. To convince Japan to join the League of Nations, the United States reneged on its idealist promises by granting Chinese territory to Japan. Germany wasn't invited to the negotiating table, and when the Allied powers threatened to undo the armistice, Germany was essentially coerced into signing the treaty.

Another weakness in the Treaty of Versailles was the League of Nations' lack of legitimacy, caused by the refusal of several world powers to participate in the League. Although U.S. President Woodrow won the Nobel Peace Prize for proposing the League of Nations, the U.S. Senate refused to ratify the treaty. When the League was created, Germany refused to join the organization due to widespread anger at the Treaty of Versailles, but it later joined, in 1926. Similarly, the Soviet Union didn't become a member until 1934, and it was expelled five years later for invading Finland. Without buy-in from the major powers, the League of Nations struggled to enforce its rulings or take decisive action when faced with clear-cut acts of aggression. For example, after Japan invaded China in 1937, the League of Nations failed to pass a meaningful resolution.

A Problematic Peace Settlement

The Treaty of Versailles created an unsustainable peace by imposing terms that undermined the German Weimar Republic's economic system and political legitimacy. Germany owed the Allied powers more than 132 billion marks, which amounts to $440 billion in 2019. In addition to this financial strain, Germany lost approximately 25,000 square miles of territory, and it was forced to cede valuable coal mines to France. These terms left Germany in a greatly weakened economic position. So when the Great Depression hit Germany in the early 1930s, the economy's recovery was particularly slow. In regard to political legitimacy, the Treaty of Versailles was intensely unpopular in Germany because it forced Germany to accept sole blame for World War I. Although every German political party criticized its terms from the beginning, the Treaty of Versailles was forever linked to the Weimar Republic's government. The Nazi Party later used this connection in its rise to power in 1933, claiming the Weimar Republic's government had sabotaged the otherwise invincible German military.

Problems with the Mandate System

Former Austro-Hungarian, German, and Ottoman colonies were also angered by the **mandate system**, which generally transferred control to Allied powers rather than providing the colonies with the right to self-determination. The mandate system also angered rival European powers because it primarily benefited Britain and France. In particular, Britain and France gained control over former Ottoman territories in the Middle East, providing those powers with immensely valuable petroleum interests. Britain oversaw mandate territories in Iraq and Palestine, while France gained mandate territories in Lebanon and Syria.

In addition, economic, diplomatic, and political crises thwarted several of the democratic successor states created under the Treaty of Versailles. Yugoslavia was formed by combining Austria-Hungary's Balkan territories, and it suffered from waves of sectarian violence between ethnic Croats, Serbs, and Slovenes. In 1929, King Alexander I revoked the constitution and banned political parties. The Kingdom of Hungary also succeeded the Austro-Hungarian Empire, and it faced a series of diplomatic and military crises with Yugoslavia, Romania, and Czechoslovakia over border disputes. The Second Polish Republic was created in territory that had been occupied by the Russian Empire. Although Poland successfully formed a democratic government, it struggled economically due to the devastation caused by World War I.

Global Economic Crisis

Causes of the Great Depression

Weaknesses in Economies Worldwide

Many factors contributed to the **Great Depression**, and this global economic crisis fueled the surge of extremist political ideologies in Europe. On October 29, 1929, the New York Stock Exchange collapsed due to rampant speculation, skyrocketing consumer debt, and unsustainable levels of production during an economic boom known as the **Roaring Twenties**. Consequently, the American public panicked and attempted to withdraw all its money, a request that the banks couldn't fulfill. This resulted in a banking crisis that created significant liquidity problems and a crisis of faith in the American financial sector. The Great Depression immediately spread from the United States to Europe because their economies were interconnected. The United States was Europe's largest creditor, and facing a cash shortage, American banks called in loans made during World War I and Europe's recovery. Unable to pay their debts, several countries were pushed to the brink of bankruptcy almost overnight, including Britain and Germany. The United States responded by restricting capital outflows, accelerating the contraction of European economies since they didn't have an alternative source of foreign investments.

Interrelated Financial Markets

During the early 1930s, European states enacted monetary and trade policies that deepened and prolonged the Great Depression. In terms of monetary policy, national banks failed to lower interest rates or inject liquidity, and as the money supply continued to contract, national currencies depreciated. Governments then passed nationalistic tariffs to prevent the outflow of capital and protect domestic industries. These economic barriers severely disrupted trade patterns, and international trade fell by

approximately 50 percent during the Great Depression. The Great Depression's economic fallout for Europe was disastrous. Unemployment doubled in Britain, and a series of hunger marches severely disrupted the British political system in the early 1930s. Numerous Italian industries and banks collapsed, and the government created the **Industrial Reconstruction Institute** to assume control over private industries. Germany defaulted on its foreign loans and reparations, and unemployment levels approached 30 percent in 1932.

Attempts to Recover from the Great Depression

To stimulate an economic recovery, European countries attempted to form new political alliances and adopt new economic theories. A unique British political alliance called the **First National Government** took power in 1931, and it included members from all the major parties, including the Conservative Party, the Liberal Party, and the Labour Party. The First National Government turned to John Maynard Keynes's groundbreaking economic theories. **Keynesianism** called for greater public intervention in economies, particularly in increasing government expenditures to stimulate demand. Keynes also successfully advocated for major changes to Britain's monetary policy, such as leaving the gold standard, increasing the money supply, and lowering interest rates. Scandinavian countries implemented cooperative social action policies, which created a more effective partnership between trade unions and capitalists. Like Britain, Scandinavia also dropped the gold standard and increased government spending on infrastructure and social services. Economists believe these changes are the reason why Scandinavia and Britain recovered earlier than other European countries.

As France's economy failed to recover in the early 1930s, communist, socialist, and progressive movements formed a political alliance known as the **Popular Front**. This left-wing movement swept the 1936 elections and enacted policies to increase workers' bargaining power, benefits, and compensation. However, the Popular Front collapsed in 1938 due to political infighting and a limited economic recovery. Despite its short time in power, the Popular Front is widely credited with preventing a fascist takeover in France. Similar extreme fascist movements had recently taken over the German and Spanish governments, which added to the immense pressure on Western European democracies to end the Great Depression. While some European countries, like Britain and the Scandinavian countries, did experience a tepid economic recovery by the mid-1930s, the Great Depression lasted until the outbreak of World War II in 1939.

Fascism and Totalitarianism

Rise of Fascism During Interwar Period

Fascism Movements

Fascist movements gained steam in the 1920s and 1930s due to the aftermath of World War I, economic turmoil during the Great Depression, issues with democracy, communist threats, and the ability to broadcast propaganda over modern technologies. **Fascism** is an extreme political ideology that features nationalism, political violence, rigid social structures, authoritarian governance, and the total mobilization of economic resources in the national interest. World War I spurred the growth of fascist movements by popularizing the idea of total mobilization of civilian resources and by spreading postwar bitterness, especially in Italy and Germany. Combined with the devastation of World War I, the Great Depression destabilized European societies. Fascist movements seized on this opportunity and characterized the transition to liberal democracy as a failed experiment in governance. Although fascists generally critiqued capitalism for elevating individual protections above the national interest, fascist movements were staunchly opposed to communism because they rejected egalitarianism and internationalism. Following the Russian Revolution, fascists gained traction with capitalists and political centrists by characterizing their movement as the only way to defend against the Bolsheviks' international ambitions.

Fascist regimes leveraged modern radio and film technologies to quickly disseminate propaganda. Radio and film created the mass media environment, functioning as a megaphone for charismatic leaders' nationalistic propaganda. **Fascist propaganda** generally aimed to indoctrinate the population, popularize violence, and scapegoat minority groups. In effect, propaganda served as the glue that bound fascist societies together under the control of an unquestioned and all-powerful leader. For example, the Nazi Minister of Propaganda Joseph Goebbels broadcast Hitler's nationalist speeches to 80 million people, and the German filmmaker Leni Riefenstahl helped created a cult of personality around Hitler. Similarly, Mussolini ordered architects to use Roman motifs in order to connect contemporary Italian nationalism with historic greatness.

Rise to Power of Mussolini and Hitler

Benito Mussolini and **Adolf Hitler** exploited unstable political situations and incited violence to establish fascist regimes in Italy and Germany, respectively. Although Italy had been a member of the Allied powers in World War I, England and France had been the primary beneficiaries of the Treaty of Versailles, which infuriated the Italian public. In addition, the Italian economy was burdened by the staggering debt it amassed during World War I. On October 27, 1922, 30,000 fascists marched on Rome and demanded the Italian Prime Minister Luigi Facta's resignation. Fearing for his life, King Victor Emmanuel III succumbed to the fascists and named Benito Mussolini as prime minster. Mussolini then consolidated political power through constitutional maneuvering and political violence. The **blackshirts** (*squadristi*) terrorized left-wing protestors and assassinated political opponents, and by 1925, Mussolini controlled a one-party fascist police state.

Similarly, the German public viewed the Treaty of Versailles as a national humiliation, and the Weimar Republic's economy was in shambles due to massive wartime debt, reparation payment, and the Great Depression. The fascist National Socialist (Nazi) party failed to win a majority of votes in the 1932 parliamentary elections, but liberal politicians and business leaders persuaded President Paul von Hindenburg to appoint Nazi leader Adolf Hitler as Chancellor of Germany. On February 27, 1933, the *Reichstag* (parliamentary building) was set ablaze, and Hitler blamed communist elements without any evidence. Hitler immediately revoked civil liberties, banned the Communist Party, and ordered his paramilitary to attack and arrest communists. One month later, Hitler strong-armed the German Parliament into passing the **Enabling Act**, which provided the legal justification for his fascist dictatorship.

Spanish Civil War

The **Spanish Civil War** (1936–1939) functioned as a dress rehearsal for World War II as Mussolini and Hitler supported an uprising of Spanish nationalists against a liberal democracy. On July 17, 1936, General Francisco Franco of Spain attempted a coup d'état with an alliance of fascists, conservatives, and Catholic conservatives. The coup failed to take control of any major cities, but the nationalists did seize important military assets. Both Hitler and Mussolini saw the conflict as an opportunity for their forces to gain experience in combat with new weapons, such as modern aircrafts, warships, and tanks. In addition to 70,000 troops, Germany and Italy provided the nationalists with funding, training, artillery, machine guns, and rifles. The Soviet Union and Mexico intervened on behalf of Spain's Republican government, and they supplied the republicans with funding, aircraft, tanks, artillery, rifles, and military advisers. While the Western democracies supported the republicans and condemned the fascists' intervention, they didn't intervene in the conflict. However, more than 50,000 American, British,

Canadian, French, and Soviet volunteers fought for the republicans. The Spanish Civil War was a brutal conflict, with both sides committing atrocities. Most infamously, Nazi pilots indiscriminately bombed Guernica in April 1937, leveling the town and killing hundreds of civilians. After nearly three years of fighting, the nationalists prevailed, and Francisco Franco's dictatorship ruled Spain until his death in 1975.

Central and Eastern European Interwar Dictatorships

The same factors that propelled fascist movements undermined Central and Eastern European democracies, which were replaced with authoritarian dictatorships. Democracy never truly got off the ground in Hungary. After the 1920 parliamentary elections, **Miklós Horthy** assumed the title of regent of Hungary. Parliamentary elections continued under Horthy, but his cult of personality kept him in power for more than two decades. Horthy gradually consolidated political, economic, and social power under his authoritarian style of governance, and he entered Hungary into an alliance with Italy and Germany's fascist regimes. Poland's democracy ended with **Józef Piłsudski's coup d'état** in 1926, and his Sanation political movement maintained one-party authoritarian rule. Faced with rampant ethnic violence and secessionist threats, King Alexander I of Yugoslavia revoked the constitution and named himself as the sole source of executive power. Romania was ruled by twenty-five different governments in the 1930s due to unrelenting violent clashes between the fascist **Iron Guard** and constitutional monarchists. Austria's democracy lasted until 1933 when **Chancellor Engelbert Dollfuss** unilaterally abolished the Austrian Parliament. Dollfuss modeled his authoritarian regime on Mussolini's fascist regime. By 1934, the **First Czechoslovak Republic** was the sole functional democracy in Central and Eastern Europe.

Totalitarian Rule in the Soviet Union

Stalinization in the Soviet Union

Joseph Stalin succeeded Vladimir Lenin as leader of the Soviet Union in 1924, and he immediately began enacting an aggressive economic and political program known as **Stalinism**. In general, Stalinism sought to abandon Lenin's New Economic Policy, complete the transition to communism, and consolidate all political power into a totalitarian system of government with Stalin at its head. Stalinism was implemented through a series of **Five Year Plans** that centralized all economic decisions and attempted to rapidly industrialize the Soviet Union. The Five Year Plans collectivized agriculture, meaning that all food production and distribution were placed under state control. Collectivization supported Stalin's urbanization and industrialization programs, and the accompanying seizure of land destroyed Stalin's greatest political threat, wealthy landowners (*kulaks*). The Five Year Plans also centralized industrial production, and this was remarkably successful. By the beginning of World War II, the Soviet Union had transformed from an agrarian society to boasting the second-highest industrial output in the world, trailing only the United States.

The Price of Stalinization

On the other hand, the centralization of all economic decisions came at a staggering human cost. Agricultural collectivization removed food from local communities, exacerbating natural famines and creating man-made ones. Between 1932 and 1933, approximately 1.5 million Kazakhs and 5 million Ukrainians died from a famine known as the **Holodomor**. Furthermore, Stalin initiated the **Great Purge** (1936–1938) to establish totalitarian control over the Soviet government. During the Great Purge, Stalin's secret police arrested and executed alleged dissidents, including *kulaks*, Communist Party rivals, military leaders, and counter-revolutionaries. Historians estimate that between 600,000 and 1.2 million people died in the Great Purge. As a result, Stalin attained unchecked and absolute power over a wildly oppressive totalitarian political system by the late 1930s.

Europe During the Interwar Period

Factors Leading to World War II

Rearming and Expanding of Fascist States

Fascists and ultra-nationalistic regimes in Germany and Italy grew increasingly aggressive in the interwar period, adopting racist policies and militarizing and annexing foreign territory. Nazi Germany branded the "Aryan race" as the superior master race in order to strengthen national unity and justify the persecution of all people who stood accused of threatening Aryans' right to rule, especially Jews. Three years after commencing Germany's rearmament, Hitler again violated the Treaty of Versailles in March 1936, by remilitarizing the Rhineland to protect Germany's western border. In March 1938, Germany peacefully annexed Austria based on the pretense of uniting the two Aryan countries. Hitler then threatened to annex the Sudetenland, a territory in Czechoslovakia with a large Germanic population. Believing this would appease Hitler, France and Britain forced their ally Czechoslovakia to give up its valuable territory under the Munich Agreement of 1938. By the spring of 1939, Hitler had seized half of Czechoslovakia, effectively causing its dissolution.

The fascist developments in Italy mirrored those in Germany. Mussolini invaded Ethiopia in October 1935, to strengthen Italy's hold over the Horn of Africa. During the Second **Italo-Ethiopian War** (1935– 1937), Italy committed several war crimes, including using chemical weapons on civilian populations. An estimated 350,000 civilians died in the conflict. In October 1936, Mussolini entered into the Rome-Berlin axis, and this fascist military alliance jointly intervened in the Spanish Civil War. In 1938, the Italian government published the *Manifesto of Race*. This manifesto described Italians as honorary Aryans, prohibited interracial marriages with Jews and Africans, and restricted Italian Jews' economic and political rights.

Rationale for Appeasement

Although the Western democracies' decision to appease Nazi Germany proved disastrous in hindsight, there were several understandable reasons for this policy in the moment, such as fear of another global conflict and distrust of the Soviet Union. Approximately 1.4 million French and 900,000 British soldiers had died in World War I, and both countries' economies continued to be weighed down by wartime debt. As such, both countries desperately hoped to avoid repeating the nightmare of global conflict. Similarly, the American public had been hesitant to join World War I, believing it was a purely European quarrel. Although the United States had been the primary beneficiary of World War I, taking preemptive action against fascism lagged far behind isolationism in terms of public opinion. Consequently, the U.S. Congress passed multiple Neutrality Acts in the run-up to World War II.

Additionally, fascism had significant support within the Western democracies because tolerating fascism was seen as preferable to allying with the totalitarian Soviet Union. While Hitler had curbed some aspects of capitalism, the German economy had seen remarkable growth. Some Western business leaders had gone so far as to advocate for adopting fascist policies. In contrast, the Soviet Union's mere existence threatened Western democracies' political and economic systems. Likewise, the Soviet Union had little in common with either the Western democracies or fascist regimes. Given the relative proximity and military strength of Nazi Germany, Joseph Stalin entered into a Non-Aggression Pact with Nazi Germany on August 23, 1939. The pact guaranteed peaceful relations between the powers, and it included plans to divide Eastern Europe and Scandinavia into Nazi and Soviet spheres of influence after World War II.

In the end, Western democracies' appeasement and the Soviet Union's Non-Aggression Pact collapsed in the face of Nazi aggression. Hitler never stopped making demands on the Western democracies. At every turn, he asked for an inch, took a mile, and then promised it wouldn't happen again. The final straw was Germany's invasion of Poland on September 1, 1939, which marked the beginning of World War II. Britain and France issued ultimatums to Hitler, which were ignored, and both powers declared war on Germany two days later. On June 22, 1941, Nazi Germany launched a surprise invasion of the Soviet Union because Hitler feared that the Soviet Union would eventually ally itself with Britain.

World War II

Technology and Innovation Affected World War II

Blitzkrieg Warfare

Within the first two years of **World War II**, Germany conquered most of Western Europe, and Japan seized control over much of East Asia and the Pacific. Germany's military deployed a strategy known as *blitzkrieg* (lightning war), in which armored units with air support conducted swift and powerful assaults. By October 1939, Germany had defeated Poland and begun focusing on France. Prior to the outbreak of World War II, France militarized and fortified the **Maginot Line** on its eastern border with Germany. On May 10, 1940, Germany shocked France by circumventing the Maginot Line, trapping Allied forces at the English Channel, and heading south to Paris. On June 10, 1940, Italy invaded France, and Germany conquered Paris four days later. France surrendered to Germany on June 22, 1940. This left Britain as the only major European power standing in Germany's way. On July 10, 1940, Germany's elite air force, the *Luftwaffe*, launched large-scale bombing campaigns of British cities. The Battle of Britain lasted until October 31, 1940, but the *Luftwaffe* continued conducting the Blitz (night raids) into May 1941. Many historians regard Germany's failure to eliminate Britain's air defense or force Britain to sign an armistice as a critical turning point.

Japan invaded China before the outbreak of World War II, conquering Manchuria, Shanghai, and Nanjing by 1937. Following a series of Chinese counter-offensives in 1940, fighting reached a stalemate, and Japan turned its attention to European colonies in Southeast Asia. In September 1940, Japan conquered northern Indochina and began threatening American, British, and Dutch colonial possessions in southern Indochina. The Western powers responded by placing financial sanctions on Japan, and after the two sides failed to reach a negotiated settlement, Japan began preparing a preemptive strike on the United States and Britain. On December 7, 1941, Japan launched a surprise attack on an American naval base in Pearl Harbor, Hawaii, and Japanese forces invaded the British colony of Hong Kong on the following day. The United States had already begun providing financial and military assistance to the Allied powers in 1940 through its Lend-Lease program, but Japan's **attack on Pearl Harbor** directly led to America fully joining into the conflict. The **Axis powers** describes the alliance of Germany, Japan, and Italy during this global conflict. In opposition, the main **Allied powers** consisted of Great Britain, the Soviet Union, the United States, and China. Countries occupied by the Axis powers during World War II include France, Poland, Netherlands, Czechoslovakia, Luxembourg, Norway, Yugoslavia, and Greece.

Allied Powers Rally and Surge to Victory

The Allied powers turned the tides of war through a combination of British and American technological innovation, exceptional political leadership, civilian resistance, and the Soviet Union's unwavering perseverance. British innovations in radar helped keep the nation afloat during the Battle of Britain, and the United States developed modern aircraft carriers and battleships. These naval innovations facilitated the American victory over Japan at the **Battle of Midway** in 1942, and, as a result, the United States gained a decisive advantage in the Pacific theater. British and American advances in computer science resulted in the Allied breaking of Japanese naval codes and German encryption devices, including the legendary **Enigma machine**. British Prime Minister **Winston Churchill**, Soviet Premier **Joseph Stalin**, and U.S. President **Franklin Delano Roosevelt** agreed to a cooperative military strategy. All three political leaders were also able to convince their entire civilian populations to participate in the total war effort despite mounting losses, which enabled an overwhelming amount of civilian resources to be repurposed for the military. Soviet civilians demonstrated incredible bravery after Germany launched **Operation Barbarossa** in 1941. Historians disagree on the exact figure, but somewhere between 13 million and 19 million Soviet civilians died in World War II. Despite this massive loss of life, Soviet civilians' resistance helped slow German advances and support Soviet counter-offensives.

The Allied powers won several critical battles and campaigns in 1942 and 1943. Most notably, Britain drove Italian and German forces out of North Africa, the United States defeated Japan at the Battle of Midway, the Soviet Union defeated Germany at Stalingrad, and the joint Allied invasion of Sicily and Italy effectively toppled Mussolini's regime. On June 6, 1944, American and British forces launched the **D-Day** operation to free German-occupied France. With the support of local French resistance forces, the Allied powers liberated Paris on August 25, 1944. Following a series of Soviet victories on the Eastern Front, the Soviets invaded Germany in February 1945. Less than a month later, American and British forces crossed the Rhine River and entered western Germany. On May 7, 1945, Germany agreed to a total and unconditional surrender. In the Pacific theater, earlier American victories had provided the Allied powers with bases to launch air raids on Japan. From June 1944 until August 1945, Allied forces relentlessly firebombed Japanese cities. When Japan still refused to surrender, the United States dropped nuclear weapons on Hiroshima and Nagasaki in the hopes of preventing the need for a full-scale invasion. On August 15, 1945, Japan gave its unconditional surrender, ending World War II.

Lasting Legacy of the Conflict's Military Technologies

The military technology produced during World War II altered the course of history through the mass production of small arms and development of nuclear weapons. Industrialized warfare exponentially increased the production of modern semi-automatic rifles and assault rifles. Many historians argue that the Soviet-made Kalashnikov (AK-47) assault rifle "democratized" warfare due to its cheap price and ease of use. Small arms flooded the market after World War II, and they were amongst the United States and the Soviet Union's top exports in the decades that followed. Along with arming state militaries, Soviet and American weapons often fell into the hands of revolutionaries and genocidal regimes. For example, the Khmer Rouge won the Cambodian Civil War with AK-47s and then conducted a genocide that killed approximately 1.5 million people. The development of nuclear weapons led to their proliferation and a rising risk of global nuclear war. To compete with the United States, the Soviet Union raced to develop nuclear weapons and completed the project in 1949. The two global superpowers then competed in an arms race, resulting in the production of 70,000 nuclear weapons. Cold War tensions nearly sparked a devastating nuclear war on several occasions, most notably during the Cuban Missile Crisis of 1962. Several world powers have since developed nuclear weapons in the twentieth century, including Britain, France, China, India, Pakistan, Israel, and North Korea.

The Holocaust

Germany's Plans for a "New Racial Order"

Nazi Germany attempted to create a "New Racial Order" dominated by Aryans that culminated in the **Holocaust**, a mass genocide of European Jews, homosexuals, people of color, people with disabilities, and Romani people. This pursuit motivated Germany's annexation of central and eastern European territory in the run-up to World War II because Hitler wanted to establish *Lebensraum* (living space) and

protect Aryans from the "subhuman" Poles and Slavs. German Jews were aggressively targeted because Hitler trafficked in conspiracy theories that scapegoated Jews for Germany's defeat in World War I and its economic struggles. Immediately after rising to power, Hitler began isolating German Jews by restricting their employment opportunities, boycotting businesses, restricting interracial marriage, burning books, and lastly, revoking citizenship rights under the **Nuremberg Laws of 1935**.

Violence against Jews culminated in *Kristallnacht* (the Night of Broken Glass). On November 9–10, 1938, German police, soldiers, and civilians destroyed an estimated 7,500 Jewish businesses and 1,000 synagogues. *Kristallnacht* also marked the first large-scale removal of Jews from ghettos to concentration camps, namely Buchenwald and Dachau. At these **concentration camps** hundreds of thousands of Jews died from starvation, forced labor, and lack of sanitation. On January 20, 1942, Nazi leaders held the **Wannsee Conference** to develop, plan, and coordinate the "final solution to the Jewish question." The Wannsee Conference escalated the Holocaust because the "final solution" meant the creation of extermination camps, such as Auschwitz and Treblinka. **Extermination camps** differed from concentration camps because they were equipped with gas chambers designed for mass murder. The systematic mass murder of Jews began in 1942 and continued until Allied forces liberated the extermination camps in 1944 and 1945.

Human Cost of World War II and the Holocaust

World War II caused more death and destruction than any conflict in human history. Approximately 25 million soldiers and 50 million civilians died as a result of fighting and war-related causes, like disease and famine. The war essentially wiped out entire generations of Russian and German men. An estimated 13.7 percent of the Soviet population and 8.2 percent of the German population lost their lives, with younger generations suffering a disproportionate impact. Additionally, Nazis murdered approximately six million Jews during the Holocaust, accounting for nearly two thirds of Europe's Jewish population. Although Jews were the Nazis' primary target, other groups experienced significant suffering. Approximately 350,000 non-Jewish Poles, 250,000 Romani people, and 225,000 people with disabilities died in the Holocaust. The Nazis also arrested an estimated 50,000 homosexual people and 10,000 people of color, but there aren't any statistics about their death rate.

This violence and destruction resulted in massive waves of forced migration in Europe. Examples include half of Germany's Jews emigrating prior to the Holocaust; more than two million Poles escaping the Nazi occupation; and the Soviet Union expelling hundreds of thousands of Estonians, Finns, Latvians, Lithuanians, and Ukrainians. After the war, a significant number of refugees settled in Western Europe and the United States; however, millions were forced to live in refugee camps established by international humanitarian relief organizations with protection from Allied forces. The chaos of World War II also disrupted class hierarchies, particularly due to the number of women joining the workforce. Labor shortages and the need to sustain industrial production created new opportunities for women, and an unprecedented number of women achieved financial independence in the conflict's aftermath.

Twentieth Century Cultural, Intellectual, and Artistic Developments

Scientific and Technological Impact on Society

Europeans' confidence in scientific progress somewhat declined before World War I. In particular, some scientific theories created uncertainty about humanity's relationship to the world. For example, Charles Darwin's theory of evolution continued to be controversial in the early twentieth century because it posed a scientific challenge to deep-seated religious beliefs about humanity's creation. Similarly, Sigmund Freud's theory of psychoanalysis presented troubling arguments about how people's subconscious could dictate their actions and thoughts. At the same time, scientific and technological innovations were undeniably driving progress and revolutionizing European societies. Prior to World War I, electricity powered urbanized cities made of steel; industrialized factories produced cheaper and more plentiful consumer goods; radio and film thrilled audiences; and railroads, telegraphs, and telephones connected people over long distances. So while some scientific theories injected doubt about the desirability of scientific progress, Europeans remained confident that science and technology could solve societal problems.

During the 1920s and 1930s, the discovery of **quantum mechanics** overturned some aspects of Newtonian physics and enabled the harnessing of nuclear power, resulting in changes to other scientific fields, military strategy, economics, and society. Albert Einstein, Werner Heisenberg, Erwin Schrödinger, Enrico Fermi, and Niels Bohr all won Nobel Prizes for their contributions to this revolutionary breakthrough in physics. Just as quantum mechanics challenged objective knowledge by focusing on infinitesimal and theoretical particles, the burgeoning fields of biochemistry and neuroscience did the same in biology in the latter half of the twentieth century. The development of nuclear weapons forever changed warfare, raising the stakes of any conflict between nuclear-armed states. European economies also changed as some states built nuclear reactors to reduce energy costs and carbon emissions. Overall, societal anxiety increased due to the existential threat of nuclear war and fear of nuclear meltdowns, such as the meltdown at the Soviet Union's Chernobyl's plant in 1986.

The World Wars' Political and Cultural Consequences

The world wars had several important political and cultural consequences, including the creation of a "lost generation," greater economic opportunities for women, and democratization. World War I produced a "lost generation" due to its then-unprecedented violence and chaos. Approximately 10 million soldiers and 7.7 million civilians died as a result of the fighting, and large swathes of Europe burned to the ground. Aside from the lives literally lost, the "lost generation" also refers to the survivors suffering from cynicism, disillusionment, and a sense of meaninglessness. On the other hand, the world wars also spurred the women's rights movement because wartime production mobilized every possible source of labor. The mass enlistment of men opened new opportunities for women, and the women's rights movement leveraged their greater economic power to secure political rights. Likewise, democratization increased across Europe. After the fascist regimes' defeat in World War II, universal suffrage was in place throughout Western Europe.

Cold War and Contemporary Europe

Contextualizing Cold War and Contemporary Europe

Context of Cold War Polarization

World War II devastated Europe. All the belligerent nations mobilized their resources and manpower to deploy total war military strategies. More than 75 million people lost their lives during World War II, and tens of millions more were displaced from their homes. Furthermore, critical infrastructure had been destroyed, and European governments were drowning in debt. The two remaining global superpowers—the United States and the Soviet Union—capitalized on this opportunity to expand their global influence. The United States provided aid to Western Europe through the **Marshall Plan**, and restructured the international monetary system through the creation of international financial organizations, like the **International Monetary Fund (IMF)** and the **World Bank**. In return, the United States received considerable economic and influence in Europe. Additionally, the United States led the formation of a powerful military alliance, the **North Atlantic Treaty Organization (NATO)**, to defend

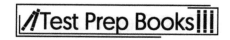

against a Soviet invasion of Europe. The Soviet Union similarly leveraged political instability to install communist regimes in Central and Eastern Europe. The Soviet satellite states then joined the **Warsaw Pact**, a Soviet-led military alliance, and participated in the **Council for Mutual Economic Assistance (COMECON)**, which increased the Soviet Union's economic influence in Central and Eastern Europe.

The Cold War lasted from the end of World War II until the Soviet Union dissolved in 1991. Throughout the Cold War, a non-physical boundary known as the Iron Curtain separated the Western European democracies from the Central and Eastern European communist regimes. In addition to underlying geopolitical disputes, this polarized state order was driven by ideological differences. The Western democracies prioritized individual rights and freedoms in their government and capitalist economies, while the Soviet Union centralized all power under a totalitarian government to promote egalitarianism. Both sides of the Cold War highlighted these differences in propaganda campaigns to demonstrate their ideological superiority. While the superpowers never formally waged a "hot war" against each other, they did compete in a nuclear arms race and regional proxy hot wars, such as the Korean War and the Vietnam War. Following the Soviet Union's collapse, the European Union spread from Western to Eastern Europe.

Cultural Context of the Cold War

European countries underwent rapid socioeconomic changes during the Cold War. American financial assistance, industrial innovations, and new agricultural products led to a postwar economic boom in Western Europe. This economic boom facilitated a "**baby boom**" and attracted immigrants from Africa and Asia. **Decolonization** in the 1960s and 1970s caused another spike in immigration, which broadened Europe's religious diversity. When economic growth slowed, nationalist political parties stoked anti-immigrant animus, sowing societal discord. Traditional social patterns were also disrupted by new voices gaining political power and social influence. **Second-wave feminists** helped pass laws to broaden divorce grounds, expand access to birth control, and reduce discrimination in the workplace. European gay and lesbian activists also achieved groundbreaking victories, like the decriminalization of homosexuality and legalization of same-sex civil unions in many countries. Diverse intellectual and cultural movements also transformed European cultures. The legacy of the destructive world wars and anxiety over potential nuclear annihilation raised questions about progress, logic, rationality, and religion. In the aftermath of World War I, **Dadaists** produced art satirizing logic and reason. Following World War II, existentialist philosophers like Jean-Paul Sartre questioned religion's monopoly on moralism and criticized capitalism. These challenges to societal norms forced traditional institutions like Christian churches to initiate reforms, such as the **Second Vatican Council**. Combined with new communication and transportation technologies, such as the internet and commercial air travel, the collapse of the Soviet Union paved the way for globalized capitalism to dominate the twenty-first century.

Rebuilding Europe

Marshall Plan

The reconstruction of Europe after World War II benefited immensely from American financial assistance. Most of this assistance was provided through the **Marshall Plan**, which the U.S. Congress passed in 1948. American foreign policymakers believed European economic turmoil threatened the United States' national security because a weakened Europe would be more susceptible to a communist revolution or Soviet invasion. To ward off this threat, the United States provided Scandinavian and Western European states with $12 billion (approximately $100 billion in 2019) between 1948 and 1952. Britain, France, and West Germany received the majority of funds, but fifteen other states also participated in the program. The United States created a supranational agency, the **Organization for**

European Economic Coordination (OEEC), to carry out the Marshall Plan, and most of the aid went to rebuilding infrastructure and boosting industrial productivity.

The Marshall Plan was a resounding success. Many economists credit the Marshall Plan with contributing to the "economic miracle" in Europe. From 1948 to 1952, Europe experienced the most rapid economic growth in history. American aid also allowed Europe to spend tax revenue on social services and infrastructure rather than cutting the budget in order to service wartime debts. Furthermore, Western and Central European communist parties lost significant support, and Europe became more politically integrated through its joint participation in the OEEC. The Marshall Plan also had a significant impact on European culture. Europeans benefited from the revitalization of European industries through the mass production of consumer goods, which reduced prices and expanded the variety of available goods. Additionally, free trade agreements brought more American imports into Europe. As a result, consumerism became a larger part of European culture. In practical terms, Europeans began to view themselves as an integral part of the marketplace, and the consumption of goods increasingly defined their day-to-day experiences.

Cold War

The Iron Curtain
Ideological and geopolitical tension between the Soviet Union and Western democracies resulted in the **Cold War**, and Europe was divided along a non-physical boundary that was referred to as the **Iron Curtain**. After the Soviet Union drove Nazi Germany out of Central and Eastern Europe in World War II, Soviet forces remained in those territories until the end of the Cold War. Large occupying forces enabled the Soviet Union to exert extreme economic and political pressure on the affected countries, which were referred to as **Soviet satellites**. Although the Soviet satellite states were technically independent, the Soviet Union oversaw the formation of loyal communist governments. Soviet satellite states included Albania, Bulgaria, Czechoslovakia, East Germany, Hungary, Poland, and Romania. All the Soviet satellite states lay east of the Iron Curtain; along with the Soviet Union, they were referred to as the **Eastern Bloc**.

Although the United Nations was created for the purpose of maintaining international cooperation, Cold War tensions proved to be a serious obstacle. As Security Council members, France, Britain, and the United States regularly vetoed Soviet proposals, and the Soviet Union did the same in return. In the General Assembly, Western democracies mostly voted with the United States, while the Soviet satellite states provided unwavering support to the Soviet Union. Still, the United Nations provided a platform for dialogue between the superpowers, reducing the likelihood of a misunderstanding spiraling out of control into a nuclear war.

Cold War Conflicts
During the Cold War, the Soviet Union and Western democracies fought each other through propaganda campaigns, covert actions, a nuclear arms race, and "hot wars" across the globe. Propaganda campaigns either promoted each country's achievements, whether real or imagined, or attempted to undermine ideological adversaries. For example, the Soviet Union disseminated posters about the Western democracies' hypocrisy in regard to European colonialism and racial segregation in the United States. Covert actions typically involved using military force for a political purpose without revealing the identity of the country carrying out those actions. For example, in 1973, American covert actions overthrew the democratically elected president of Chile, Salvador Allende, to contain the spread of socialism in Latin America. The arms race between the United States and the Soviet Union skyrocketed the threat of a

global nuclear war that would've ended life on earth. For example, after the United States stationed nuclear missiles in Italy and Turkey, the Soviet Union stationed nuclear missiles in Cuba. During the Cuban Missile Crisis of 1962, the superpowers were on the brink of a devastating nuclear exchange until U.S. President John F. Kennedy and Soviet leader Nikita Khrushchev reached a last-minute agreement to remove missiles from Cuba and Turkey.

The Soviet Union and the Western democracies provided weapons, financing, and troops to proxy forces in several "hot wars," including the Korean War, the Vietnam War, the Yom Kippur War, and the Soviet-Afghan War. The Korean War began after communist North Korea invaded South Korea in 1950 with Soviet support, and the United States led United Nations coalition forces to drive back the advancing North Korean forces. Communist China's intervention turned the conflict into a war of attrition, and the belligerents signed an armistice in 1953. In the early 1950s, North Vietnamese communists rebelled against French imperial control, and the United States intervened in 1964. The Soviet Union and China provided financial, logistical, and military support to the North Vietnamese, and after the war became a controversial political issue, the United States withdrew in 1973.

Two years later, North Vietnam defeated South Vietnam, uniting the country. The Yom Kippur War commenced with a coalition of Arab states invading Israeli territory in the Suez Canal and the Golan Heights in October 1973. The United States provided military supplies to Israel, while the Soviet Union did the same for the Arab coalition. Fighting ended after two weeks, and the United Nations helped negotiate the ceasefire agreement. In December 1979, the Soviet Union invaded Afghanistan and overthrew the government. Over the next decade, the United States provided Afghan guerilla fighters (*mujahideen*) with financial, logistical, and military support. The Soviet-Afghan War lasted until 1989, and the financial and diplomatic costs for the Soviet Union contributed to its collapse.

Two Superpowers Emerge

Economic and Political Consequences of the Cold War
American Influence on Western Europe

The United States exerted significant military, political, and economic influence over Western Europe. In 1949, the United States spearheaded the formation of a powerful military alliance, the **North Atlantic Treaty Organization (NATO)**, to protect Western Europe from a Soviet invasion. The twelve founding members of NATO were: Belgium, Britain, Canada, Denmark, France, Iceland, Italy, Luxembourg, the Netherlands, Norway, Portugal, and the United States. As the alliance's strongest military power, the United States played a leading role in NATO's military strategy. For example, the United States placed and maintained 7,000 nuclear weapons in NATO countries during the Cold War.

The United States' political influence in Western Europe was a product of its economic status. After World War II, the United States oversaw the restructuring of the international monetary and trade system. This involved the creation of new international organizations, such as the International Monetary Fund (IMF), World Bank, the General Agreement on Tariffs and Trade (GATT), and the World Trade Organization (WTO). The IMF seeks to promote monetary cooperation and achieve sustainable economic growth, while the World Bank provides governments with loans for capital-intensive projects. Both the IMF and the World Bank are headquartered in Washington, DC, and the United States has historically played an outsized role in setting the terms for loans and other monetary agreements. Since Western Europe required an immense amount of capital for infrastructure projects in the postwar period, the United States gained political influence through its relationship to the World Bank. Similarly, the United States benefited from GATT's lowering of the barriers to international trade. As a result,

American industries profited from exporting more products to Western Europe. The WTO replaced GATT in 1995, and it too focuses on increasing international trade.

Soviet Influence on Central and Eastern Europe

The Soviet Union dominated its Central and Eastern European satellite states through the Communist Information Bureau (Cominform), Council for Mutual Economic Assistance (COMECON), and the Warsaw Pact. At the end of World War II, the Soviet Union established communist regimes in the Central and Eastern European nations it occupied. All the communist regimes under Soviet control participated in Cominform, which coordinated the implementation of communist policies. For example, Cominform required the satellite states to centralize economic planning, expand social welfare programs, and specialize in the production of certain goods as directed by Soviet officials. Additionally, Cominform focused on suppressing all anti-communist activities. In practice, this meant curtailing freedom of expression, restricting political rights, and prohibiting emigration beyond the Iron Curtain.

In order to maintain its stranglehold over Central and Eastern Europe, the Soviet Union barred its satellite states from accepting the United States' offer to participate in the Marshall Plan. Instead, the Soviet Union created the COMECON in 1949, which provided industrial assistance and coordinated trade. Likewise, the Soviet Union responded to the formation of NATO by creating a military alliance known as the Warsaw Pact. Since the Soviet-dominated Warsaw Pact controlled military deployments, it further extended the Soviet Union's control over Central and Eastern Europe.

Nikita Khrushchev's De-Stalinization Policies

Soviet leader Nikita Khrushchev's **de-Stalinization policies** attempted to introduce limited economic and political reform in the 1950s. De-Stalinization initiatives included releasing political prisoners from gulags and ending the economy's reliance on forced labor. In addition, Khrushchev sought to deconstruct Stalin's cult of personality, meaning the public's veneration of Stalin as a paternal and God-like figure. Khrushchev believed this intimate connection between Stalin and the Soviet Union undermined the state's long-term development, so he ordered the renaming of cities and buildings named after Stalin. For example, Khrushchev changed the name of Stalingrad to Volgograd in 1961. However, de-Stalinization failed to stimulate economic growth or prevent revolts in Central and Eastern Europe. In 1956, a student protest in Hungary escalated into a revolt that toppled the Soviet-controlled government.

The Soviet Union crushed the revolt with overwhelming force, killing 2,500 protestors. An additional 200,000 refugees fled Hungary as the Soviet Union installed an even more repressive communist regime. Similarly, the Soviet Union rejected political liberalization efforts in Czechoslovakia during the **Prague Spring of 1968**. The Warsaw Pact ordered 650,000 troops to invade and occupy Czechoslovakia, and the new Soviet-controlled government reinstituted extreme censorship. This oscillation between liberalization and repression continued until a wave of nationalist movements in the late 1980s triggered the Soviet Union's collapse. The mostly peaceful nationalist revolutions produced some notable successes, like the democracies in Latvia and Estonia. On the other hand, political instability, authoritarianism, rampant corruption, and sectarian violence have undermined many former Soviet republics and satellite states, including Armenia, Belarus, Georgia, Serbia, and Ukraine.

Postwar Nationalism, Ethnic Conflict, and Atrocities

Post–World War II Nationalism and Separatism

The relative peace in Europe that followed World War II was intermittently interrupted by nationalist and separatist movements. During "the Troubles," Irish nationalists staged an uprising to end British rule

of Northern Ireland. Beginning in the late 1960s, Irish nationalists formed paramilitary units, such as the **Provisional Irish Republican Army (IRA)**, and they carried out bombings and assassinations. British military forces and loyalist paramilitaries waged a bloody counter-insurgency against the nationalists. The Troubles ended with the Good Friday Agreement of 1998, in which the nationalists agreed to British rule in Northern Ireland in exchange for police reform and the withdrawal of British forces. Similarly, Basque separatists called the ETA and Flemish separatists advocated for greater autonomy in Spain and Belgium, respectively. Following several decades of violence, the ETA disarmed in 2011 after gaining limited autonomy. Flemish separatists pursued autonomy in Flanders through political organizing, and those efforts are ongoing.

Following the collapse of the Soviet Union and Yugoslavia, nationalist movements sparked military conflicts and "ethnic cleansing" in Central and Eastern Europe. Ethnic cleansing occurred in the Balkans during the breakup of Yugoslavia. In the **Bosnian War** (1992–1995), Bosnian Serb Christians systematically murdered 25,000 Bosnian Muslims (Bosniaks) and forcibly displaced more than 1 million Bosniaks and Bosnian Croats. During the **Kosovo War** (1998–1999), the Serbian military attempted to ethnically cleanse Albanians living in Kosovo. Serbian forces committed numerous war crimes, including forcible displacement, mass rape, massacre of civilians, and destruction of settlements and religious centers. More than 10,000 Albanian civilians were killed, and more than 1.2 million were displaced. In Eastern Europe, Russia invaded Chechnya, a former Soviet republic, on two separate occasions in the 1990s. Russia completed the annexation of Chechnya in 2000. In August 2008, Russia invaded Georgia to support separatist groups. The **Russo-Georgian War** ended with the separatist groups successfully seceding from Georgia and Russian forces occupying the newly "independent" territories.

Contemporary Western Democracies

Development of European Welfare States
The postwar economic boom allowed Western European democracies to create sweeping social welfare programs. The programs were so all-encompassing they're sometimes referred to as "cradle-to-grave" welfare. Although individual countries follow different social models, Western European welfare programs generally include universal health care, free childcare, free higher education, subsidized housing, generous unemployment insurance, legally required vacation and sick days, and pensions. Furthermore, Western European states guarantee collective bargaining rights, protect labor and consumer rights, and make a commitment to pursuing full employment. However, generous social welfare programs and pro-labor policies have come under fire in recent years. Western European economies have struggled to adjust to globalization and automation, and, as growth slows, budgetary pressures mount. Consequently, governments face a difficult choice between cutting popular social welfare programs and raising already steep tax rates. In the twenty-first century, high government spending contributed to destabilizing financial crises in Greece, Spain, Ireland, and Italy.

Fall of Communism

Soviet Reform Efforts
In response to a lengthy economic downturn, Soviet leader **Mikhail Gorbachev** adopted a set of reforms—known as perestroika and glasnost—in the mid-1980s. **Perestroika** was a broad set of policies aimed at restructuring the Soviet economy. For the first time since Lenin's New Economic Policy, Soviet citizens were allowed to own and operate businesses outside of the state's centralized control. Perestroika also subjected Soviet-owned enterprises to bankruptcy proceedings if revenues didn't match expenses. Most controversially, Gorbachev allowed foreigners to invest in Soviet enterprises and

cooperatives. Glasnost sought to increase government transparency, reduce corruption, and introduce some liberalization measures. The loosening of censorship laws and travel bans facilitated greater contact between Soviet and Western culture. All these reforms weren't enough to rejuvenate the Soviet economy or political system, but they did introduce Soviet citizens to economic and political freedom for the first time in decades, if not ever. As such, many historians believe perestroika and glasnost actually accelerated the Soviet Union's collapse because they showcased the advantages of capitalism and democracy.

Collapse of the Soviet Union

Faced with mounting pressure from nationalist movements, the Soviet Union started to crumble in the late 1980s and officially collapsed in 1991. Several Soviet republics in the Baltic region—Latvia, Lithuania, and Estonia—pushed for political reform in 1988, and one year later, Poland held democratic elections that ousted the Soviet-controlled communist regime. On November 9, 1989, East Germany announced plans to demolish the Berlin Wall, and by the end of 1989, the Soviet satellite states had all regained their independence. In 1990, Germany completed its reunification, and the Soviet Union dissolved into fifteen separate countries in 1991. During the early 1990s, Czechoslovakia peacefully splintered into the Czech Republic and Slovakia. Yugoslavia also abandoned communism and dissolved into five new countries: Bosnia and Herzegovina, Croatia, the Federal Republic of Yugoslavia, Macedonia, and Slovenia. As a result, Central and Eastern Europe had completed their transition to capitalism by the mid-1990s. From 2004 to 2017, numerous Soviet republic and satellite states joined the European Union, including Bulgaria, Czechia (the Czech Republic), Estonia, Hungary, Latvia, Lithuania, Poland, Romania, and Slovakia.

Twentieth Century Feminism

Early Women's Rights Movements

Women's role in society underwent a major change in the early twentieth century due to the wartime labor shortage. When millions of men left their jobs to fight in World War I, women joined the workforce in record numbers to sustain the levels of production necessary for sustaining industrialized warfare. Prior to this period, the overwhelming majority of women were confined to traditional household responsibilities, and they lacked basic political and legal rights. So as women's societal role grew to include more work responsibilities, European women's rights movements began advocating for equality under the law. As a result, during and immediately after World War I, women were granted the right to vote in many European countries, including Austria, Azerbaijan, Czechoslovakia, Georgia, Germany, Luxembourg, the Netherlands, Poland, and Sweden. Immediately after the Russian Revolution, the Soviet Union enshrined gender equality in its constitution. Communists considered women to be an underutilized labor source for the economy and the military, so employment and educational opportunities were expanded accordingly. Furthermore, Vladimir Lenin passed laws to provide women with the right to abortion, extensive grounds for divorce, prohibitions on marital rape, and free childcare.

Second-Wave Feminism

During the latter half of the twentieth century, Western Europe caught up with the Soviet Union in terms of gender equality as a result of feminist societal critiques and new methods of birth control. French feminist Simone de Beauvoir's *The Second Sex* (1949) served as a foundational text for second-wave feminism. While first-wave feminism primarily focused on women's suffrage, second-wave feminism championed reproductive rights, sexuality, and career advancement. European second-wave feminists successfully advocated for prohibitions on marital rape, access to birth control, and the

legalization of abortion. Improved control over family planning provided women with more choice in how to balance their work and family responsibilities. Birth control and legalized abortions contributed to the growing sexual liberation movement, which changed cultural norms about women remaining single and cohabitation outside of marriage. Family planning also expanded through the creation of new scientific methods of fertilization, such as in vitro fertilization. Furthermore, second-wave feminism advanced women's professional and educational opportunities. Beginning in the 1960s, women's enrollment in colleges skyrocketed, and by the end of the twentieth century, it was common for women to work in nearly every profession at the highest levels.

Second-wave feminists also successfully pushed for the passage of laws to expand the types of marriage and the grounds for divorce, increasing women's independence. In the 1960s and 1970s, many Western European countries passed laws to recognize "common law marriages," meaning that long-term cohabitation provided rights similar to marriage. Civil unions and domestic partnerships were also popularized during this period, which allowed couples to enter into legal contracts that functioned like traditional marriages. In addition, the grounds for divorce were broadened in nearly all Western European countries. Prior to the 1960s, women could rarely obtain a divorce without the consent of their husband. Divorce reform allowed women to escape domestic violence and general unhappiness. Although twentieth-century women's rights movements revolutionized women's societal status, serious issues still lingered into the twenty-first century, such as sexual harassment and the gender pay gap.

Women Increase Representation in Government

As women gained more economic, political, and social independence, an increasing number of European women attained political office. **Margaret Thatcher** achieved a major breakthrough in 1979 by becoming the first women to serve as British prime minister. Nicknamed the "Iron Lady," Thatcher kept her Conservative Party in power for more than a decade, and she enjoyed the longest tenure of any twenty-first-century prime minister. In 1990, **Mary Robinson** became the first female president of Ireland, and she helped pass landmark pieces of legislation that decriminalized homosexuality and increased access to contraceptives. Édith Cresson became the first and only woman ever elected as prime minister of France in 1991, but her term lasted less than a year due to a corruption scandal. Women's representation in legislative bodies increased throughout the twentieth centuries, but men continue to hold a disproportionate number of seats. For example, in 2019, a record number of women won seats in the British House of Commons, but the body was still composed of 68 percent men. As of 2019, nearly all European legislative bodies have less than 40 percent women members.

Decolonization

Post-World War I Plans for Decolonization

Since imperialism had been a major cause of World War I, after the war U.S. President Woodrow Wilson promoted the right to national self-determination. **Self-determination** meant allowing people to choose their government without any interference from a foreign power. This policy was an idealistic and ambitious one because it would have required European powers and Japan to relinquish valuable territorial assets. After Wilson announced America's commitment to self-determination in 1918 during his famous **"Fourteen Points" speech**, the non-European world expected to be freed from colonialism. However, diplomatic infighting at the Versailles Peace Conference brought an early end to Wilson's idealism. The Ottoman Empire's territories in the Middle East were transferred to France and Britain under the mandate system, and many of those territories were not granted independence for more than a decade. Likewise, Japan was allowed to retain all of Germany's East Asian colonies it conquered during the war, including Chinese territory. China had joined the Allies to regain this territory, and it refused to sign the Treaty of Versailles in protest of the territory's annexation. Overall, most of Asia and Africa did not receive the right to self-determination until the 1950s and 1960s.

Reasons for Delayed Decolonization

Western European states cooperated, interfered, or clashed with national independence movements in their African and Asian colonies throughout the latter half of the twentieth century. Britain cooperated with a number of independence movements due to the instability inherent in maintaining the colonial economic and political system. The leader of the Indian National Congress, **Mohandas Gandhi**, organized boycotts of British goods and encouraged his followers to commit nonviolent acts of civil disobedience before, during, and after World War II. British control over the Indian subcontinent eventually became untenable, and the British Raj was dissolved into the newly independent countries of India and Pakistan in 1947. Five years later, Britain attempted to interfere with Gamal Abdel Nasser's Egyptian national movement to protect the pro-British monarchy. However, after the United States refused to support a British expedition to recapture the valuable Suez Canal, Britain withdrew from Egypt. Afterward, Britain granted several colonies independence through negotiated settlements, including Ghana (1957), Malaysia (1957), Nigeria (1960), Kuwait (1961), South Africa (1962), Kenya (1963), Yemen (1967), Bahrain (1971), Qatar (1971), and the United Arab Emirates (1971).

European resistance to independence movements occasionally led to war. Aside from the desire to continue profiting from colonialism, Western European powers feared the spread of communism and an expansion of Soviet influence in the newly independent countries. With the looming threat of a disruption to its Cold War strategic interests, Western Europe occasionally waged incredibly bloody counter-insurgencies against Asian and African nationalist movements. In the immediate aftermath of World War II, Indonesian nationalists and communists revolted against the Dutch colonial government. An Indonesian revolutionary named Sukarno led the fight for independence. Britain supported the Dutch counter-insurgency efforts, but the **Indonesian National Revolution** (1945–1949) succeeded in freeing the Dutch East Indies. From 1954 to 1962, French colonial forces battled against the Algerian National Liberation Front's (FLN's) guerilla warfare.

Both sides used torture and committed crimes against civilians. More than 140 FLN soldiers, 25,000 French soldiers, and 55,000 civilians died during the **Algerian War of Independence** (1954–1962). In Vietnam, the revolutionary politician **Ho Chi Minh** organized the Viet Minh political party, which took over control of North Vietnam after World War II. Once Ho Chi Minh assumed leadership of the newly freed Democratic Republic Vietnam, he sought to overthrow the French colonial government in South Vietnam. The United States intervened in 1955, and Ho Chi Minh organized the Viet Cong guerilla military forces. The Viet Cong outlasted the American military who withdrew in 1973, and Vietnam was united in 1975.

The European Union

Development of Transnational Government

During the latter half of the twentieth century, European states overcame their national rivalries and established a transnational government focused on economic development. The **European Coal and Steel Community (ECSC)** represented the first step toward greater economic and political cooperation. At its founding in 1952, the ECSC included six states—Belgium, France, Italy, Luxembourg, the Netherlands, and West Germany—and they jointly established a common market for coal and steel. The common market eliminated barriers to trade, such as tariffs and protections for domestic industries. In addition to spurring the postwar recovery, the deepened economic ties were intended to prevent a

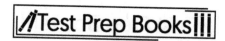

future military conflict amongst the member states. Five years later, the ECSC's six member states signed the Treaty of Rome to form the European Economic Community (EEC), which created a larger common market and customs union. Between 1973 and 1986, Denmark, Greece, Ireland, Portugal, Spain, and the United Kingdom all joined the EEC.

To ensure that political cooperation kept pace with economic integration, the EEC member states signed the **Maastricht Treaty** in 1992. This marked the beginning of the European Union (EU). Following the collapse of the Soviet Union, the EU expanded into Central and Eastern Europe. As of 2019, the EU has 28 member states with more than 500 million residents. The EU's common market allows citizens to freely move across member states' borders, and nearly all member states adopted the euro as their official currency. Furthermore, the EU established a supranational government based in Brussels. EU citizens directly elect members of the European Parliament, and in conjunction with the Council of the European Union, the European Parliament is responsible for passing regulations and directives. Regulations are immediately and automatically binding on all member states, even if there's a conflict with a domestic law, while directives need to be adopted by members' domestic legislatures before they're enforceable.

Challenges to the European Union
The conflict between supranational governance and national sovereignty has forced EU member states to strike a tricky balance. In general, the EU is criticized for bureaucracy and a lack of transparency, but the EU also faces left-wing and right-wing critiques, though the reasons behind each group's anger is different. Left-wing skeptics believe the free movement of capital unjustly favors wealthy investors, while right-wing skeptics oppose the free movement of people and aspects of the EU's immigration policy. Opposition to the EU rose to a fever pitch in the United Kingdom during the 2010s. Specifically, the nationalists advocating for a British exit ("Brexit") from the EU objected to a lack of national control over refugee resettlement, government spending, and trade deals. On June 23, 2016, "Brexit" supporters narrowly won a referendum on the United Kingdom's membership status, but as of July 2019, the British Parliament has struggled to reach a deal with the EU on Britain's withdrawal. Lingering issues include the financial penalties owed to the EU, new trade deals between the United Kingdom and the EU, and the border status of Ireland (an EU member) and Northern Ireland (a UK province).

Migration and Immigration

Postwar Immigration Patterns
Immigration into Europe increased in the 1950s and 1960s due to the postwar economic boom and decolonization. Tens of millions of Europeans were killed or grievously injured during World War II, and the labor shortage was filled with African, Asian, and southern European migrant workers who were seeking improved economic opportunities. To attract migrant workers, some Western European countries passed laws to streamline the immigration process. For example, the **British Nationality Act of 1948** removed work visa requirements for immigrants from a former British colony. This measure effectively increased immigration from India, Pakistan, Kenya, and the West Indies. Decolonization similarly spurred immigration because formerly colonized people feared reprisals from the new regimes. For example, after the Algerian War of Independence (1954–1962), the National Liberation Front (FLN) consolidated all political power and threatened to persecute anyone who had supported France in the war. As a result, nearly a million French citizens and Algerian loyalists fled the country and immigrated to France.

Anti-Immigration Backlash

An economic downturn in the 1970s tightened the European labor market, and anti-immigration sentiments increased in Europe. Immigrants were especially targeted by nationalist political parties. In 1972, Jean-Marie Le Pen founded the **French National Front**, and its platform called for expelling non-European immigrants. During the 1980s, the **Austrian Freedom Party** adopted the slogan "Austria First!" and advocated for halting all immigration. In addition to the fear of economic competition, nationalist political parties objected to how immigration had led to more religious diversity in Europe. Prior to the 1950s, European countries were overwhelmingly Christian, but by the 1980s, there were millions of Hindus and Muslims living in Europe.

Muslim immigrants faced especially intense harassment. The French National Front and Austrian Freedom Party both accused Muslim immigrants of replacing the European legal system with Sharia law. This sparked a debate over religion's role in European culture and government, with anti-immigration activists claiming that Muslim immigrants lacked Western values. During the twenty-first century, several European nationalist movements challenged the European Union's plans to accept Muslim refugees displaced by the Arab Spring and the Syrian Civil War. Anti-immigration furor and Islamophobia fueled the "Brexit" movement, and the French National Front's Marie Le Pen nearly won the 2017 French presidential election.

Technology

Consequences of Medical and Technological Innovations

New medical theories and innovations extended human life expectancy during the twentieth century. The discovery of ABO and Rhesus blood groups enabled safer blood transfusions and facilitated the development of new surgeries, such as cardiac surgery, laparoscopic surgery, and organ transplants. Theories about electromagnetic radiation led to the invention of X-rays and CAT scans, which help doctors diagnose injuries and illnesses. New fertility treatments have helped countless couples conceive children when they otherwise wouldn't have been able to. Hundreds of millions of lives have been saved through the invention of new antibiotics, like penicillin, as well as vaccines for influenza, HPV, measles, mumps, polio, and smallpox. As a result, European life expectancies increased by more than a decade over the twentieth century.

However, some scientific innovations were controversial. Genetically modified organisms (GMOs) have faced criticism on philosophical, political, and religious grounds. Opponents of GMOs accuse scientists of playing God and patenting life, while supporters point to how genetically modified crops have produced higher yields and improved nutritional value. Another major controversy involves birth control and abortion. Feminists believe access to birth control and abortion is a human right because it enables women to have bodily autonomy. In contrast, opponents of abortion pose religious arguments about how life begins at conception. The legal status of abortions remains a hot button issue in several European countries, particularly in Ireland and Poland.

Globalization

U.S. Technology

The United States was at the forefront of developing new communication and transportation technologies. For example, American businessman Henry Ford pioneered the mass production of cars, and the American military developed the technology that would later become the internet. In addition, the American economy was the strongest in the world for much of the twentieth century, so American

products were widely available in Europe. Given the United States' role in World War II and its contributions to the postwar recovery, American imports were generally greeted with enthusiasm. However, European socialists and communists criticized America's commercial influence as imperialistic, and green parties resisted the rising consumption of consumer goods. As such, boycotts of American products were relatively common, but they never broke the deep commercial ties between the United States and Europe.

New Technologies Increased Connections

The world became significantly more interconnected in the twentieth century due to the advent of new communication and transportation technologies. During the early twentieth century, the telephone replaced the telegraph, and it allowed people to instantaneously communicate for the first time. By the end of World War I, the radio had become the dominant form of entertainment and commercial advertising. In the latter half of the twentieth century, television allowed companies to instantaneously disseminate images to a mass audience, and computers exponentially increased people's ability to store and process information. The widespread adoption of the internet in the 1990s marked yet another revolution in communication, connecting computers from all over the world in a digital space.

Modern cell phones included internet access, effectively allowing people to communicate, in a handful of different ways, at any time and from anywhere. While all these new forms of communication quickened the spread of information, innovations in transportation shortened travel times. The mass production of cars in the early twentieth century reduced the price to the point where middle-class families could afford them. This led to the development of suburbs and major changes to urban planning. Following World War II, commercial aviation expedited travel over long distances. By the end of the twentieth century, people and ideas could travel around the world in record time.

Challenges to Globalization

Toward the end of the twentieth century, Western and Central European green parties raised questions about the consequences of unbridled consumerism. Beginning in the 1970s, green parties pushed for more sustainable development to prevent the depletion of natural resources and destruction of ecosystems. Calls for reform grew louder after the fall of the Soviet Union, which constituted a decisive victory for capitalism. In response to the explosive growth and unchecked power of multinational corporations, green parties began to question the wisdom of globalization. During the late 1980s and early 1990s, green party activists allied with socialists and anarchists to stage high-profile protests of international intergovernmental organizations. For example, on June 18, 1999, a large coalition of anti-globalization activists held the "Carnival Against Capital" in several dozen cities to protest austerity, the IMF, the World Bank, and multinational corporations.

Twentieth and Twenty-First Century Culture, Arts, and Demographic Trends

Changes to European Culture
Existentialism and Postmodernism

The unimaginable suffering inflicted by the Great Depression and the world wars toppled the public's confidence in the ability of science and rationality to deliver progress. Consequently, artistic movements shifted away from realism to existentialism and postmodernism. **Existentialism** focused on subjective feelings and authentic self-expression, while **postmodernism** prioritized experimentation and challenged traditional understandings of reality, truth, and progress. The United States played an outsized role in promoting these new artistic movements, partially because it served American geopolitical and ideological interests during the Cold War. While Soviet art continued to be dominated by realism, the United States used existential and postmodern art to showcase the benefits of freedom. Most controversially, the U.S. Central Intelligence Agency (CIA) provided clandestine funding to American and European artists, including Jackson Pollock and Robert Motherwell.

Religious Trends

Despite the disruptions caused by military conflicts, fascism, communism, and secularism, religion continued to play an influential role in European culture throughout the twentieth century. When the Nazis seized control over Protestant churches, Central European pastors established the Confessing Church to protect the free exercise of religion. One of the Confessing Church's founding members, **Dietrich Bonhoeffer**, overtly condemned Nazism, and he was executed in 1945 over his alleged role in a plot to assassinate Adolf Hitler. Another founding member, **Martin Niemöller**, initially supported Nazism and anti-Semitism, but he later disavowed those beliefs. When Niemöller challenged the Nazi's growing influence over Protestant churches, he was sent to the Dachau concentration camp.

Niemöller survived his imprisonment, and he spent the rest of his life working as a pacifist and activist for nuclear disarmament. Eastern European Christian churches similarly struggled against totalitarian policies in the Soviet Union. The communists effectively suppressed the Russian Orthodox Church, closing thousands of churches and coercing its leadership into supporting communist propaganda. Although the Soviet Union attempted to replace Christianity with atheism, the Russian Orthodox Church still had more than 50 million followers in the 1980s. Christian leaders around the world supported the Polish Solidarity movement led by trade unions. In 1989, Solidarity forced the Soviet leadership to allow free elections in Poland, which accelerated the Soviet Union's collapse.

In response to the rising tide of secularism and rapid social changes, the Catholic Church attempted to modernize after World War II. **Pope John XXII** initiated a major reform effort at the **Second Vatican Council** (1962–1965). Perhaps most importantly, the Second Vatican Council permitted churches to hold masses in vernacular languages, rather than Latin, to forge a deeper connection between the Catholic Church and its parishioners. The Second Vatican Council also issued a formal condemnation of war and attempted to redefine the Catholic Church's relationship to other denominations by inviting observers from the Eastern Orthodox Church and Protestant churches. Following his election to the papacy in 1978, John Paul II continued the Catholic Church's opposition to violence. Specifically, John Paul II was an outspoken critic of capital punishment, Soviet totalitarianism, South African apartheid, the Rwandan genocide, and the United States' invasion of Iraq in 2003. In addition, John Paul II helped organize the World Day of Prayer for Peace, and adherents of more than 120 different religious groups attended the event, including Buddhists, Jews, Muslims, and Protestants.

Artistic Movements

Existentialism and postmodernism revolutionized visual arts, producing movements with new aesthetic standards, subjective perspectives, and relationships to Western values. In the early twentieth century, the artistic innovations of **Pablo Picasso** and **Georges Braque** created **cubism**, an abstract art movement that uses multiple perspectives to dissect and reassemble objects. Cubism influenced the futurist art movement, and futurist depictions of modern technology and violence were particularly popular in fascist Italy. **Dadaism** responded to the violence of World War I, satirizing logic, progress, and capitalism. During the interwar period, the **surrealist art movement** emphasized the unconscious mind, element of surprise, and seemingly illogical relationships between objects. Following World War II, **abstract expressionism** became popular in New York and spread to Paris. Abstract expressionists like **Jackson Pollock** and **Robert Motherwell** completely departed from earlier aesthetic standards, creating

spontaneous-looking art that broadened viewers' freedom of interpretation. Like Dadaism, **Pop Art** satirized capitalism, and these works were typically ironic portrayals of popular cultural objects.

Shifting aesthetic standards also influenced new architectural, musical, and literary movements. The German Bauhaus school, combining functionality with simple forms, laid the groundwork for modern architecture during the interwar period. Modernism became the dominant architectural form in the 1940s and 1950s. **Modernist architects** embraced minimalism and used new construction materials, such as reinforced concrete and steel. **Postmodern architects** critiqued modernism's formality by introducing stylistic flourishes. During the early twentieth century, the composers Arnold Schoenberg, Igor Stravinsky, and Richard Strauss produced orchestral works that reinterpreted classical styles with innovative harmonies, melodies, rhythms, and touches of individualistic self-expression. With the advent of radio and film, pop music emerged in the 1950s. Pop music was defined by its mass appeal, individualism, and incorporation of diverse styles. Examples of European pop music include Elton John, ABBA, and the Beatles.

Throughout the twentieth century, European literary movements adopted innovative literary conventions and challenged traditional norms. Responding to the rapidly changing world of the twentieth century, Franz Kafka wrote surreal stories with themes of absurdity, alienation, and anxiety. James Joyce popularized a literary style known as stream of consciousness in his groundbreaking work *Ulysses* (1922). Erich Maria Remarque's *All Quiet on the Western Front* (1928) detailed the horrors experienced by German soldiers in World War I, and the novel's enormous commercial success established war memoirs as a popular literary genre. Virginia Woolf pioneered feminist critiques of society, and she explored issues related to morality, class, and war during and after World War I. Jean-Paul Sartre played a critical role in the development of existentialist philosophy, and his works featured incisive critiques of conformity under capitalism and the immorality of European colonialism.

Creation of a Consumer Culture

The postwar economic boom produced a consumer culture and enhanced domestic comforts during the 1950s and 1960s. Mass production had been perfected in its application to industrialized warfare, incorporating the latest automated technologies, and European countries transitioned from the mass production of weapons to consumer products in the conflict's aftermath. The invention of intermodal freight transport and construction of modern highway systems further increased industrial efficiency and reduced the prices of consumer goods. People also paid less for food due to creation of new fertilizers, pesticides, high-yield crops, and industrial farming equipment, like tractors and combine harvesters. Widely available goods and food at historically low prices launched consumerism into the fabric of European culture. In addition, Europeans' standard of living increased due to the introduction of new domestic comforts. Nearly all homes built in the postwar period included access to electricity and indoor plumbing. The invention of plastics had numerous low-cost applications within the household, ranging from plumbing to furniture, and the development of synthetic fibers produced more versatile and stain-resistant clothing.

Increase in the Birth Rate

The economic expansion after World War II contributed to a phenomenon known as the "**baby boom**." Economic prosperity caused a spike in marital rates, and, when combined with relatively ineffective methods of contraception, the European birth rate dramatically increased as families had more children. Governments also adopted natalist policies to promote population growth. In general, **natalist policies** supported or incentivized families to have more children, through such measures as tax credits and free childcare. The European countries with highest birth rates were Austria, Czechoslovakia, Finland, France, Iceland, and Norway.

Political and Social Movements

A variety of political and social movements transformed European culture in the twentieth century, including the women's rights movement, the gay and lesbian rights movement, and the civil rights movements. During the early twentieth century, the women's rights movement won the right to vote in nearly all European countries. Over the latter half of the twentieth century, second-wave feminists successfully expanded the grounds for divorce, secured the passage of anti-discrimination laws, increased access to birth control and abortion, and enhanced protections against domestic violence. The gay and lesbian movement advocated for the decriminalization of homosexuality and for marital rights. During the late 1950s and 1960s, Germany and Czechoslovakia decriminalized homosexuality, and Sweden declassified homosexuality as an illness in 1979. Denmark became the first European country to allowed same-sex couples to enter into registered partnerships in 1989, and from 2001 to 2017, sixteen European countries legalized civil unions for same-sex couples. However, twelve Central and Eastern European countries have passed prohibitions on same-sex marriage since 1991.

Revolts of 1968

Numerous European civil rights movements flourished in the 1960s, and their critiques of authoritarianism, capitalism, imperialism, racism, and sexism culminated in the revolts of 1968. The Northern Ireland Civil Rights Association was organized in the late 1960s, and it used civil disobedience to fight discrimination against Catholics in employment, housing, and politics. The United Kingdom and Irish loyalists strongly resisted those efforts, and the struggle for civil rights escalated into a violent conflict known as "the Troubles," which lasted until 1998. Student protests erupted in Poland and Czechoslovakia in 1968, and they challenged Soviet authoritarianism, imperialism, and political suppression. Neither protest achieved its goals. The Polish government arrested and prosecuted the protest's leaders, while the Soviet Union invaded Czechoslovakia in August 1968. Student protests also rattled West Germany in 1968. The students objected to poor conditions, racism, and sexism in Germany's higher education system, but Germany passed emergency legislation that effectively undermined the movement. French anti-capitalist protests against bourgeois materialism led to a general strike in May 1968, and the strike won some labor concessions and protections.

Practice Questions

Questions 1–3 refer to the passage below.

At the same time, the Soviet was an organized expression of the will of the proletariat as a class. In its fight for power the Soviet applied such methods as were naturally determined by the character of the proletariat as a class: its part in production; its numerical strength; its social homogeneity. In its fight for power the Soviet has combined the direction of all the social activities of the working class, including decisions as to conflicts between individual representatives of capital and labor. This combination was by no means an artificial tactical attempt: it was a natural consequence of the situation of a class which, consciously developing and broadening its fight for its immediate interests, had been compelled by the logic of events to assume a leading position in the revolutionary struggle for power.

The main weapon of the Soviet was a political strike of the masses. The power of the strike lies in disorganizing the power of the government. The greater the "anarchy" created by a strike, the nearer its victory. This is true only where "anarchy" is not being created by anarchic actions. The class that puts into motion, day in and day out, the industrial apparatus and the governmental apparatus; the class that is able, by a sudden stoppage of work, to paralyze both industry and government, must be organized enough not to fall the first victim of the very "anarchy" it has created. The more effective the disorganization of government caused by a strike, the more the strike organization is compelled to assume governmental functions.

Excerpt from Our Revolution: Essays on Working Class and International Revolution, 1904–1917 by Leon Trotsky, 1918

1. Based on the information contained in the passage, which of the following best describes the meaning of the word "proletariat"?
   a. Proletariat refers to working class people who share material interests.
   b. Proletariat refers to the collection of people who participated in the Soviet political movement.
   c. Proletariat refers to the socioeconomic class of people who are in conflict with labor.
   d. Proletariat refers to people who identify as either anarchists or revolutionaries.

2. Which of the following occurred in the immediate aftermath of the massive political strikes that caused Tsar Nicholas II to abdicate his throne?
   a. The Soviet established a dictatorship of the proletariat in Russia.
   b. The Soviet toppled the Provisional Government.
   c. The Soviet competed with the Provisional Government over political power.
   d. The Soviet fought a bloody civil war against monarchists, capitalists, and foreign powers.

3. According to the passage, why must the protestors be highly organized?
   a. Organization ensures a smooth transition from democracy to communism.
   b. Organizations facilitates the creation of a new regime based on anarchistic principles.
   c. Organization creates more leverage for the protestors when they're demanding reform.
   d. Organization allows the protestors to effectively seize and wield political power.

Questions 4–6 refer to the passage below.

As Commander-in-Chief of the Army and Navy, I have directed that all measures be taken for our defense.

But always will our whole nation remember the character of the onslaught against us. No matter how long it may take us to overcome this premeditated invasion, the American people in their righteous might will win through to absolute victory.

I believe that I interpret the will of the Congress and of the people when I assert that we will not only defend ourselves to the uttermost but will make it very certain that this form of treachery shall never again endanger us.

Hostilities exist. There is no blinking at the fact that our people, our territory and our interests are in grave danger.

With confidence in our armed forces—with the unbounding determination of our people—we will gain the inevitable triumph—so help us God.

I ask that the Congress declare that since the unprovoked and dastardly attack by Japan on Sunday, December 7th, 1941, a state of war has existed between the United States and the Japanese Empire.

Excerpt from President Roosevelt's speech to a Joint Session of Congress asking for a formal declaration of war against Japan, December 8, 1941

4. Before the events that precipitated this speech, what was the program that was already providing financial and military assistance to the Allied powers?
    a. Munich Agreement
    b. Lend-Lease program
    c. Treaty of Versailles
    d. Marshall Plan

5. Why was the Japanese bombing of Pearl Harbor considered premeditated?
    a. Because of the distance from Japan to Hawaii
    b. Because of the breaking of Japanese naval codes
    c. Because of the Japanese invasion of Hong Kong
    d. Because of the American victory at Midway

6. What do the events in the passage signify?
    a. The invasion of China by Japanese forces
    b. United States' foreign policy changing from neutrality to military support for the Allied powers
    c. A continuation of isolationism as a foreign policy by the United States
    d. The beginning of United States choosing to implement total war strategies along with the other allied powers

Questions 7–9 refer to the passage below.

As far as the Jews are concerned, I want to tell you quite frankly that they must be done away with in one way or another. The Fuehrer said once: "Should united Jewry again succeed in provoking a world war, the blood of not only the nations which have been forced into the war by them, will be shed, but the Jew will have found his end in Europe." I know that many of the measures carried out against the Jews in the Reich at present are being criticized. It is being

tried intentionally, as is obvious from the reports on the morale, to talk about cruelty, harshness, etc. Before I continue, I want to beg you to agree with me on the following formula: we will principally have pity on the German people only, and nobody else in the whole world. The others, too, had no pity on us. As an old National Socialist, I must say: this war would only be a partial success if the whole lot of Jewry would survive it, while we would have shed our best blood in order to save Europe. My attitude toward the Jews will, therefore, be based only on the expectation that they must disappear. They must be done away with.

Excerpt from Governor-General of the Nazi-occupied Polish territory Hans Frank's speech at a meeting of Nazi political leaders, December 16, 1941

7. The author's attitude toward Jewish people most likely contributed to the development of which of the following?
   a. Concentration camps
   b. Ethnic ghettos
   c. *Kristallnacht*
   d. The Final Solution

8. The author alludes to which of the following conspiracy theories?
   a. A conspiracy about Jewish people instigating World War I and sabotaging Germany.
   b. A conspiracy about Jewish people secretly directing the National Socialist political party.
   c. A conspiracy about Jewish people provoking ethnic conflicts in Germany.
   d. A conspiracy about Jewish people controlling international trade and finance.

9. Which of the following best summarizes the Nazis' future plans for race relations in Europe?
   a. The Nazis sought to enrich the Aryan race by enslaving Poles, Romani, and Slavs.
   b. The Nazis hoped to create *Lebensraum* in Central and Eastern Europe, which would be shared with the Soviet Union in accordance with the Non-Aggression Pact of 1939.
   c. The Nazis planned to establish Aryan dominance over Europe through the elimination or subjugation of races they deemed subhuman.
   d. The Nazis considered Italian and Japanese people to be honorary Aryans.

Questions 10–12 refer to the passage below.

About nine o'clock the enemy indulges in what is usually described, most disrespectfully, as "a little morning hate"—in other words, a bombardment. Beginning with an hors d'oeuvre of shrapnel along the reserve trench—much to the discomfort of Headquarters, who are shaving—he proceeds to "search" a tract of woodland in our immediate rear, his quarry being a battery of motor machine guns, which has wisely decamped some hours previously. Then, after scientifically "traversing" our second line, which has rashly advertised its position and range by cooking its breakfast over a smoky fire, he brings the display to a superfluous conclusion by dropping six "Black Marias" into the deserted ruins of a village not far behind us. After that comes silence; and we are able, in our hot, baking trenches, assisted by clouds of bluebottles, to get on with the day's work.

This consists almost entirely in digging. As already stated, these are bad trenches. The parapet is none too strong—at one point it has been knocked down for three days running—the communication trenches are few and narrow, and there are not nearly enough dugouts. Yesterday three men were wounded; and owing to the impossibility of carrying a stretcher along certain parts of the trench, they had to be conveyed to the rear in their ground-sheets—

147

bumped against projections, bent round sharp corners, and sometimes lifted, perforce, bodily into view of the enemy.

Excerpt from British Captain Ian Hay Beith's firsthand account of trench warfare during World War I, published in True Stories of the Great War *(vol. 1), 1917*

10. Which of the following best explains why the author's primary job is digging?
    a. The author was a laborer, rather than a soldier, so they weren't responsible for fighting.
    b. Soldiers were digging graves for those killed in combat.
    c. Soldiers needed to maintain, repair, and extend the defensive positions.
    d. Soldiers needed to dig a path for stretchers to save the lives of wounded soldiers.

11. Based on the passage, it can be inferred that the stretcher couldn't cross certain parts of the trench due to which of the following?
    a. The parapet was collapsing, and the soldiers didn't want to risk the remnants falling on the stretcher.
    b. The lack of dugouts meant that soldiers carrying the stretcher couldn't seek shelter during enemy bombardments.
    c. Sections of the trench weren't protected by motor machine guns.
    d. Sections of the trench were extremely narrow or were damaged from enemy bombardments.

12. Which of the following most accurately describes why trench warfare was so deadly?
    a. The trenches were difficult to maintain, and when the parapets collapsed, soldiers were left defenseless against enemy bombardments.
    b. Defensive forces wasted critical manpower on the digging of tunnels, which increased the mortality rate when enemy forces invaded the trenches.
    c. Armies used outdated military tactics to attack defensive positions that were protected with modern weaponry.
    d. Trench warfare was highly efficient, allowing militaries to outflank and rout enemy forces.

Questions 13–14 refer to the passage below.

Small arms, cannon, and ammunition are so plentiful, that they have merely to be unpacked. In view of all this, it is no wonder that the regiments marching in were everywhere greeted with jubilation, and that those marching out took leave of their garrisons with joyful songs. No one thinks of death and destruction, everyone of happy victory and joyful reunion. German discipline, once so slandered, now celebrates its triumph...

The army is increased to many times its ordinary strength by the mobilization. It draws from everywhere millions of soldiers, workmen, horses, wagons, and other materials. The entire railway service is at its disposal.... Not only is our great army mobilized, but the whole folk is mobilized, and the distribution of labor, the food question, and the care of the sick and wounded are all being provided for. The whole German folk has become a gigantic war camp, all are mobilized to protect Kaiser, folk, and fatherland, as the closing report of the Reichstag put it.

Excerpt from internal memorandum issued by the German government, outlining Germany's military mobilization efforts prior to World War I, published in The Story of The Great War *(vol. 1), 1916*

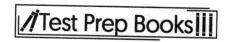

13. Based on the passage, Germany was engaging in what military strategy?
   a. Attrition warfare
   b. *Blitzkrieg*
   c. Nationalized mobilization
   d. Total war

14. Which of the following best describes how Germany produced such a surplus of weapons?
   a. Germany imported massive amounts of weapons from their ally Austria-Hungary.
   b. Germany adopted industrial innovations to mass produce weapons.
   c. Germany utilized new sources of labor, such as migrant workers from the Americas.
   d. Germany leveraged scientific innovations related to nuclear power, reducing production costs.

Short Answer Question

1. Use the passage below to answer all parts of the question that follows.

> National pride might be on the whole beneficent, if it took the direction of emulation in the things that are important to civilization. If we prided ourselves upon our poets, our men of science, or the justice and humanity of our social system, we might find in national pride a stimulus to useful endeavors. But such matters play a very small part. National pride, as it exists now, is almost exclusively concerned with power and dominion, with the extent of territory that a nation owns, and with its capacity for enforcing its will against the opposition of other nations. In this it is reinforced by group morality. To nine citizens out of ten it seems self-evident, whenever the will of their own nation clashes with that of another, that their own nation must be in the right. Even if it were not in the right on the particular issue, yet it stands in general for so much nobler ideals than those represented by the other nation to the dispute, that any increase in its power is bound to be for the good of mankind. Since all nations equally believe this of themselves, all are equally ready to insist upon the victory of their own side in any dispute in which they believe that they have a good hope of victory. While this temper persists, the hope of international cooperation must remain dim.

Excerpt from <u>Political Ideals</u> by Bertrand Russell, 1917

a) Describe one way in which the passage reflects the historical context of its time period.

b) Explain one way in which nationalism is dangerous for civilization based on the historian's arguments.

c) Evaluate how the historian's philosophical orientation would've informed his opinion about the events taking place in Germany during the 1930s.

Document-Based Question

1. Evaluate whether the League of Nations' innate weakness or the punitive measures placed on Germany had a greater impact on the outbreak of World War II.

Document 1

> With the increasing military preparations and operations throughout Eastern Europe and the evident purpose of all these quarreling nations to ignore any idea of disarmament and to rely upon force to obtain and retain territory and rights, the League of Nations is being discussed with something like contempt by the cynical, hard-headed statesmen of those countries which

are being put on a war-footing. They are cautious and courteous out of regard for the president. I doubt if the truth reaches him, but it comes to me from various sources.

These men say that in theory the idea is all right and is an ideal to work toward, but that under present conditions it is not practical in preventing war. They ask, what nation is going to rely on the guarantee in the covenant if a jealous or hostile neighbor maintains a large army. They want to know whether it would be wise or not to disarm under such conditions. Of course the answers are obvious. But, if the guarantee is not sufficient, or accepted as sufficient, protection, what becomes of the central purpose of the League and the chief reason for creating it?

Excerpt from government memorandum written by U.S. Secretary of State Robert Lansing, March 25, 1919

Document 2

The fact that the National Socialist movement and its struggle for internal power were the preparatory stage of the outer liberation from the bonds of the Dictate of Versailles is not one on which I need enlarge in this circle. I should like however to mention at this point how clearly all thoughtful regular soldiers realize what an important part has been played by the National Socialist movement in reawakening the will to fight [*Wehrwillen*], in nurturing fighting strength [*Wehrkraft*], and in rearming the German people. In spite of all the virtue inherent in it, the numerically small *Reichswehr* would never have been able to cope with this task, if only because of its own restricted radius of action. Indeed, what the Fuehrer aimed at—and has so happily been successful in bringing about—was the fusion of these two forces.

Excerpt from Nazi General Alfred Jodl's speech to the German High Command, November 7, 1943

Document 3

Such were the overpowering expectations that President Wilson raised. How completely he disappointed them and how weak and futile was the League of Nations he made is too long and too distressful a story to tell here. He exaggerated in his person our common human tragedy, he was so very great in his dreams and so incapable in his performance. America dissented from the acts of its president and would not join the League Europe accepted from him. There was a slow realization on the part of the American people that it had been rushed into something for which it was totally unprepared. There was a corresponding realization on the part of Europe that America had nothing ready to give to the old world in its extremity. Born prematurely and crippled at its birth, that League has become indeed, with its elaborate and unpractical constitution and its manifest limitations of power, a serious obstacle in the way of any effective reorganization of international relationships.

Excerpt from A Short History of the World by H.G. Wells, British writer, 1922

Document 4

At this ratio (of 20 paper marks=1 gold mark), a reparation liability of 3½ milliard gold marks (assuming exports on the scale of 6 milliards) is equivalent to 70 milliard paper marks, and a liability of 4½ milliards (assuming exports of 10 milliards) is equivalent to 90 milliard paper marks. The German Budget for the financial year April 1, 1921, to March 31, 1922, provided for an expenditure of 93.5 milliards, exclusive of reparation payments, and for a revenue of 59 milliards. Thus the present reparation demand would by itself absorb more than the whole of the existing revenue. Doubtless expenditure can be cut down, and revenue somewhat

increased. But the budget will not cover even the lower scale of the reparation payments unless expenditure is halved and revenue doubled.

If the German Budget for 1922–23 manages to balance, apart from any provision for reparation, this will represent a great effort and a considerable achievement. Apart, however, from the technical financial difficulties, there is a political and social aspect of the question which deserves attention here. The Allies deal with the established German government, make bargains with them, and look to them for fulfilment. The Allies do not extract payment out of individual Germans direct; they put pressure on the transitory abstraction called Government, and leave it to this to determine and to enforce which individuals are to pay, and how much. Since at the present time the German Budget is far from balancing even if there were no reparation payments at all, it is fair to say that not even a beginning has yet been made toward settling the problem of how the burden is to be distributed between different classes and different interests.

Excerpt from A Revision of the Treaty by John Maynard Keynes, British economist, 1922

Document 5

I. Open covenants of peace, openly arrived at, after which there shall be no private international understandings of any kind but diplomacy shall proceed always frankly and in the public view.

II. Absolute freedom of navigation upon the seas, outside territorial waters, alike in peace and in war, except as the seas may be closed in whole or in part by international action for the enforcement of international covenants.

III. The removal, so far as possible, of all economic barriers and the establishment of an equality of trade conditions among all the nations consenting to the peace and associating themselves for its maintenance.

IV. Adequate guarantees given and taken that national armaments will be reduced to the lowest point consistent with domestic safety.

V. A free, open-minded, and absolutely impartial adjustment of all colonial claims, based upon a strict observance of the principle that in determining all such questions of sovereignty the interests of the populations concerned must have equal weight with the equitable claims of the government whose title is to be determined.

VI. The evacuation of all Russian territory and such a settlement of all questions affecting Russia as will secure the best and freest cooperation of the other nations of the world in obtaining for her an unhampered and unembarrassed opportunity for the independent determination of her own political development and national policy and assure her of a sincere welcome into the society of free nations under institutions of her own choosing; and, more than a welcome, assistance also of every kind that she may need and may herself desire. The treatment accorded Russia by her sister nations in the months to come will be the acid test of their good will, of their comprehension of her needs as distinguished from their own interests, and of their intelligent and unselfish sympathy.

VII. Belgium, the whole world will agree, must be evacuated and restored, without any attempt to limit the sovereignty which she enjoys in common with all other free nations. No other single act will serve as this will serve to restore confidence among the nations in the laws which they have themselves set and determined for the government of their relations with one another. Without this healing act the whole structure and validity of international law is forever impaired.

VIII. All French territory should be freed and the invaded portions restored, and the wrong done to France by Prussia in 1871 in the matter of Alsace-Lorraine, which has unsettled the peace of the world for nearly fifty years, should be righted, in order that peace may once more be made secure in the interest of all.

IX. A readjustment of the frontiers of Italy should be effected along clearly recognizable lines of nationality.

X. The peoples of Austria-Hungary, whose place among the nations we wish to see safeguarded and assured, should be accorded the freest opportunity to autonomous development.

XI. Rumania, Serbia, and Montenegro should be evacuated; occupied territories restored; Serbia accorded free and secure access to the sea; and the relations of the several Balkan states to one another determined by friendly counsel along historically established lines of allegiance and nationality; and international guarantees of the political and economic independence and territorial integrity of the several Balkan states should be entered into.

XII. The Turkish portion of the present Ottoman Empire should be assured a secure sovereignty, but the other nationalities which are now under Turkish rule should be assured an undoubted security of life and an absolutely unmolested opportunity of autonomous development, and the Dardanelles should be permanently opened as a free passage to the ships and commerce of all nations under international guarantees.

XIII. An independent Polish state should be erected which should include the territories inhabited by indisputably Polish populations, which should be assured a free and secure access to the sea, and whose political and economic independence and territorial integrity should be guaranteed by international covenant.

XIV. A general association of nations must be formed under specific covenants for the purpose of affording mutual guarantees of political independence and territorial integrity to great and small states alike.

US President Woodrow Wilson's "Fourteen Points" speech to Congress, January 8, 1918

Document 6

While reorganizing the interior, I undertook the second task: to release Germany from its international ties. Two particular characteristics are to be pointed out: secession from the League of Nations and denunciation of the disarmament conference. It was a hard decision. The number of prophets who predicted that it would lead to the occupation of the Rhineland was large, the number of believers was very small. I was supported by the nation, which stood firmly behind me, when I carried out my intentions. After that the order for rearmament. Here again there were numerous prophets who predicted misfortunes, and only a few believers. In 1935 the introduction of compulsory armed service. After that militarization of the Rhineland, again a process believed to be impossible at that time. The number of people who put trust in me was very small. Then beginning of the fortification of the whole country especially in the west.

One year later, Austria came. This step also was considered doubtful. It brought about a considerable reinforcement of the Reich. The next step was Bohemia, Moravia and Poland. This step also was not possible to accomplish in one campaign. First of all, the western fortification had to be finished. It was not possible to reach the goal in one effort. It was clear to me from the first moment that I could not be satisfied with the Sudeten-German territory. That was only partial solution. The decision to march into Bohemia was made. Then followed the erection of the Protectorate, and with that basis for the action against Poland was laid, but I wasn't quite clear at that time whether I should start first against the east and then in the west, or vice-versa.

Excerpt from German Führer Adolf Hitler's speech to the German High Command, November 23, 1939

Document 7

Instead of "open covenants openly arrived at," the treaty was made in secret conference; we did not gain the freedom of the seas, but helped Great Britain to strengthen her command of the seas by eliminating her greatest rival; we witnessed no removal of economic barriers—not even among the Allies, as the president himself recommended an American tariff on dyes; disarmament was decreed for Germany and Austria only; self-determination of small nations became a dead letter at once as to Ireland, German Austria, the German Tyrol, Danzig, Egypt, India, the Boers, Korea, Persia, and numerous others, especially where the question involved the self-determination of Germans; Hungary's borders were at once invaded by Rumania, Serbia and Czecho-Slovakia; Russia was not permitted to determine her own fate, as Kolchak was formally recognized and supported by the powers; Belgium remains a vassal of England and France; in addition to righting the wrong of 1871 by the recession of Alsace-Lorraine, the Saar Valley was taken away from Germany and a plebiscite was ordered in Schleswig, Silesia, and German-Poland under the guns of the Entente; Italy's borders were not readjusted along national lines, for the Brenner Pass, the Vorarlberg, parts of Dalmatia and a lease on Fiume provided; the autonomous development of Austria-Hungary was interpreted to mean that the German-speaking part of Austria was forbidden to unite with Germany; the independence of the Balkan states was made subject to the invisible government of the Big Four; autonomy for Turkish vassal states and the internationalization of the Dardanelles was construed to mean that these states should become mandatories of the Allies and the strait to be under Allied control; Polish freedom celebrated its advent with Jewish pogroms, while the League of Nations became a league of victors, in which Japan was bribed to enter by the cession to her of the Shantung peninsula.

Excerpt from 1683–1920: The Fourteen Points and What Became of Them by Frederick Franklin Schrader, American journalist, 1920

Answer Explanations

1. A: Under Marxist economic theory, the proletariat is the working class, which is in direct conflict with the ruling class (bourgeoisie) due to the inherent conflict between their collective material interests (relationship to property). Marxism heavily influenced the leaders of the Soviet, including the passage's author, Leon Trotsky. In the passage, Trotsky repeatedly uses the Marxist conception of the proletariat to describe the collective working class. Thus, Choice *A* is the correct answer. While the proletariat generally did support the Soviet political movement, the definition is more closely related to the working class. So, Choice *B* is incorrect. Choice *C* is incorrect because it confuses the class interests of the proletariat and the bourgeoisie. The proletariat's class interest is labor, and the bourgeoisie' class interest is capital. Although some members of the Russian proletariat were anarchists and revolutionaries, those characteristics don't define the proletariat. So, Choice *D* is incorrect.

2. C: The passage mentions how a "political strike of the masses" can cause enough disruption to overthrow the government. This occurred during the Russian Revolution in March 1917. After the Russian military refused to break a general strike of industrial workers, Tsar Nicholas II abdicated his throne. Immediately afterward, the Provisional Government assumed control over official state power, but the Soviet held widespread influence amongst the broader public. As a result, the Provisional Government and the Soviet competed over political power until the Soviet's leaders successfully overthrew the Provisional Government on November 7, 1917. Thus, Choice *C* is the correct answer. Choice *A* is incorrect because the Soviet didn't establish a dictatorship of the proletariat until after overthrowing the Provisional Government. The strikes didn't immediately topple the Provisional Government, so Choice *B* is incorrect. The Russian Revolution also occurred after the Provisional Government was overthrown. As such, Choice *D* is incorrect.

3. D: The argument describes how protests can undermine and overthrow governments by spreading anarchy, but if the protest movement isn't organized, then anarchy will continue after the revolution. As such, the protests must be organized to such a degree that they're capable of filling the power vacuum and wielding political power. Thus, Choice *D* is the correct answer. The Russian Revolution was a transition from absolute monarchy to communism, not democracy to communism, and in any event, the passage never mentions democracy. So, Choice *A* is incorrect. Choice *B* is incorrect because the author describes how anarchy undermines governmental functions. There's nothing in the passage about how anarchy would work as a governing strategy, so Choice *C* is incorrect.

4. B: The United States was already supplying financial and military assistance to the Allied powers before the bombing of Pearl Harbor through the Lend-Lease program. Therefore, Choice *B* is correct. The Munich Agreement refers to territory in Czechoslovakia changing hands in 1938, so Choice *A* is incorrect. Choice *C* is incorrect because the Treaty of Versailles was an agreement that was instrumental in ending World War I. Choice *D* is not the correct answer choice because the Marshall Plan provided financial assistance to Europe after the war was over.

5. A: The attack on Pearl Harbor was considered premeditated because of the long distance from Japan to Hawaii. Logistically the Japanese needed time to devise the plan and put that plan into action. Thus, Choice *A* is the correct answer choice. Choice *B* is incorrect because the Allied forces did not break the Japanese naval codes until later in the war. The Japanese invasion of Hong Kong happened the day after the attack on Pearl Harbor but did not relate directly to the bombing of Pearl Harbor. Therefore, Choice *C* is incorrect. Choice *D* is incorrect because the American victory over Japan at Midway occurred in 1942 months after the attack on Pearl Harbor.

6. B: After World War I, the United States was moved toward isolationism and even enacted a series of Neutrality Acts. This was one of the reasons the United States did not join the Allied powers earlier in the war. After the attack on Pearl Harbor, the United States declared war on Japan and then Germany a few days later. Therefore, Choice *B* is the best answer choice. Choice *A* is not the correct answer because Japan had already invaded China before the outbreak of World War II. When the United States joined the war, this represented an abandonment of isolationism, so Choice *C* is incorrect. Choice *D* is not the correct answer choice because even though the United States did implement total war strategies as part of their war effort, the passage does not specifically address total war efforts.

7. D: The author is Hans Frank, the Governor-General of the Nazi-occupied Polish territory. At the beginning and end of the passage, he argues that Jewish people "must be done away with," and he expresses his support for extreme policies throughout the passage. These sentiments are consistent with the Nazis' "final solution to the Jewish question," which involved the construction of death camps to exterminate European Jews. The Final Solution was adopted at the Wannsee Conference on January 20, 1942, a little more than one year after Frank's speech. Thus, Choice *D* is the correct answer. Beginning in 1938, Nazis forcibly relocated Jewish people to concentration camps. However, the passage is describing a more extreme policy, so Choice *A* is incorrect. The Nazis established segregated Jewish ghettos in the late 1930s. These ghettos developed prior to Frank's speech, and he is clearly calling for the Nazis to take more aggressive actions against Jewish people. So, Choice *B* is incorrect. On November 9–10, 1938, Nazi supporters destroyed Jewish businesses and synagogues during an event known as *Kristallnacht* (Night of Broken Glass). Frank's speech was advocating for a long-term solution rather than merely supporting another *Kristallnacht*, so Choice *C* is incorrect.

8. A: Adolf Hitler promulgated conspiracy theories to scapegoat Jewish people for Germany's struggles during the interwar period. Specifically, Hitler blamed an international cabal of Jewish people for starting World War I, and he claimed that Jewish people sabotaged the German war effort. The passage indicates this when Hans Frank quotes Hitler as saying, "Should united Jewry *again* succeed in provoking a world war..." This means Hitler blamed the Jews for starting the previous world war, World War I. Thus, Choice *A* is the correct answer. Hitler personally exercised total control over the National Socialist (Nazi) political party, so he never accused Jews of directing it. As such, Choice *B* is incorrect. The Nazis did blame Jewish people for the ethnic conflicts in Germany, but the passage is describing a different conspiracy. In the second sentence, the author quotes Hitler's claims about Jewish people provoking another world war. So, Choice *C* is incorrect. Likewise, Choice *D* refers to an actual Nazi conspiracy theory about Jewish people controlling international finance, but the passage alludes to a conspiracy theory about World War I. So, Choice *D* is incorrect.

9. C: The Nazis sought to create a "New Racial Order" dominated by Aryans. To cement Aryans' status as the dominant race, the Nazis implemented the Holocaust to exterminate "subhuman" European Jews, which is described in the passage. In addition, Poles and Slavs were also considered to be "subhuman," and the Nazis enacted plans to displace, subjugate, and eliminate them from the *Lebensraum*. Thus, Choice *C* is the correct answer. The Nazis did enslave some Poles, Romani, and Slavs, but this was only part of the Nazis' plans for a "New Racial Order." So, Choice *A* is incorrect. Choice *B* correctly identifies the *Lebensraum* as a part of the Nazis' future plans for race relations in Europe, but that constituted a living space for Germans alone. In the Non-Aggression Pact of 1939, Hitler promised to give the Soviet Union other territory in Central and Eastern Europe. Since the Soviet Union had a large Slavic population, Hitler considered them to be an impediment to Aryans' dominance over Europe. This partially motivated Hitler to break the Non-Aggression Pact by launching a surprise invasion of the Soviet Union on June 22, 1941. So, Choice *B* is incorrect. The Nazis considered Italians and Japanese people to be honorary Aryans, but Choice *D* doesn't mention the relationship of Aryans to other races, so it's incorrect.

10. C: The author states that his primary job is digging because the trenches are in disrepair. He cites several issues with the trenches, including a weak parapet, narrow communication trenches, and a lack of dugouts. As such, the soldier is maintaining, repairing, and extending the trenches, which are defensive positions. Thus, Choice *C* is the correct answer. The author is a British captain, and there is nothing in the passage to support his being a laborer rather than a solider. So, Choice *A* is incorrect. Soldiers were being killed and wounded according to this passage, but grave digging isn't the type of digging the speaker is describing. Therefore, Choice *B* is incorrect. Likewise, repairing and extending trenches was more closely related to military tactics than saving the lives of wounded soldiers, so Choice *D* is incorrect.

11. D: At the end of the passage, the author states that a stretcher couldn't be carried across the trench, but they were able to move the bodies anyway. Earlier in the passage, the author describes how parts of the trench were too narrow, and the parapet had been damaged during enemy bombardments. The stretcher likely couldn't fit in the trench due to its narrowness and the damage. This is why the wounded soldiers' bodies needed to be bent around sharp corners and otherwise contorted on their way out of the trench. Thus, Choice *D* is the correct answer. The author describes the parapet as weak, not completely collapsed, so it's unlikely they couldn't use the stretcher due to the risk of pieces falling on the body. So, Choice *A* is incorrect. Choice *B* is incorrect because the primary issue is the stretcher being too bulky for the trench. The lack of dugouts was a problem for all soldiers, not a problem related to the stretcher. Motor machine guns didn't cover the entire trench, so it didn't impact the decision on whether to use the stretcher. They still moved the body, so they weren't waiting for the motor machine guns to return. As such, Choice *C* is incorrect.

12. C: Trench warfare was incredibly deadly due to the combination of modern weaponry and outdated military tactics. Trenches were protected with the latest military technologies, such as barbed wire and machine guns. In addition, the advancing forces also used modern weapons, like long-range artillery, chemical weapons, and aircrafts. Trench warfare was itself an outdated military tactic, and military commanders made it worse by carrying out traditional frontal attacks on fortified positions. Thus, Choice *C* is the correct answer. Trenches were difficult to maintain, but modern weaponry and outdated attacks had a larger impact on the soaring casualty rates. So, Choice *A* is incorrect. Although defensive forces dedicated significant manpower to digging trenches and tunnels, the mortality rate would've been high regardless of the lost manpower due to the inherent dangers involved in trench warfare. So, Choice *B* is incorrect. Trench warfare was highly inefficient, as evidence by the stalemate it produced in World War I, so Choice *D* is incorrect.

13. D: The passage is discussing Germany's mobilization during World War I. It describes the production of massive amounts of weapons, dramatic increases in personnel, the use of railways for military purposes, and the mobilization of civilian resources. This large-scale mobilization of resources is consistent with a military strategy known as "total war." Thus, Choice *D* is the correct answer. World War I was sometimes referred to as a war of attrition because trench warfare produced a stalemate. Accordingly, attrition warfare isn't related to the mobilization of resources, so Choice *A* is incorrect. *Blitzkrieg* (lightning war) involved using armored units and aerial bombardments to achieve fast, decisive victories, and Nazi Germany deployed this military strategy during World War II. So, Choice *B* is incorrect. Nationalized mobilization is not a relevant term. As such, Choice *C is* incorrect.

14. B: At the beginning of the passage, the memorandum describes Germany's mass production of weapons during World War I. Like all the belligerent powers fighting in World War I, Germany leveraged new automated technologies and cutting-edge industrial techniques to mass produce weapons. Thus, Choice *B* is the correct answer. Germany was allied with Austria-Hungary during World War I, but Germany's mobilization didn't depend on importing Austro-Hungarian weapons. So, Choice *A* is incorrect. Germany did utilize new sources of labor, like women, to mass produce weapons; however, migrant workers from the Americas were not a common labor source, so Choice *C* is incorrect. Germany leveraged new scientific innovations related to mass production, not nuclear power, during their mobilization efforts. So, Choice *D* is incorrect.

Short Answer Response

1.

a) The passage focuses on the deleterious effects of nationalism, and at the time of the passage's publication in 1917, World War I was ravaging Europe. Nationalism heavily contributed to the underlying tensions that led to World War. As described in the passage, nationalism fueled an obsession with extending nations' power and influence. Prior to the outbreak of World War I, European powers entered into an imperial competition known as the "Scramble for Africa." By 1914, European powers controlled nearly 90 percent of the African continent. After the assassination of the Archduke Franz Ferdinand of Austria-Hungary, European powers were partially motivated to enter the conflict to protect their colonial empires. Since the general public wasn't usually the direct beneficiary of imperialism and global military conflicts, governments leveraged nationalism in order to rally the necessary support. In effect, nationalism fanned the flames that would later consume Europe during World War I.

b) The historian makes an argument that nationalism is dangerous for civilization because it convinces people to support actions they otherwise wouldn't find sensible, including violence. According to the historian, nationalism results in nine out of ten people blindly following their country into a war. Whether their country is actually in the right or wrong is immaterial because nationalists consider any increase in power to be a positive development. This phenomenon was readily apparent in European citizens' attitude toward World War I. At the beginning of the conflict, countries were able to deploy total war military strategies. This included the mobilization of all civilian resources for the war, and citizens all over Europe cooperated with rations and conscription. Resistance increased as the fighting turned into a stalemate and millions of people died, but nationalism's ability to popularize total war showcases the danger it poses to civilization.

c) The historian is philosophically opposed to nationalism, so he would've strongly opposed the rise of Nazism from the outset. During the early 1930s, Nazi political leaders used nationalism to exploit the public's mounting anger over the Treaty of Versailles and economic turmoil. For example, Adolf Hitler regularly characterized the Treaty of Versailles as a national humiliation and issued demands for the restoration of Germany's historic greatness. These nationalist appeals swayed public opinion and led to Hitler's appointment as the Chancellor of Germany in 1933. Almost immediately upon taking office, Hitler consolidated all political power under his personal authority and ordered Nazi paramilitary units to carry out anti-Semitic and violent policies. Even as the Nazi regime grew more extreme with each passing year, it enjoyed substantial popular support throughout Germany due to nationalist fervor. Like his critiques of the prior government, Hitler used nationalism to justify everything from military invasions to the Holocaust. While much of the world took nearly a decade to appreciate the threat posed by Nazism, the historian would've immediately recognized the horrors extreme nationalism could unleash.

Dear AP European History Test Taker,

We would like to start by thanking you for purchasing this study guide for your AP European History exam. We hope that we exceeded your expectations.

Our goal in creating this study guide was to cover all of the topics that you will see on the test. We also strove to make our practice questions as similar as possible to what you will encounter on test day. With that being said, if you found something that you feel was not up to your standards, please send us an email and let us know.

We would also like to let you know about other books in our catalog that may interest you.

SAT

This can be found on Amazon: amazon.com/dp/1628458984

ACT

amazon.com/dp/1628458844

AP English Literature and Composition

amazon.com/dp/1628459476

We have study guides in a wide variety of fields. If the one you are looking for isn't listed above, then try searching for it on Amazon or send us an email.

Thanks Again and Happy Testing!
Product Development Team
info@studyguideteam.com

FREE Test Taking Tips DVD Offer

To help us better serve you, we have developed a Test Taking Tips DVD that we would like to give you for FREE. **This DVD covers world-class test taking tips that you can use to be even more successful when you are taking your test.**

All that we ask is that you email us your feedback about your study guide. Please let us know what you thought about it – whether that is good, bad or indifferent.

To get your **FREE Test Taking Tips DVD**, email freedvd@studyguideteam.com with "FREE DVD" in the subject line and the following information in the body of the email:

    a. The title of your study guide.

    b. Your product rating on a scale of 1-5, with 5 being the highest rating.

    c. Your feedback about the study guide. What did you think of it?

    d. Your full name and shipping address to send your free DVD.

If you have any questions or concerns, please don't hesitate to contact us at freedvd@studyguideteam.com.

Thanks again!

CPSIA information can be obtained
at www.ICGtesting.com
Printed in the USA
BVHW061545090321
602096BV00009B/503